D1602705

Whitehead's Metaphysics

Whitehead's
Metaphysics

AN INTRODUCTORY EXPOSITION

IVOR LECLERC

INDIANA UNIVERSITY PRESS
Bloomington & London

Library of Congress Cataloging in Publication Data

Leclerc, Ivor.
   Whitehead's metaphysics.

   Includes bibliographical references and index.
   1. Whitehead, Alfred North, 1861-1947—Metaphysics.
I. Title.
B1674.W354L4   1975   110   74-23296
ISBN 0-253-20181-0   75 76 77 78 79 1 2 3 4 5

To My Mother

ABBREVIATIONS

THE following are the abbreviations of titles and the editions of Whitehead's works used in footnote references:

A E   *The Aims of Education and Other Essays*, Williams & Norgate, 1929.

A I   *Adventures of Ideas*, Cambridge University Press, 1933.

C N   *The Concept of Nature*, Cambridge University Press, 1920.

F R   *The Function of Reason*, Princeton University Press, 1929.

M T   *Modes of Thought*, Cambridge University Press, 1938.

P R   *Process and Reality*, Cambridge University Press, 1929.

P Rel   *The Principle of Relativity*, Cambridge University Press, 1922.

P N K   *An Enquiry Concerning the Principles of Natural Knowledge*, Cambridge University Press, 1919; 2nd edition, 1925.

R M   *Religion in the Making*, Cambridge University Press, 1926.

S M W   *Science and the Modern World*, Cambridge University Press, 1926.

Adventures of Ideas (1933), *Modes of Thought* (1938), *Process and Reality* (1929), *Religion in the Making* (1926), and *Science in the Modern World* (1925) have also been published by The Macmillan Company in the United States. Page numbers in square brackets refer to these American editions. (The pagination of *Adventures of Ideas* and *Modes of Thought* is the same as that of the Cambridge editions.)

PREFACE

The aim of this book is to provide an introduction to the philosophical system of *Process and Reality* and other works of Whitehead's later period. One effective way of coming to an understanding of a philosopher's thought is through an appreciation of the problems with which he was basically concerned. This method is especially appropriate in Whitehead's case, and is that here adopted. But it must inevitably rest upon some view as to what those problems were, and regarding this there is as yet no general agreement among Whitehead scholars.

It is the particular thesis of this book that in developing the system which he elaborated in such detail in *Process and Reality*, Whitehead's problems were specifically metaphysical, and not those which characterized his earlier investigations in the philosophy of natural science. I have tried to make clear that Whitehead's basic problems belong to the great tradition of philosophical inquiry, first opened up by the Greeks. I have set out to explain how and why Whitehead posed the questions in a way different from that of antecedent thought, and that this is the root of the originality and novelty of his philosophy. In adopting this view and this approach to Whitehead, his ideas and terminology become fairly readily explicable; and it is then possible at an early stage to enter into a systematic exploration of the fundamental notions or categories of his metaphysics.

In connection with this, a few words will be apposite about my procedure of exposition. In contrast to Whitehead's, in which all his ideas are presupposed in the discussion of each of them, I have introduced his notions and concomitant terms one at a time, elucidating them in the context of the particular issues involved. At each stage I have endeavoured to make the discussion of the problems as full as possible without bringing in issues with which I intend dealing subsequently. I have found it no easy matter to avoid over-simplification on the one hand, and on the other a treatment too elaborate for an introductory exposition. I leave it to my readers to decide as to the extent to which I have been successful in this.

The first chapter briefly surveys the development of Whitehead's thought, indicating how his preoccupation with the philosophy of science led him to metaphysics as the fundamental inquiry. Chapter II is the key chapter of the book, and shows what Whitehead was essentially concerned to do. Chapter IV and the other chapters of Part Two follow directly from this, taking up progressively the issues and problems arising from the philosophical position explained in Chapter II. In dealing with these problems and in arriving at his solutions, Whitehead followed an explicit procedure and appealed to particular criteria, as I show throughout. Chapter III contains Whitehead's justification for that procedure and those criteria. The main notions of Whitehead's scheme are gradually elaborated in Parts Two and Three, and in Part Four an attempt is made, especially in the final chapters, to draw together the whole preceding investigation into a presentation of Whitehead's general metaphysical conception of the universe.

Whitehead's Metaphysics

No great philosopher's thought can be properly understood without some study of his own works. Whitehead's writings are often rather difficult because of his distinctive style, combining great complexity with extraordinary brevity and precision of statement. It has accordingly been an explicit aim of this book to facilitate the reader's efforts to deal with the original by familiarizing him with important passages. I have thus purposely quoted Whitehead's own words rather extensively, interpreting and unravelling the key statements relevant to the problems at issue. This has the secondary advantage that the reader will also more readily be able to assess the accuracy of my interpretations when encountering these passages in their original contexts.

I.L.

CONTENTS

Contents

PART FOUR

THE NATURE OF ACTUALITY
A METAPHYSICAL DESCRIPTION

PART ONE

INTRODUCTION

CHAPTER I

Whitehead's Philosophical Endeavour

---

§ I

The proper understanding of a philosopher's thought requires a clear appreciation of the problems and issues with which he was essentially concerned, and of the context in which they presented themselves to him. This is certainly a most important requirement for the understanding of Whitehead's metaphysics, for its difficulty has been greatly exaggerated by incorrect or misleading approaches.

Viewed chronologically, it is evident that Whitehead's earliest philosophical preoccupation was with the philosophical problems of modern science, which had become acute with the new developments which had taken place toward the beginning of the twentieth century. His writings during this period[1] were devoted exclusively to those problems. It is indubitable that also in his later writings they continue to play a significant part, but the relevant question is whether they in fact continue to be central. In this connection it is of particular interest to consider a statement Whitehead made in his preface to the second edition of *An Enquiry into the Principles of Natural Knowledge*, written in 1924 at the close

[1] P N K, C N, P Rel, and the various papers collected in A E.

of his earlier period, a statement which gives a fair indication of his attitude as he entered upon his later period. He said there that he hoped 'in the immediate future to embody the standpoint of these volumes in a more complete metaphysical study'.[1]

This statement can be interpreted as meaning that his metaphysics constitutes a development or expansion of his earlier theories into a more comprehensive scheme, so as to embrace fields other than the explicitly scientific. This has in fact been a widely accepted view of the relation of Whitehead's metaphysics to his earlier philosophy of science; it has been regarded as constituting the key to the understanding of his metaphysical doctrines.[2] His metaphysics, it is held, is correctly to be conceived as a philosophy of twentieth-century physics, as an attempt at providing the fundamental theory for the physics of relativity, electro-magnetism and quanta; and indeed by some as not being intelligible except in the light of an appreciable knowledge of modern physics. This view is not without considerable plausibility, and appears to be substantiated by the fact that in most of his later writings Whitehead frequently returns to a consideration of the philosophical problems of modern science, discussing their solutions in terms of his metaphysical concepts.

It is the thesis of this book, however, that this interpretation of Whitehead's statement in the 1924 preface to the *Principles of Natural Knowledge*, together with the concomitant view of the relation of his later to his earlier theories, is not correct. It results in a distortion of the part played by the philosophical problems of science in Whitehead's later philosophical thought, and thus in a failure to appreciate the vital shift of his centre of interest which inaugurated his later period. This shift did not consist merely in a widening of his field; his later theory is not simply

[1] P N K, 2nd edition, 1925.

[2] An able and detailed presentation of the approach from the earlier works has been given by Nathaniel Lawrence in his *Whitehead's Philosophical Development: A Critical History of the Background of Process and Reality* (University of California Press, Berkeley and Los Angeles, 1956)—received after this book was written. I have discussed it at some length in an article 'Whitehead's Philosophy' in *The Review of Metaphysics*, Vol. XI, September 1957, pp. 87–112.

an expanded development of his earlier. It should be noted that in that preface Whitehead speaks of *embodying* the standpoint of the earlier works in a metaphysics; that word is significant. As we shall see, in turning to metaphysics Whitehead turned to a new set of problems, different from those which had previously been his primary concern. The result of this new preoccupation was by no means to leave his earlier theories unaltered. Their 'embodiment' involved in the end a much more considerable change in Whitehead's theories about the problems of science than he himself had at first anticipated, and than most commentators have subsequently allowed. His entire approach to these problems underwent a considerable change, so much so indeed that, as Professor Victor Lowe has reported,[1] in his later years Whitehead used to remark that he doubted whether there was such a subject as the 'philosophy of science'. What Whitehead meant by this will be shown later.[2]

It is not my intention here to attempt any full account of Whitehead's philosophical development,[3] but merely to indicate some main points in it in order to bring out and emphasize the new set of problems and issues which occupied him in his later period. A clear grasp of these is indispensable to a proper understanding of his metaphysical theories.

Whitehead's philosophical interest had originated with a realization, already during the 1890's, that the new physical theories involved the complete breakdown of the Newtonian cosmology.

The story of the breakdown extends over more than a century. For by far the greater part of that period men of science were quite unaware that the ideas which they were introducing, slowly, one after the other, were finally to accumulate into a body of thought inconsistent with the Newtonian ideas dominating their thoughts and shaping their modes of expression. The story commences with the wave theory of light and ends with the wave theory of matter.[4]

[1] Cf. *Whitehead and the Modern World*, V. Lowe, C. Hartshorne, and A. H. Johnson, p. 18.   [2] § 46 below.
[3] There is an excellent account of it by Victor Lowe in the volume *The Philosophy of Alfred North Whitehead*, edited by P. A. Schillp.
[4] A I 200.

Whitehead appreciated earlier and more clearly than most that the continued inconsistent adherence to the fundamental concepts of the Newtonian cosmology would increasingly prove frustrating to the development of science, and that the replacement of these concepts was a matter of urgency.

The first requirement was to distinguish precisely the foundational concepts of the classical Newtonian scheme. Classical physics was concerned to discover the laws of motion of material bodies and to formulate them in exact mathematical terms. Thus in this scheme the fundamental notions are matter, space, and time.

The material, the space, the time, the various laws concerning the transition of material configurations are taken as ultimate stubborn facts, not to be tampered with.[1]

But even from the point of view of classical physics these notions involved serious difficulties. It is assumed that there are self-identical material particles in motion, that is, changing their spatial relations at successive times. As we shall see later,[2] however, the concept of a self-identical entity undergoing spatio-temporal adventures is far from being as self-evident and acceptable as has usually been supposed. But apart from this, the ultimate fact for Newtonian physics is not a material particle in motion, nor the multitude of physical entities constituting the universe as in motion. Newtonian physics is concerned to express in precise mathematical terms the transitions of a particle or of the configurations of material particles. To do so it must take the relative spatial positions of the particles at one durationless instant of time, and then at a later instant. For classical dynamics, therefore, the configuration of material particles at a durationless instant of time is the ultimate fact. There is a succession of such facts, each at a durationless instant. But there is no particle in transition, in a state of change, as an ultimate fact. As Whitehead has put it,[3]

the ultimate fact embracing all nature is (in this traditional point of view) a distribution of material throughout all space at a durationless instant of time, and another such ultimate fact will be another distribution of the same material throughout the same space at another durationless instant of time. The difficulties of this extreme statement are evident and were pointed out even in classical times when the concept first took shape. . . . No room is left for velocity, acceleration, momentum, and kinetic energy, which certainly are essential physical quantities.

The point is that velocity, acceleration, etc., all involve the notion of a state of change, but this is precisely what has evaporated from the ultimate 'Newtonian' facts. 'A state of change at a durationless instant of time is a very difficult conception'—indeed it is self-contradictory. For 'it is impossible to define velocity without some reference to the past and the future'.[1] Nevertheless, for Newtonian physics the ultimate facts had this particular character which Whitehead subsequently, in *Science and the Modern World*, described as that of 'simple location'.[2]

Newtonian physics is based upon the independent individuality of each bit of matter. Each stone is conceived as fully describable apart from any reference to any other portion of matter. It might be alone in the Universe, the sole occupant of uniform space. But it would still be that stone which it is. Also the stone could be adequately described without any reference to past or future. It is to be conceived fully and adequately as wholly constituted within the present moment.[3]

But, Whitehead insists, this concept of the ultimate facts as simply located material particles is inconsistent with the notions of motion, velocity, momentum, etc., and accordingly 'there is a fatal contradiction inherent in the Newtonian cosmology'.[4] Clearly, therefore, Whitehead maintains, the indispensable requirement is a different conception of the ultimate facts; these facts must be conceived as involving transition as an essential feature; 'we must therefore in the ultimate fact, beyond which science ceases to analyse, include the notion of a state of change'.[5]

This criticism of the fundamental notions of Newtonian physics has all the more point since modern physics has in effect, despite

[1] P N K 2.   [2] Cf. S M W 61 ff.   [3] A I 200–1.   [4] M T 199.   [5] P N K 2.

the continued use by scientists of the older terminology and concepts, moved to a new conception.

Modern physics has abandoned the doctrine of Simple Location. The physical things which we term stars, planets, lumps of matter, molecules, electrons, protons, quanta of energy, are each to be conceived as modifications of conditions within space-time, extending throughout its whole range. There is a focal region, which in common speech is where the thing is. But its influence streams away from it with finite velocity throughout the utmost recesses of space and time. Of course, it is natural, and for certain purposes entirely proper, to speak of the focal region, thus modified, as the thing itself situated there. But difficulties arise if we press this way of thought too far. For physics, the thing itself is what it does, and what it does is this divergent stream of influence. Again the focal region cannot be separated from the external stream. It obstinately refuses to be conceived as an instantaneous fact. It is a state of agitation, only differing from the so-called external stream by its superior dominance within the focal region.[1]

It is beyond the scope of this book to enter further into a discussion of this analysis of the fundamental ideas of science. Our purpose is served if we have some appreciation of the kind of problem with which Whitehead was dealing in his earlier period, and of his way of tackling it.

His endeavour was to formulate a conception of the ultimate facts of physical science, and specifically of modern physical science, such as would be consistent with experience, and free from the inner contradictions of the older theory. In pursuing this aim Whitehead adopted the empirical, piecemeal procedure of science in face of any scientific problem. He conceived himself as concerned with more fundamental problems than the usual scientific ones, but not with problems essentially different, requiring a different procedure. At this period his conception of the distinction between philosophy and science had not yet been clearly worked out. The investigation of nature, he then thought, has one aspect more fundamental than the rest, namely the inquiry into the foundational notions which are involved. This

[1] A I 201–2.

is 'natural philosophy', or 'philosophy of nature', or 'philosophy of science'—Whitehead made no clear distinction. His use of the term 'philosophy' here indicates some appreciation that this inquiry, which has traditionally been pursued as 'philosophy', is in some respects different from 'science'. But Whitehead was still not properly clear as to that distinction, and in so far as he had a definite idea he was anxious to avoid any intrusion of 'metaphysics' (as he then conceived it) in this inquiry. 'In the philosophy of science we seek the general notions which apply to nature, namely, to what we are aware of in perception.'[1] Science as such is concerned with the investigation of the more specific details of nature in terms of the fundamental general notions. Thus the philosophy of science is 'the philosophy of the thing perceived, and it should not be confused with the metaphysics of reality of which the scope embraces both perceiver and perceived'.[2] In summary Whitehead's view was that

the primary task of a philosophy of natural science is to elucidate the concept of nature, considered as one complex fact for knowledge, to exhibit the fundamental entities and the fundamental relations between entities in terms of which all laws of nature have to be stated, and to secure that the entities and relations thus exhibited are adequate for the expression of all the relations between entities which occur in nature.[3]

What then are the fundamental entities, the ultimate facts, if we reject the concept of simply located particles of matter? The theory which Whitehead proposed was that the ultimate facts with which science deals are 'events': 'the ultimate facts of nature in terms of which all physical and biological explanation must be expressed, are events connected by their spatio-temporal relations'.[4] Nature as it is given for sense-awareness is not constituted by simply located bits of matter.

The immediate fact for awareness is the whole occurrence of nature. It is nature as an event present for sense-awareness, and essentially passing. There is no holding nature still and looking at it. . . . Thus

[1] C N 28.   [2] C N 28.   [3] C N 46.   [4] P N K 4.

the ultimate fact for sense-awareness is an event. This whole event is discriminated by us into partial events. We are aware of an event which is our bodily life, of an event which is the course of nature within this room, and of a vaguely perceived aggregate of other partial events.[1]

The configuration of entities at an instant, which is admittedly necessary for the mathematical calculations and measurements involved in scientific theory, can be displayed as derivable from 'events' by a process of 'extensive abstraction'. Much of Whitehead's work at this time was concerned with the careful, logically exact elaboration of the theory of 'extensive abstraction'. For our present purposes, however, it is not necessary to discuss this theory.

By taking 'event' as the ultimate facts Whitehead was able to fulfil the requirements that a state of change be an intrinsic feature of the ultimate facts. Furthermore, with the recognition that it is an intrinsic feature of events to extend over each other, the character of essential relatedness is also accounted for. But if we are given only these features we will be unable to distinguish between events. Nature must therefore include some other features. Whitehead pointed out that 'sense-awareness also yields to us other factors in nature which are not events. For example, sky-blue is seen as situated in a certain event. . . . My present point is that sky-blue is found in nature with a definite implication in events,. but is not an event itself. Accordingly in addition to events, there are other factors in nature directly disclosed to us in sense-awareness'.[2] These factors he called 'objects', and the elaboration of his theory brought him to the recognition of a number of species of 'objects': perceptual objects, sense objects, physical objects, and scientific objects.

It is of special importance to us to note that in putting forward this theory of 'events' and 'objects' in place of the old simply located material particles, the main considerations in Whitehead's mind were the requirements of scientific theory. And further, his procedure in developing it was essentially that which scientists

[1] C N 14–15.   [2] C N 15.

have adopted in arriving at any of their theories, such as those of atoms, electrons, quanta, electro-magnetic fields, etc. In science theories are advanced in a rather piecemeal fashion, in the light of certain restricted conditions, and specifically to meet those conditions, coherence with other theories frequently being a subordinate consideration.

But while this, which can most fittingly be described as a scientific attitude, characterized Whitehead's procedure in his earlier period, his theory had nevertheless necessarily to be a comprehensive one, because of the fundamental nature of his task. In its origin his theory had been concerned more especially with the requirements of dynamics; but other aspects of scientific theory entered as prominent considerations in elaborating it into a more complete scheme. With this a most important change began occurring in his approach, resulting in the vital shift of his centre of interest mentioned above. In order to achieve the more complete scheme, and to ensure the coherence of his concepts, Whitehead was steadily driven to taking into account considerations other than the purely scientific, considerations which he later came to recognize as being properly *philosophical* ones. The clarification of the obscurities contained in his conceptions, and the more precise working out of the relations, for example, between several events, and between events and objects, brought to light many very special problems and issues which were essentially different from scientific ones. Whitehead's earlier period closed with his clear realization that he would have to take full and explicit account of these specifically philosophical issues and problems, and that this would involve him in a comprehensive *metaphysical* inquiry, in which his previous results would be 'embodied'.

§ 2

THE METAPHYSICAL INQUIRY

It is thus not the case that Whitehead simply lost interest in the fundamental scientific problems. It was precisely these which drove him to the philosophical inquiry for their solution. In his earlier period Whitehead had thought that the spatio-temporal relations of events 'are in the main reducible to the property of events that they can contain (or extend over) other events which are parts of them. In other words, in the place of emphasizing space and time in their capacity of disconnecting, we shall build up an account of their complex essences as derivative from the ultimate ways in which those things, ultimate in science, are interconnected'.[1] In a note appended to the second edition of the *Principles of Natural Knowledge* Whitehead wrote that

the book is dominated by the idea that the relation of extension has a unique preeminence and that everything can be got out of it. During the development of the theme, it gradually became evident that this is not the case. . . . But the true doctrine, that 'process' is the fundamental idea, was not in my mind with sufficient emphasis. Extension is derivative from process, and is required by it.[2]

Also, pursuing further the implication of denying as fundamental the disconnecting or 'separative' character of space-time, and in the endeavour to build up a clearer account of the ways in which the 'complex essences' of events are derivative from their interconnections, Whitehead realized that to events must be ascribed the essential feature of 'unity', a unity which is the outcome of the 'prehensive'[3] character of space-time. Thus 'unity' and 'process' became increasingly recognized as fundamental features of events, and Whitehead moved, in the earlier part of his later

[1] P N K 4.   [2] P N K, 2nd edition, p. 202.
[3] 'Prehensive' is his term in this context for the way in which things are 'together' in space-time, as opposed to the 'separative', that in which they are held apart. Cf. S M W 80 ff.

period, to 'the analysis of process as the realization of events disposed in an interlocked community. The event is the unit of things real'.[1]

This is a most significant development. Earlier, with the conception of extension as the fundamental feature of events, Whitehead had thought of an event as simply any happening, of no specific duration or rapidity: 'the endurance of a block of marble is an event'.[2] These extensive events, he then held, were what constituted the ultimate facts for science. Now he was laying the emphasis on the unity, with the result that an event, as the fundamental fact, came to be rather differently conceived: 'the event is the unit of things real'. In this conception, an 'event' is a much more complex, and concrete, entity than in the earlier theory. When Whitehead had originally put forward his theory of 'events' to replace the old concept of simply located matter, it was to meet the requirements of only certain aspects of scientific theory, more especially that of dynamics. Accordingly it was fairly abstract; and in order to take account of other aspects of scientific theory it had to be considerably 'filled out'. For example, the wave theory, of light and of matter, was not readily interpretable in terms simply of the 'extension' of events. It was considerations such as these that brought him to conceive of events as 'processes of unifying'. It was no longer possible to consider so abstract a conception as was his earlier theory of events as an adequate characterization of the ultimate facts. In other words, the features which he had distinguished, and principally signified by the term 'event', were but some abstract features of the ultimate facts; they did not characterize what was the full concrete nature of these facts. Nor was the expanded concept of events as 'processes of unifying' much of an improvement.

The name '*event*' given to such a unity, draws attention to the inherent transitoriness, combined with the actual unity. But this abstract word cannot be sufficient to characterize what the fact of the reality of an event is in itself.[3]

[1] S M W 189.   [2] P Rel 21.   [3] S M W 116.

This then is the problem which from the point of view of scientific theory is the fundamental one to be tackled: 'what the fact of the reality of an event is in itself'. This is the problem which is clearly brought to the fore by modern science: 'what are the concrete facts which exhibit this mathematical attribute of wave-vibration?'[1]

That this is the fundamental problem was recognized by Whitehead from yet another point of view: the obscurities and difficulties of his earlier concepts are clearly bound up with their abstractness, and it is not possible to define or in any precise way understand in what respects they are abstract except on the basis of an adequate comprehension of the concrete nature of the ultimate facts.

This problem of the nature of the ultimate concrete fact, it was now completely clear to Whitehead, was far from being a scientific one. The task which he had previously set himself, of developing a new concept of ultimate fact to replace the classical concept of simply located particles of matter, could not be carried out along the lines, and by the procedure he had hitherto attempted. The task, he now saw, is a specifically philosophical one; more precisely, it is a metaphysical one—taking 'metaphysics' here broadly as the investigation of the 'ultimate nature of reality' (this will be clarified in the next two chapters). This inquiry involves its own special set of issues and problems, to be dealt with by its own methods.

The final problem is to conceive a complete [παντελής] fact. We can only form such a conception in terms of fundamental notions concerning the nature of reality. We are thrown back upon philosophy.[2]

Whitehead's mature conception of 'complete fact' is presented in *Process and Reality*. The 'fundamental notions' in terms of which this conception is formed 'involve some divergence from antecedent philosophical thought',[3] and are often expressed in a somewhat novel and unfamiliar terminology, with the result that they have usually been found not very easy to grasp. This

---

[1] A I 200.   [2] A I 203.   [3] P R 24 [27].

difficulty is intensified by the structure of the book, which is admirable for its purpose—namely, to investigate all the major philosophical problems in elaborate detail in terms of his fundamental notions—but which does not 'introduce' those notions by showing in any extensive way how they have been arrived at. The book starts off with a highly compressed, summary statement of the fundamental concepts, a statement so compressed, as Whitehead himself acknowledges, that the rest of the book is required for 'rendering this summary intelligible',[1] and in the subsequent discussion of each of these notions all the rest are presupposed.

Nor does Whitehead, in any other of his writings, provide an 'introductory exposition'. What is often mistaken for this are his discussions of the philosophical problems involved in modern science, especially in *Science and the Modern World* and the two lectures *Nature and Life*.[2] For in these writings a consideration of the philosophical problems of science leads up to his 'fundamental notions' as solutions to those problems. The impression is often gained, even from Whitehead's express statements, that these notions have been arrived at by inference from the scientific situation. For example, he states[3] that

it is equally possible to arrive at this organic conception of the world if we start from the fundamental notions of modern physics, instead of, as above, from psychology and physiology. In fact by reason of my own studies in mathematics and mathematical physics, I did in fact arrive at my convictions in this way. Mathematical physics presumes in the first place an electro-magnetic field of activity pervading space and time. The laws which condition this field are nothing else than the conditions observed by the general activity of the flux of the world, as it individualizes itself in the events.

But the last sentence makes it clear, as indeed Whitehead frequently insists,[4] that the data of mathematical physics are here being *interpreted* in terms of a certain system of philosophical

---

[1] P R 24[27].　　[2] Also published as Chapters VII and VIII in *Modes of Thought*.
[3] S M W 189–90.
[4] As will be shown in § 6 below. Cf. also A I 198, 284, F R 57, etc.

concepts, concepts which have been otherwise arrived at, namely by a specifically philosophical procedure. In fact, this 'interpretation' is the essential purpose of these writings. That is, they are concerned to investigate the ultimate problems of science in the light of, and in terms of his fundamental philosophical notions.

These writings are therefore not properly 'introductory' to Whitehead's philosophical concepts. An introductory exposition is highly desirable. It is required to show how Whitehead arrived at his metaphysical concepts by bringing out what the specific philosophical issues were which he primarily had in mind, what the problems were which led him to those concepts as their solution, and the procedure, the method, he followed. This is the kind of exposition of Whitehead's ideas attempted in this book. It must be pointed out, however, that what we shall be doing is not an inferential construction of Whitehead's procedure. On the contrary, it will be an exposition of what he has himself explicitly stated, chiefly in *Process and Reality*, in a variety of contexts, and often in brief and summary references, and which thus, for 'introductory' purposes, require to be specially brought out and assembled.

CHAPTER II

The Ontological Principle

---

§ 3

THE BASIC METAPHYSICAL PROBLEM

In declaring that 'the final problem is to conceive a complete [παντελής] fact' Whitehead is placing himself fully in the great philosophical tradition. This is further evidenced by the next sentence in the passage quoted in the previous chapter:[1] 'we can only form such a conception in terms of fundamental notions concerning the nature of reality'. For in these two sentences Whitehead is stating the basic and essential metaphysical problem of which Aristotle has given the classic formulation:[2]

And indeed the question which was raised of old and is raised now and always, and is always the subject of doubt, namely, what being is [τί τὸ ὄν], is just the question: what is substance [οὐσία]? For it is this that some assert to be one, others more than one, and that some assert to be limited, others unlimited. And so we also must consider chiefly and primarily and almost exclusively what that is which *is* in this sense.

When Whitehead says the problem is 'to conceive a complete fact' he means thereby what Aristotle meant in declaring the problem to be: 'what that is which *is* in this sense'. Aristotle's phrase 'what that is' can be transcribed 'the nature of that', so

---

[1] P. 14 above.   [2] *Metaphysics*, Z, I, 1028^b 2–8. Translated by W. D. Ross.

17

that in his formulation the metaphysical problem is that of finding 'the nature of that which *is* in this sense'. Whitehead's statement can be reformulated in the same terms: the problem is to find 'the nature of a complete fact'.

By 'a complete fact' Whitehead means precisely what Aristotle meant by the *that* which '*is* in this sense'. This becomes clear when we analyse the respective phrases in detail. In Greek the phrase which Sir David Ross has translated as 'what that is which *is* in this sense' reads: εἰπεῖν περὶ τοῦ οὕτως ὄντος θεωρητέον τί ἐστιν. This is an extremely difficult phrase to translate adequately. The 'that' refers to *being*, and Joseph Owens has accordingly rendered this passage: '*what* Being in this sense *is*'.[1] 'This sense' refers to οὐσία, and H. Tredennick has thus translated this passage: 'to investigate the nature of "being" in the sense of substance'.[2] The word 'substance' is most unsatisfactory as a translation of οὐσία,[3] and I shall therefore keep to the use of the Greek word. These three translations together help to bring out the full meaning of Aristotle's sentence. For our immediate purposes the wording of the Ross translation is the most useful.

The problem, Aristotle says, is: 'what that is which *is* in this sense'. That is to say, the problem is to discover or determine the nature of something, namely, of 'that which *is*'. The clause 'in this sense' specifies the sense of '*is*': as we have noted, it refers to οὐσία, to 'being' in the sense of οὐσία. By this he means 'being' or 'existence' in the primary and full sense of the term. This is brought out partly by the word οὐσία itself, and partly by the sentence as a whole: we are concerned with a 'that' in the sense of οὐσία. Οὐσία is a noun formed from the verb εἶναι, 'to be'. It is a word which combines the abstractness of 'being' expressed by the word 'beingness', with the concreteness of a particular individual. This is the special precise meaning which the term

[1] J. Owens, *The Doctrine of Being in the Aristotelian Metaphysics* (Toronto, Pontifical Institute of Mediaeval Studies, 1951), p. 193.

[2] Loeb Classical Library.

[3] On this see the extremely good discussion by Owens. *op. cit.*, Chapter 4, pp. 65–74.

οὐσία came to have in Aristotle's metaphysics.[1] It is Aristotle's term for that particular entity or individual thing which exists in the complete sense of the word 'exist'. As Etienne Gilson has put it:[2]

Whatever other name it may bear, reality always is for him [Aristotle] a particular and actually existing thing, that is, a distinct ontological unit which is able to subsist in itself and can be defined in itself: not man in himself, but this individual man whom I can call Peter or John.

It is exactly this which Whitehead means in using the phrase 'a complete fact'. He has indicated[3] that this is his rendering of Plato's τῷ παντελῶς ὄντι.[4] Whitehead uses the word 'fact' here and not 'being' in order to bring out that it is a particular concrete thing he has in mind, for the word 'being' does not necessarily connote this. On the contrary, 'being' is thoroughly ambiguous.[5] It *can* be understood as signifying a concrete existent, but it can also have the meaning—to use Gilson's words—of 'a property common to all that can rightly be said to be'. This 'being as such' is readily capable of hypostatization; it can then be regarded as itself an ultimate existent, 'more real' than the concrete existing things. Further, even if 'being' be not thus hypostatized, it is very easy to confuse its use as a gerund with that as a past participle in, for example, the phrase 'the being of a thing'. In the former it would refer to the 'nature' or 'essence' of the thing; in the latter to 'the fact that' the thing exists. All this ambiguity has, in much of the philosophical thought of the past, led to grave difficulties and error through the implicit shifting from one meaning to the other.

[1] Cf. Owens, *op. cit.*, *passim*, and E. Gilson, *Being and Some Philosophers* (Toronto, Pontifical Institute of Mediaeval Studies, 1949), p. 42.

[2] Gilson, *op. cit.*, p. 42.   [3] A I 203, note.   [4] Cf. *Sophist*, 248 E.

[5] Cf. Gilson, *op. cit.*, p. 2–3, on what he speaks of as 'the fundamental ambiguity of the notion of *being*': 'In a first acceptation, the word being is a noun. As such, it signifies either *a being* (that is, the substance, nature, and essence of anything existent), or being itself, a property common to all that which can rightly be said to be. In a second acceptation, the same word is the present participle of the verb "*to be*". As a verb, it no longer signifies something that is, nor even existence in general, but rather the very act whereby any given reality actually is, or exists.' Cf. also p. 49.

Whitehead has accordingly avoided the word 'being' in this context. The word 'fact' is, however, also unsatisfactory, but for other reasons. Its chief disadvantage is that it has no direct etymological connection with 'being', 'existing', and this is specifically what Whitehead intends here, as his reference to Plato makes clear. What he means by a 'complete fact' is a 'complete existent', that which exists in the complete sense of the word 'exist'. This is the same as what Gilson was expressing in the passage above by 'a distinct ontological unit which is able to subsist in itself and can be defined in itself'. It is this that Descartes had in mind in defining the *that* with which we are concerned as that 'which requires nothing but itself in order to exist'.[1] Spinoza and Leibniz used very similar words in this connection. It is clear that the factor of 'being', of 'existence', is absolutely central. But it is not 'existence' as such, in the abstract; it is the *existence of a particular*, a 'that'. Moreover, the 'that' which is in question is the that which is possessed of 'full existence', the that which exists 'in and of itself'.

§ 4

THE ONTOLOGICAL PRINCIPLE

Whitehead is thus in full agreement with Aristotle as to what constitutes the ultimate metaphysical problem. To them both it is the problem of determining the nature of 'that' which is the 'complete existent', the 'fully existing' entity. Aristotle points out (in the passage we have been discussing) that the perennial metaphysical problem is that of the nature of 'being'; not, however, simply 'being' as such, but 'being' in the sense of a 'complete existent', οὐσία. This is the core of his polemic, in his *Metaphysics*, against Plato. He insists that the 'that', the ὄντως ὄν, which is the primary concern of metaphysics is, in Gilson's words, 'a particular

---

[1] *Principles of Philosophy*, I, 51, Haldane & Ross transl.

and actually existing thing'; it cannot, as Plato held, be a 'form' or 'the Forms'. 'Forms', Aristotle maintains against Plato, are 'forms of' something; they are not themselves individually existent things. That is, forms only *exist as* the forms of the things which are the complete existents, those things whose existence or being is not a 'dependent' existence as is that of the forms.

The recognition that it is these 'fully existent' things which are the primary concern of the metaphysical inquiry, Whitehead also maintains to be of absolutely fundamental importance if the inquiry is not to go seriously astray from the beginning. Accordingly he states it as a specific 'principle', and makes explicit appeal to it throughout:[1]

The general Aristotelian principle is maintained that, apart from things that are actual, there is nothing—nothing either in fact or in efficacy.

Whitehead here uses the phrase 'the things that are actual' for what in the previously quoted passage he had called 'complete facts'. In *Process and Reality* Whitehead employs the word 'actual' explicitly to indicate these particular things. In explaining his usage he points out that 'Descartes [in *Meditation* I] uses the phrase *res vera* in the same sense as that in which I have used the term "actual". It means "existence" in the fullest sense of that term, beyond which there is no other'.[2] Thus the 'things that are actual' are the things which exist in the fullest sense of 'existence'.

This Aristotelian principle—which Whitehead terms the 'ontological principle'—asserts that these 'actual things' are the truly and fully existent things, and that whatever else exists, does so in a sense dependent upon, and derivative from, that of 'actual' things. This principle clearly requires detailed discussion.

That there is 'being' or 'existence' in senses other than that of the existence of οὐσία or an 'actual' thing, both Whitehead and Aristotle acknowledge. We speak, for example, of the existence or being of forms, of characters, thoughts, ideas, etc. etc. Grammatically these appear as nouns, and are distinguished as in some respects 'things'. In English the word 'entity' has come to be used

[1] P R 54 [64].   [2] P R 103 [116].

for 'thing' in this very general sense.[1] It is derived from the Latin *esse*, 'to be', and denotes anything which 'is' or 'exists', in any sense of 'being' or 'existing'; anything of which we can say: 'it is . . .'. Since we do think about and thus distinguish a large number of 'entities' which do indubitably 'exist' in some sense or other, Whitehead explicitly and technically accepts this usage of 'entity' in this completely general sense; philosophically he regards it as entirely justified.

Then, to distinguish those entities with which metaphysics is primarily concerned from all others, Whitehead employs the term 'actual'. The word 'actual', in Whitehead's usage, connotes 'existence' in the 'full' as opposed to the 'dependent' sense. Accordingly, a 'thing which is actual', an 'actual thing', or more precisely, an 'actual entity', is an entity which is a 'fully existent' entity. That is to say, the word 'actual' in the phrase 'actual entity' is intended to distinguish, as fully existent, the entity in question from all other entities. This use of 'actual' is in conformity with present-day English usage, but as we shall see later,[2] Whitehead provides an additional, properly philosophical justification for his use of this word in this special technical sense.

The term 'actual entity' is thus Whitehead's equivalent of Aristotle's οὐσία. Whitehead has coined this term because the traditional term 'substance', which has been used not only as the translation of Aristotle's οὐσία, but also generally in traditional philosophy for the ultimate existent, is so extremely unsatisfactory and misleading. Etymologically it fails to bring out or suggest that on which both Aristotle and Whitehead insist in their respective terms, namely, the ultimate sense of 'existence' or 'being' as the fundamental feature of this entity. On the contrary, both etymologically and by long philosophical tradition

---

[1] Cf. C N 5: ' "Entity" is simply the Latin equivalent for "thing" unless some arbitrary distinction is drawn between the two for technical purposes.' Also S M W 178–9: 'The notion of "entity" is so general that it may be taken to mean anything that can be thought about. You cannot think about a mere nothing; and the something which is an object of thought may be called an "entity". In this sense a function is an entity.'

[2] § 10 below.

22

the word 'substance' stresses other features which Aristotle as well as Whitehead reject as not being fundamental. Leibniz too had strongly felt the unsatisfactoriness of the term 'substance' and coined the term 'monad'. Although more satisfactory, Whitehead has preferred not to adopt it, partly because it has become so exclusively associated with Leibniz's philosophy, but mainly because etymologically it lays the emphasis on an aspect, that of 'unity', which Whitehead does not regard as the most fundamental.

For similar reasons Whitehead also avoids the traditional terms 'the real' and 'reality'. The term 'actual entity' expresses more precisely than its alternatives what, by the ontological principle, is the ὄντως ὄν ('beingly being'), the 'really real'. It is to be observed that Whitehead gains this precision by taking advantage, for technical purposes, of the English language possessing other words as equivalents for the verb 'to be' and its derivatives. The verb 'to exist' is of special importance in this connection; with it the ambiguities of the word 'being' can be more readily avoided.[1]

The 'ontological' principle, as the etymology of the word indicates, is the principle concerned with 'existence' or 'being'. Note that Whitehead speaks of it as *the* ontological principle, meaning thereby that it is the ultimate principle concerning 'being' or 'existence'; it constitutes the fundamental assertion about 'existence' or 'being'. This is that 'existence' or 'being', in the sense in which metaphysics is primarily concerned with it, is the existence or being of 'actual entities' or οὐσίαι. These are all that, in the full sense of 'to be' or 'exist', *are:* 'apart from the things that are actual, there is nothing—nothing either in fact or in efficacy'. Whitehead's phrase 'apart from' is ambiguous: in one sense it means that actual entities alone exist, in the full 'actual' sense of 'exist'. But in a second sense it means that whatever other entities exist, they do not exist 'apart from', i.e. in separation from, actual entities but as dependent upon actual entities.

---

[1] This enables him to achieve a clearer and unambiguous formulation of the essential metaphysical problem and of the nature of metaphysics, as will be further shown in the next chapter.

Further, involved in the ontological principle, and specifically intended in its statement here, is the rejection of the view that there is some kind of entity—for example, some kind of hypostatized 'being'—which is not a concrete existing thing, an 'actual entity', but which is yet somehow 'more real' than concrete actual entities. This is part of what Whitehead has in mind when writing (in the above-quoted passage) that by 'actual' in 'actual entity' he 'means "existence" in the fullest sense of the term, *beyond which there is no other*'.

It is of the utmost importance to be clear about the full meaning and implications of the ontological principle. Basically it is the affirmation, first, that some entities are 'actual', i.e. fully existent entities—or that at least one entity is 'actual'; and secondly, that actual entities 'form the ground from which all other types of existence are derivative and abstracted'.[1] That is to say, since actual entities are all that, in the strict full sense, exist or are, all other entities 'exist' only in a sense derivative from the existence of actual entities. Thus according to the ontological principle, 'the actual world is built up of actual [entities]', and 'whatever [other] things there are in any sense of "existence", are derived by abstraction from actual [entities]'.[2]

In its basic sense, therefore, the ontological principle is the statement of the explicit recognition or appreciation that the fully existent, i.e. 'actual', entities are all that, in the complete sense of 'existence' or 'being' *are*. This statement is not, however, a mere tautology. It means that in the *full* sense of 'to be' or 'to exist', other than actual entities there just simply is *nothing*—non-entity, non-being, non-existence, sheer nothingness. As Whitehead has put it, 'in separation from actual entities there is nothing, merely nonentity—"The rest is silence"'.[3] In using the phrase 'in separation from' or 'apart from' actual entities, Whitehead is acknowledging the existence of other types of entities, but is making it clear that they do not exist as themselves independent actualities. That is to say, although other types of entity do exist, they are (i.e. exist as) either 'ingredients in' actual entities, or, in a sense

[1] P R 103 [116].   [2] P R 101 [113].   [3] P R 58 [68].

to be explained more fully later, 'derivative from' actual entities. So that whatever there is, in any sense of 'is' or 'exist', either is an actual entity or has its locus in some actual entity or actual entities. Thus every other type of entity is referable to some actual entity for its existence. Only by recognizing this dependence can other types of entities be said to 'be' or 'exist' in any sense whatever.

The recognition of the ontological principle has been somewhat fitful in the history of philosophy. It has been departed from or ignored as often as it has been adhered to. Its recognition—but not necessarily explicit formulation as a 'principle'—has, however, been characteristic of all the great metaphysicians. For example, in his excellent summary of Leibniz's philosophy, Gottfried Martin writes:[1]

> The monad becomes the central concept of Leibniz's ontology: for him all reality is involved in the existence of individual monads one by one. Real existence is only possible as the individual existence of a monad or of a modification of an individual monad. This is Leibniz's fundamental ontological thesis.

The importance and value of the explicit formulation of the ontological principle can hardly be overstressed. In the first place, it clarifies what that is which is the primary concern of metaphysics, and keeps it clearly in view; and secondly, it assists in preventing a confusion of other types of entity with actual entities, or in other words, it assists in guarding against mistaking other types of entities for actual entities. Whitehead has called this confusing or mistaking the 'Fallacy of Misplaced Concreteness'.[2] It is an insidious fallacy, responsible for a great deal of error in philosophical thought throughout its entire history. It is a fallacy which is facilitated and promoted by language, for any 'entity' can be the grammatical subject of a sentence, and is thus very readily treated implicitly, if not explicitly, as an actuality.[3] We

[1] G. Martin, *Kant's Metaphysics and Theory of Science*, translated from the German by P. G. Lucas (Manchester University Press, 1955), p. 2.

[2] Cf. P R 9 [11], S M W 64 ff. and S M W 72.

[3] Whitehead uses 'an actuality' as a synonym for an 'actual entity'.

have already noted that the word 'being', by virtue of its ambiguity, is very liable to result in this fallacy.

In taking the ontological principle as fundamental Whitehead explicitly returns to a standpoint which characterized philosophy prior to the introduction of the 'subjectivist bias' by Descartes. This had brought epistemology into the foreground; epistemology became basic to the whole philosophical enterprise. For on this standpoint all that we can be completely certain of is our experiencing, now. Accordingly the central problem becomes how we can justifiably proceed from the subjective experiencing to external existents; how one can, for example, validly infer from perception to the existence of external things. The consequence of the adoption of this standpoint is that modern philosophy has been haunted by the solipsist difficulty, from which the only escape is the irrational appeal to 'practice' or what Santayana has called 'animal faith'.

Whitehead maintains that it follows from the ontological principle that in its predominant characteristic modern philosophy has been in error.[1] For according to this principle our perceptions, our 'impressions of sensation', cannot be 'produced by the creative power of the mind' (to use Hume's phrase[2]), but must be derivative from some actual entity. In other words, our perceptions, our sensa, etc., cannot be of entirely subjective origination, 'belonging to the mind only', for if they were it would in fact mean that they came into existence *de novo*, 'out of nowhere'. But according to the ontological principle this is impossible. As Whitehead has put it, 'according to the ontological principle there is nothing which floats into the world from nowhere. Everything in the actual world is referable to some actual entity';[3] 'it is a contradiction in terms to assume that some explanatory fact can float into the actual world out of nonentity. Nonentity is nothingness. Every explanatory fact refers to the decision and to the efficacy of an actual thing'.[4] Our percepts and concepts, our sensa and 'ideas' ('explanatory

[1] This will be further discussed in some detail in Part Three below.
[2] Cf. *Treatise*, Book III, Section V.   [3] P R 345 [373].   [4] P R 63 [73].

The Ontological Principle

facts', 'reasons'), must in any complete analysis be derivative from other actualities; they cannot be subjectively generated.

This implication of the ontological principle is in full accord with the tacit presuppositions according to which we live and act. As Whitehead says, 'the common sense of mankind conceives that all its notions ultimately refer to actual entities, or as Newton terms them, "sensible objects" '.[1] Despite their explicit theories to the contrary, this presupposition frequently comes to the fore in the thought of philosophers. Thus, Whitehead points out, the ontological principle 'underlies Descartes' dictum: "For this reason, when we perceive any attribute, we therefore conclude that some existing thing or substance to which it may be attributed is necessarily present" '.[2] In this dictum Descartes is inconsistent with the subjectivism which dominates his thinking. A similar inconsistency with his dominant subjectivist sensationalism is found in Locke's doctrine that external things have the 'power' to produce sensory ideas in us.

But in this doctrine Locke is in full accord with the ontological principle. Whitehead declares that in his own statement of it[3]

the 'ontological principle' broadens and extends a general principle laid down by John Locke in his *Essay* (II, XXIII, § 7), when he asserts that 'power' is 'a great part of our complex ideas of substances'. The notion of 'substance' is transformed into that of 'actual entity'; and the notion of 'power' is transformed into the principle that the reasons for things are always to be found in the composite nature of definite actual entities—in the nature of God for reasons of the highest absoluteness, and in the nature of definite temporal actual entities for reasons which refer to a particular environment. The ontological principle can be summarized as: no actual entity, then no reason.

This is of particular significance for the whole philosophical enterprise as such. This enterprise, as we shall see in more detail in the next chapter, is the pursuit of rationalism to its fullest extent: it is the endeavour to discover the final 'reasons' for things. According to the ontological principle these 'reasons' are to be discovered in 'the composite nature of definite actual

[1] P R 99 [111].   [2] P R 54–5 [64]. Cf. also P R 103 [116].   [3] P R 25 [28].

entities'. That is, these actual entities themselves embody the 'reasons' which philosophy seeks. These particular 'reasons' are nothing other than the 'nature', the 'what' of actual entities which constitutes the essential problem of metaphysics. Thus the notions, the ideas, in terms of which we are to conceive the nature of actual entities must be derivative from the actual entities themselves. The ontological principle therefore involves the repudiation of any 'subjectivist' doctrine of 'forms of thought' belonging essentially to the knowing mind, such as was asserted by Kant in his Copernican revolution' and was before him already implicit in Descartes and in British empiricism. Whitehead by contrast adopts the 'objectivist' standpoint of Greek and mediaeval philosophy. Thereby too Whitehead accepts metaphysics as the basic philosophical inquiry.

CHAPTER III

Metaphysics and its Procedure

§ 5

THE NATURE OF METAPHYSICS

In the philosophical tradition there has been broad agreement about what metaphysics is, with, nevertheless, an appreciable difference of view as to its precise nature and method. Whitehead's conception of it can therefore not be simply taken for granted, and a somewhat detailed discussion is desirable. This is the more so since Whitehead's metaphysical notions are, in part at least, determined by his conception of the nature of the inquiry and its procedure. The argument of the following chapters will accordingly be more readily and adequately understood if we have some explicit appreciation of what Whitehead conceives himself to be doing.

Whitehead understands by 'metaphysics' that inquiry which Aristotle called 'first philosophy'. He agrees with the implications of this phrase, namely, that metaphysics is philosophy in that aspect in which it is concerned with 'first principles', 'first questions', with the basic and primary problems and issues. These are those concerning the nature of 'ultimate fact', the ὄντως ὄν: 'the final problem is to conceive a complete fact'; the problem is 'what that is which *is* in this sense'. I have called metaphysics an 'aspect' of philosophy explicitly because Whitehead uses the term 'philosophy' generically: there is one inquiry, namely 'philosophy', with a number of subdivisions, metaphysics, epistemology, cosmology, ethics, aesthetics, etc. That is to say, 'philosophy' is not a mere blanket term to cover a number of similar, though independent and autonomous inquiries. On the contrary, Whitehead rejects the view that these are independent and autonomous; he maintains that they are all interdependent, parts or aspects of one discipline, with metaphysics fundamental to them all.

Metaphysics is fundamental to the whole philosophical endeavour because, in the final analysis, the particular conception entertained of a 'complete fact' or ὄντως ὄν determines the answers to all the more special groups of problems: those of knowledge and truth, of judgement, of value, of the good, beauty, virtue, duty, of social organization, etc. etc. In each of the branches or subdivisions of philosophy some particular aspect of the whole is being stressed or specially dealt with, the connection with or dependence upon others being tacitly or explicitly presupposed. We cannot here discuss this point in further detail; some illustration of it will, however, be given later.

Our particular concern is metaphysics as that aspect of philosophy in which the central problem is 'to conceive a complete fact'. Whitehead has pointed out, as we have seen, that 'we can only form such a conception in terms of fundamental notions concerning the nature of reality'. Thus in order to conceive 'complete fact' or the ὄντως ὄν it is necessary to discover the appropriate 'fundamental notions'. This, however, is not something different: the endeavour to find the appropriate fundamental notions *is* the endeavour to conceive the nature of 'complete fact'; and this endeavour is that aspect of philosophy which is metaphysics. Whitehead has accordingly given the following definition:[1]

Speculative Philosophy is the endeavour to frame a coherent, logical, necessary system of general ideas in terms of which every element of our experience can be interpreted.

[1] P R 3 [4], and A I 285.

Metaphysics and its Procedure

Or, slightly differently,[1]

> By 'metaphysics' I mean the science which seeks to discover the general ideas which are indispensably relevant to the analysis of everything that happens.

We shall see later why Whitehead uses the term 'speculative philosophy'; it is not simply synonymous with 'metaphysics', but for the moment the distinction need not concern us. Metaphysics is the endeavour to discover the 'general ideas'. In this definition, and especially in the former formulation, Whitehead specifies more precisely what he means by 'fundamental notions'. These notions must be 'general', for they must be such that in terms of them 'every element of our experience can be interpreted'. Further, they must be coherent, logical, necessary, and framed into a system. We must consider this in detail.

What does Whitehead mean by 'general ideas'? A full account will involve the explication of all the other items, namely, 'coherent', 'necessary', etc., since these specify the particular kind of 'general ideas' in question. For it must be clear that the concern of metaphysics is not 'general ideas' as such; every kind of conceptual knowledge, all science, involves 'general ideas'. Whitehead has pointed out[2] that

> the first step in science and philosophy has been taken when it is grasped that every routine exemplifies a principle which is capable of statement in abstraction from its particular exemplifications.

He has used the word 'routine', but might as well have said 'happening', 'event', 'fact'. The point is that 'facts' etc. exhibit features which are 'general', in the sense of not being peculiar to those particular facts, but capable of exemplification in other facts. These 'general features' or 'principles' are capable of being 'conceived', 'entertained in idea', 'stated in abstraction'—the detailed philosophical explanation of this will be given later;[3] here it suffices to note that it is in accord with the ontological principle. In this connection the revealing ambiguity of the word

[1] R M 72, footnote.   [2] A I 180-1.   [3] § 35.

'principle' should be observed: it means a feature of a thing, either as such, or as conceived.

Whitehead points out further[1] that philosophy and science are both concerned with the understanding of individual facts as illustrations of general principles. The principles are understood in the abstract, and the facts are understood in respect to their embodiment of the principles.

That is to say, philosophy and science are basically the endeavour to *understand things in terms of general principles*. This understanding in terms of general principles is, in Whitehead's doctrine, what *rationalism* essentially is; it is what constitutes rationalism. 'Rationalism' is the search for 'reasons', for 'grounds', 'causes' in Aristotle's wide sense. These 'reasons' are the 'general principles' exhibited by things. Thus anything—an entity or an event—is *rationally understood* when the principles or reasons it embodies are discerned or discriminated. In other words, with the discrimination of the principles we *understand*, and can *explain* why, for what reasons, things are as they are, and events happen as they do. For example, we wish to understand why, on a particular occasion, the sun is occulted in a cloudless sky. The 'reason' is given in terms of a set or system of general principles exemplified by the relative motions of sun, moon, and earth, stated as scientific laws, and expressed in mathematical formulae.

We shall leave the distinction between science and philosophy for later discussion;[2] for the moment we shall restrict our attention to that aspect of philosophy which is metaphysics. The 'facts' with which metaphysics is concerned are the 'complete facts', the ὄντως ὄντα, οὐσίαι, what Whitehead has termed 'actual entities'. The endeavour of metaphysics is to understand the nature of its 'facts', i.e. actual entities, in terms of the general principles they embody, *qua* actual entities. That is to say, metaphysics seeks to understand the nature of an actual entity in terms of those of its general principles or features which it shares with all other actual entities whatever, those of its features which are generic to all

[1] A I 179.　　　[2] § 46 below.

actual entities. These are the features or general principles of actual entities which constitute their 'nature', 'what' they are, their 'essence'.

The *complete* generality of the features or principles of actual entities with which metaphysics is concerned must be carefully noted. For actual entities also exhibit many features or principles of varying degrees of restricted generality, ones which thus characterize only some actual entities. These more restricted general principles or features are those determining the more special characteristics of various groups and types of actual entities, those for example which account for varieties of behaviour, and which are thus the explicit concern of the special sciences. To put it another way, besides all their more special features, actual entities exhibit features which they possess *qua* actual entities, and which thus constitute their nature as actual entities.

This is a point which must be specially stressed, namely that the features which actual entities possess *qua* actual entities are those constituting their 'nature', 'what' they are. Also, these features, the generic features of actual entities, are those of complete generality. Because metaphysics is primarily and essentially concerned with these generic features of actual entities, Whitehead's consistent use of the term 'metaphysics', and the adjective 'metaphysical', is with specific reference to these features. As he explicitly states: 'the metaphysical characteristics of an actual entity—in the proper general sense of "metaphysics"— should be those which apply to all actual entities'.[1]

Thus Whitehead could define metaphysics as the study of the completely general or generic features or characteristics of actual entities, the study of actual entities *qua* actual entities. This, and particularly the latter formulation, is a great deal clearer and more specific than the traditional definition of metaphysics as the study of 'being *qua* being', the disadvantage of which hinges on the ambiguity of the term 'being'. Further, it should be noted that in not adopting the ambiguous 'being'-terminology, Whitehead has avoided the kind of difficulty in which Aristotle became

[1] P R 126 [138]. Cf. also P R 274 [294], 279 [300], 408 [441].

involved, and after him much of traditional philosophy, through the identification of 'being' in the sense of οὐσία, with the 'being of things', i.e. with their 'whatness', their 'essence'.[1]

The endeavour to discover the nature of actual entities is the endeavour to 'conceive' actual entities, and this, as Whitehead points out, can only be done in terms of certain 'fundamental notions'. That is to say, the endeavour is to find the appropriate 'ideas'. The method or procedure will be discussed in the following section. What is relevant here is that the problem is that of finding certain 'ideas' which are the 'correct', 'true', 'fitting', 'appropriate' ones. Thus it is necessary to know what kind of ideas are in question, and what are the criteria in terms of which they are to be assessed.

This is precisely what we were beginning to make clear in showing that the ideas in question, because they are the conceptions of the generic features of actual entities, must be *completely general*. Whitehead states this in his definition by the phrase 'general ideas in terms of which every element of our experience can be interpreted'. We shall examine the notion of 'interpretation' presently; in doing so we shall demonstrate that it provides further precise criteria for the assessment of the metaphysical ideas.

To continue the specification of the ideas in question: metaphysics endeavours to frame a *system* of these general ideas. This is so because the ideas it seeks must of necessity be interrelated. This necessary interrelation is what is primarily expressed by their coherence. The notions of 'system' and 'coherence' are correlative.

The 'coherence' of ideas in a system constitutes one of the most important and fundamental criteria, not only in metaphysics, but in all rationalistic enterprise. Whitehead has put this, none too strongly, by saying that 'the requirement of coherence is the great preservative of rationalistic sanity'.[2] For coherence in ideas is intrinsic to rationalism as such; it is that without which there can be no proper rationalistic understanding at all.

This can perhaps most conveniently be brought out by con-

[1] On this see the excellent discussion by Gilson, *op. cit.*, Chapter II, and *passim*.
[2] P R 7 [9]. Cf. also F R 68.

sidering the contrary of 'coherence'. 'Incoherence' is the arbitrary disconnection of principles or ideas. By 'arbitrary disconnection' is meant that the ideas or principles possess no inherent inter-relationship; that is, they do not involve each other. Thus they cannot be brought into a system, it being the very meaning of 'arbitrary disconnection' that there is no principle more general in terms of which they can be brought together—the word 'arbitrary' stresses that there is no 'reason' for the disconnection. For to give such a reason or principle would be to exhibit their interrelationship, thereby negating their supposed disconnection and incoherence. It is therefore clear that incoherence is the frustration of the rationalistic endeavour; it spells the failure of rationalistic understanding—or, at best, it means only partial understanding. The acceptance of incoherence is the essence of 'irrationalism'. In other words, there is irrationalism whenever there is the acceptance, explicit or merely tacit, of an arbitrary disconnection of principles, a 'disconnection without reason'. Irrationalism involves the denial that 'reasons' or general principles are attainable, either at all, or beyond a certain point—usually that which the special sciences happen to have reached. This is the core of 'positivism', the doctrine so widely accepted today in almost all intellectual spheres. It is the basis of the positivistic rejection of metaphysics. Because of its essential irrationalism Whitehead has attacked positivism as treason to philosophy and science alike.[1] It is evident that there can be no 'rational' defence of 'irrationalism'.

[1] Cf., for example, M T 202–3: 'We are left [by the abstractions of physics] with the notion of an activity in which nothing is effected. Also this activity, thus considered, discloses no ground for its own coherence. There is merely a formula for succession. But there is an absence of understandable causation to give a reason for that succession. Of course, it is always possible to work oneself into a state of complete contentment with an ultimate irrationality. The popular positivistic philosophy adopts this attitude.

The weakness of this positivism is the way in which we all welcome the detached fragments of explanation attained in our present stage of civilization. Suppose that a hundred thousand years ago our ancestors had been wise positivists. They sought for no reasons. What they had observed was sheer matter of fact. It was the development of no necessity. They would have searched for no reasons

Whitehead's Metaphysics

In metaphysics, Whitehead writes,[1]

incoherence is the arbitrary disconnection of first principles. In modern philosophy Descartes' two kinds of substance, corporeal and mental, illustrate incoherence. There is, in Descartes' philosophy, no reason why there should not be a one-substance world, only corporeal, or a one-substance world, only mental.

This argument in relation to Descartes and other thinkers will be discussed in some detail in the next chapter. Here we are concerned with it only as an illustration of the application of the criterion of coherence in metaphysics, and with the reason why in this inquiry it is peculiarly fundamental. This is because metaphysics is the search for 'first principles'; that is, it is the search for the ultimate 'reasons'. Metaphysics is rationalism pursued to its limit, to its fullest extent. And it is here that the very basis of rationalism is laid bare. This is the point Whitehead was making in saying that[2]

faith in reason is the trust that the ultimate natures of things lie together in a harmony which excludes mere arbitrariness. It is the faith that at the base of things we shall not find mere arbitrary mystery.

In slightly different words:[3]

That we fail to find in experience any elements intrinsically incapable of exhibition as examples of general theory, is the hope of rationalism.

underlying facts immediately observed. Civilization would never have developed. Our varied powers of detailed observation of the world would have remained dormant. For the peculiarity of a reason is that the intellectual development of its consequences suggests consequences beyond the topics already observed. The extension of observation waits upon some dim apprehension of reasonable connection. For example, the observation of insects on flowers dimly suggests some congruity between the natures of insects and of flowers, and thus leads to a wealth of observation from which whole branches of science have developed. But a consistent positivist should be content with the observed facts, namely insects visiting flowers. It is a fact of charming simplicity. There is nothing further to be said upon the matter, according to the doctrine of a positivist. At present the scientific world is suffering from a bad attack of muddled-headed positivism, which arbitrarily applies its doctrine and arbitrarily escapes from it. The whole doctrine of life in nature has suffered from this positivistic taint.' Cf. also P R 7 [8], S M W Chapter I and *passim*, F R *passim*, A I Chapters 7 and 8.

    [1] P R 8 [9–10].   [2] S M W 23.   [3] P R 57 [67]. Cf. also F R 29.

This hope is not a metaphysical premise. It is the faith which forms the motive for the pursuit of all sciences alike, including metaphysics.

This 'hope', 'faith', or 'trust', is not a premise from which metaphysical theory can start; rather 'it is an ideal which is seeking satisfaction',[1] for it is intrinsically inherent in rationalism as such. That is to say, there can be no rational endeavour at all without the acceptance, tacit or explicit, of this aim or ideal. It is evident that a 'rational' denial of it must be self-contradictory.

In Whitehead's view the fundamental importance of the requirement of coherence in metaphysics is an implication of the essential character of the inquiry: that it is the pursuit of rationalism to its limit. It is the requirement of coherence which he is stressing in saying that 'it is the ideal of speculative philosophy that its fundamental notions shall not seem capable of abstraction from each other'.[2] And this rests, in part, on the recognition of 'an essential interconnectedness of things', as is expressed for example in the following passage:[3]

In the world, there are elements of order and disorder, which thereby presuppose an essential interconnectedness of things. For disorder shares with order the common characteristic that they imply many things interconnected.

Accordingly, he maintains 'that no entity can be conceived in complete abstraction from the system of the universe, and that it is the business of speculative philosophy to exhibit this truth'.[4] The essential interconnectedness of things involves that the ideas in terms of which they are conceived must be interconnected, that they 'shall not seem capable of abstraction from each other'. Thus, Whitehead explains, ' "coherence", as here employed, means that the fundamental ideas, in terms of which the scheme is developed, presuppose each other so that in isolation they are meaningless'.[5]

---

[1] We shall see in the following section that Whitehead rejects the conception that the procedure of metaphysics is to start from premises which are assumed to be 'self-evident', 'clear and distinct', etc.

[2] P R 3 [5].   [3] A I 292.   [4] P R 3 [5].   [5] P R 3 [5].

The point is that the metaphysical ideas, as we have seen, are those of complete generality; thus there cannot be others more general. When we are concerned with ideas of less than complete generality, as for example in science, coherence is achieved by ideas of greater generality uniting the others into a system. But the completely general, metaphysical ideas 'are incapable of analysis into factors more far-reaching than themselves. [Accordingly] each must be displayed as necessary to the various meanings of groups of notions, of equal depth with itself'.[1] It is in this way that their unification into a system, and thus their coherence, is achieved. Therefore, in the *framing* of a metaphysical system, coherence is the fundamental requirement: it is what should be aimed at, and is the test constantly to be applied.

With the recognition of the importance of coherence in metaphysics, it is evident that the system of ideas must be 'logical'. Whitehead explains that 'the term "logical" has its ordinary meaning, including "logical" consistency, or lack of contradiction, the definition of constructs in logical terms, the exemplification of general logical notions in specific instances, and the principles of inference'.[2]

The other requirements of metaphysical ideas follow as explications of the foregoing. Thus it is a consequence of the complete generality of the metaphysical ideas that they must be *necessary*. That is to say, because of the complete generality of the metaphysical features of actual entities, these features (and accordingly the ideas expressing them) must be *universal*, and thus necessarily embodied in all things. This *necessity in universality* of the metaphysical principles is what is meant by saying that they are 'not contingent'. Contingency is the mark of principles of some degree of restricted generality, of a generality less than universal. The necessity of metaphysical ideas is constituted by their universality. This means, Whitehead says, that 'the philosophic scheme should be "necessary", in the sense of bearing in itself its own warrant of universality throughout all experience'.[3] The metaphysical

[1] M T I.   [2] P R 3–4 [5].   [3] P R 4 [5].

ideas 'bear their own warrant of universality throughout all experience' by virtue of it being possible to interpret all elements of experience in terms of them.

This is therefore another important test of a metaphysical scheme of ideas, namely, that all items of experience should be able to be interpreted in terms of them. It is clearly necessary to appreciate precisely what is meant by *interpretation* here. By it, Whitehead explains, he means 'that everything of which we are conscious, as enjoyed, perceived, willed, or thought, shall have the character of a particular instance of the general scheme'.[1] That is to say, since the metaphysical principles are those generic to every actual entity, and since by the ontological principle all other entities, events, etc., are derivative from actual entities, it must be possible to exhibit everything as a particular exemplification of a scheme of metaphysical ideas. Philosophical interpretation therefore constitutes one of the most important tests of the *adequacy* of a philosophical scheme.

It is evident that a scheme of metaphysical ideas must at least be *applicable*. The 'applicability' of a metaphysical scheme means that *some* items of experience are interpretable in terms of it. But the applicability of a scheme does not imply its adequacy. Though applicable, it might nevertheless be inadequate, in that it fails to provide an interpretation of some other items of experience.[2] Clearly it must be the ideal of a metaphysical scheme or system to be both 'applicable' and 'adequate'.

The foregoing characteristics of metaphysical ideas, namely, that they must be completely general or universal, and necessary, that they must form a system which is coherent, logical, applicable, and adequate, follow upon the acceptance of the ontological principle which clarifies the fundamental problem and object of metaphysical inquiry. These characteristics thus constitute the requirements which a metaphysical system has to fulfil; they constitute the criteria guiding its construction, as well as those in terms of which it is to be assessed. They are the ideals to be aimed at in the metaphysical endeavour. Whitehead points out,

[1] P R 3 [4].   [2] Cf. P R 4 [5].

however, that they can only be asymptotically approached, never fully achieved. As he puts it:[1]

> Philosophers can never hope finally to formulate these metaphysical first principles. Weakness of insight and deficiencies of language stand in the way inexorably. Words and phrases must be stretched toward a generality foreign to their ordinary usage; and however such elements of language be stabilized as technicalities, they remain metaphors mutely appealing for an imaginative leap.
>
> There is no first principle which is in itself unknowable, not to be captured by a flash of insight. But, putting aside the difficulties of language, deficiency in imaginative penetration forbids progress in any form other than that of an asymptotic approach to a scheme of principles, only definable in terms of the ideal which they should satisfy.

§ 6

THE PROCEDURE OF METAPHYSICS

The endeavour of metaphysics is to conceive the nature of 'complete fact', the ὄντως ὄν, of an 'actual entity'. That is, it seeks to discover the appropriate 'fundamental notions'; it seeks to frame a scheme of 'general ideas'. How does metaphysics proceed to the discovery of the nature of the ὄντως ὄν? By what method does it seek to find the general ideas, the universal features of actual entities?

It has been shown in the previous section that metaphysics is rationalism pursued to its limit. In Whitehead's view this does not mean, however, that the essential method of metaphysics is to proceed deductively from premises. 'Philosophy', he writes,[2] 'has been haunted by the unfortunate notion that its method is dogmatically to indicate premises which are severally clear, distinct, and certain; and to erect upon those premises a deductive

---

[1] P R 4–5 [6].   [2] P R 10 [11–12].

system of thought'. This is a view which had gained renewed prominence with Descartes, under the sway of the realization of the fundamental role of mathematics in the physical sciences. Leibniz went further and projected a 'universal calculus', which has influenced much later philosophy, not least during this century. Whitehead maintains, however, that 'philosophy has been misled by the example of mathematics', and as a result has adopted 'a false estimate of logical procedure in respect to certainty, and in respect to premises'.[1] He insists, on the contrary, that we do not have clear and distinct ideas as starting-points: 'the accurate expression of the final generalities is the goal of discussion and not its origin'.[2] Logical deduction depends upon premises, and it is precisely these which cannot be accepted as initially known and thus adopted as indubitable starting-points. Accordingly, he affirms, 'deductive logic has not the coercive supremacy which is conventionally conceded to it. When applied to concrete instances it is a tentative procedure, finally to be judged by the self-evidence of its issues'.[3]

It is the 'premises' which are finally at issue. This is what Whitehead is wishing to emphasize in saying that 'philosophy is the search for premises. It is not deduction'.[4] Philosophers such as Descartes, Spinoza, and Leibniz have misconceived the method which they have in fact followed in their metaphysical thinking. This is not the deductive procedure prominent in their expositions; their essential method is that by which they reached their premises, and this, when their thinking is carefully examined, is far from being a matter of simply 'dogmatically indicating'. Their fundamental procedure, like that of all other great metaphysicians, is that involved in their 'searching' for the first principles; it is the method by which they 'seek', 'endeavour to find' the ultimate ideas.

This activity of 'seeking', Whitehead maintains, is not something other than 'reason' or 'reasoning': it *is* reason, in its basic form. That is to say, it is not in the deductive procedures, but in the activity of 'seeking' that we have the fundamental aspect of

[1] P R 10 [12, 11].   [2] P R 10 [12].   [3] M T 144.   [4] M T 143.

'reason', of 'rationalism'. It is this which Whitehead speaks of as 'speculative reason'—as opposed to 'deductive' and 'analytical' reason. It is this aspect of 'seeking', of 'searching', that he wishes to emphasize as primary in using the word 'speculative' in 'speculative reason', 'speculative philosophy', etc. We can thus see why in the definition of metaphysics quoted in the previous section, Whitehead wrote: 'Speculative philosophy is the *endeavour to frame . . .*'; metaphysics is 'the science which *seeks to discover . . .*'

What we are particularly concerned with here is what is involved in this conception of 'speculative reason' in respect to 'method'. Whitehead points out that speculative reason must be 'in its essence untrammelled by method',[1] for by its very nature it is the search for method, as well as for 'first principles'. By this he does not mean that there can be no method, that the 'searching' is purely random; he means that the method cannot be a fixed, definite procedure, such as that of deductive logic. It is precisely the 'premises', the 'first principles', which are at issue, and they cannot themselves be arrived at by a deductive procedure which necessarily presupposes them. In this Whitehead is carrying further the old argument that new knowledge is not attainable by the method of the syllogism. The problem is the method by which the 'first principles' are arrived at, and the difficulty is precisely that those 'first principles' include 'principles of method'. Whitehead maintains[2] that the Greeks

discovered the almost incredible secret that the speculative Reason was itself subject to orderly method. They robbed it of its anarchic character without destroying *its function of reaching beyond set bounds.* That is why we now speak of the speculative Reason in the place of Inspiration. Reason appeals to the orderliness of what is reasonable while 'speculation' expresses the transcendence of any particular method. The Greek secret is, how to be bounded by method even in its transcendence. They hardly understood their own discovery, but we have the advantage of having watched it in operation for twenty centuries.

---

[1] F R 51.   [2] F R 52, my italics.

How Whitehead conceives this 'orderly method' of the speculative reason which transcends the more special methods we shall
make clear as we proceed.

Metaphysics is the search for, the endeavour to find, the
generic features of actual entities. By the ontological principle,
we have seen, the actualities themselves embody those features,
which must accordingly be sought in our 'experience' of those
actualities. As Whitehead puts it:[1]

Our datum is the actual world, including ourselves; and this actual
world spreads itself for observation in the guise of the topic of our
immediate experience. The elucidation of immediate experience is
the sole justification for any thought; and the starting-point for thought
is the analytic observation of components of this experience.

That is to say, for the discovery of the generic features of actuality
we must appeal to 'experience'. But this is precisely where the
crucial difficulties lie, not only in respect to method, but also as
to what precisely constitutes 'experience'.[2] In the first place,
the 'analytic observation of the components of immediate
experience' is far from being the relatively easy matter it is all
too frequently assumed to be. On the contrary, Whitehead insists,
it is necessary strongly to resist the supposition 'that the interroga-
tion of experience is a straightforward operation'.[3] Along with
this we must reject the associated assumption that the 'components'
—whatever they may be—are clear-cut, distinct, and readily distinguishable:[4]

There is a conventional view of experience, never admitted when
explicitly challenged, but persistently lurking in the tacit presuppositions. This view conceives conscious experience as a clear-cut knowledge of clear-cut items with clear-cut connections with each other.
This is the conception of a trim, tidy, finite experience uniformly
illuminated. No notion could be further from the truth. In the first
place the equating of experience with clarity of knowledge is against
the evidence. In our own lives, and at any one moment, there is a

[1] P R 5 [6]. Cf. also M T 208.
[2] The latter will be discussed in some detail in Part Three below.
[3] F R 54.   [4] F R 62–3.

focus of attention, a few items in clarity of awareness, but interconnected vaguely and yet insistently with other items in dim apprehension, and this dimness shading off imperceptibly into undiscriminated feeling.

This is not the place to enter into a detailed epistemological discussion; I am only concerned to bring out Whitehead's point that 'we are not conscious of any clear-cut complete analysis of immediate experience, in terms of the various details which comprise its definiteness'.[1] What the 'components' are can be settled, as we shall show, only by a difficult process of 'reasoning', the exact nature of which we are seeking to determine.

Next, Whitehead holds, we should observe that those items which do come into the clarity of consciousness do so by virtue of their variability; in other words, 'factors in our experience are "clear and distinct" in proportion to their variability, provided that they sustain themselves for that moderate period required for importance'.[2] This is because of the way in which conscious discrimination is effected: 'we habitually observe by the method of difference. Sometimes we see an elephant, and sometimes we do not. The result is that an elephant, when present, is noticed. Facility of observation depends on the fact that the object observed is important when present, and sometimes is absent'.[3]

As far as metaphysics is concerned this point is of tremendous importance, for it means that the discovery of the metaphysical features by 'experience' is attendant with peculiar difficulties. The factors which are readily discriminated are the variable, changing, and thus contingent factors; that is to say, those which are not the metaphysical ones. The latter, since they are the generic, universal features of things, are stable and invariable,

[1] P R 5 [6]. [2] M T vii.
[3] P R 5 [6–7]. Cf. also M T 41: 'The first principle of epistemology should be that the changeable, shifting aspects of our relations to nature are the primary topics of conscious observation. This is only common sense; for something can be done about them. The organic permanences survive by their own momentum: our hearts beat, our lungs absorb air, our blood circulates, our stomachs digest. It requires advanced thought to fix attention on such fundamental operations.'

and are accordingly not noticed; 'the necessities are invariable, and for that reason remain in the background of thought, dimly and vaguely'.[1] Thus we cannot rely on simple observation for their discovery. In Whitehead's words,[2]

for the discovery of metaphysics, the method of pinning down thought to the strict systematization of detailed discrimination, already affected by antecedent observation, breaks down. This collapse of the method of rigid empiricism is not confined to metaphysics. It occurs whenever we seek the larger generalities.

That is to say, the difficulty of discrimination applies not only to the metaphysical generalities, but also to the features of somewhat more restricted generality which are the special concern of science. What is most readily discriminated are the comparatively superficial details, those which are on the whole useful for the purposes of daily living. Scientific and philosophical generalities are not discoverable by 'antecedent observation' (which gives us the superficial features), but only by *observation directed by theory*.

Without such a theory, Whitehead points out, 'it is impossible to know what to look for';[3] without a theory we cannot know what, among all that is given, is relevant: 'the relevance of evidence depends upon the theory which is dominating the discussion'.[4] Not only scientific, but also 'philosophical discussion in the absence of a theory has no criterion for the validity of evidence'.[5] As far as science is concerned this has long been recognized in the doctrine of the 'working hypothesis'. Whitehead strongly reaffirms this doctrine:[6]

Such an hypothesis directs observation, and decides on the mutual relevance of various types of evidence. In short, it prescribes method.

---

[1] M T vii. In maintaining this Whitehead is at variance with a great deal of past thought. As he explicitly remarks, A I 225: 'When Descartes, Locke, and Hume undertake the analysis of experience, they utilize those elements in their own experience which lie clear and distinct, fit for the exactitude of intellectual discourse. It is tacitly assumed, except by Plato, that the more fundamental factors will ever lend themselves for discrimination with peculiar clarity. This assumption is here directly challenged.' Cf. also A I 209, and E S P 122.

[2] P R 5 [7].   [3] A I 284.   [4] A I 283.   [5] A I 284.   [6] A I 286.

To venture upon productive thought without such an explicit theory is to abandon oneself to the doctrines derived from one's grandfather.

This doctrine of the 'working hypothesis', Whitehead maintains, applies equally to metaphysics: 'speculative philosophy embodies the method of the "working hypothesis"'.[1] That is to say, the metaphysical generalities are only discoverable by observation guided by a theory as to the nature of those generalities. In saying that *speculative* philosophy *embodies* the method of the "working hypothesis"', Whitehead is asserting that this method is involved in the very nature of 'speculation', of '*speculative* reason'. The method is complex. 'Speculation' refers more particularly to the aspect of *originating* the theory. How do we come by the theory which is our 'hypothesis'? Whence do we derive it? Whitehead's reply is that ultimately it is by 'direct insight' into the nature of our datum, 'the actual world, including ourselves':[2]

We can only appeal to our direct insight—to what Descartes termed, our Inspectio. Our Judgement, that is our Judicium to which Descartes also appealed, requires an Inspection to provide the material from which decision arises.

The process of 'direct insight' cannot be fully analysed until a scheme of metaphysical ideas has been developed, in terms of which such an analysis can be made. However, it must be strongly emphasized that Whitehead does not at all hold 'direct insight' to be some separate and superior form of knowledge; it is but a phase in one whole constituting the method of the working hypothesis, the method by which, in the final analysis, all conceptual knowledge is attained.

Insight into the metaphysical generalities is only reached at an advanced stage of thought, upon the basis of a good deal of antecedent analysis involved in more special fields of knowledge:[3]

In the first place, this construction must have its origin in the generalization of particular factors discerned in particular topics of human interest; for example, in physics, or in physiology, or in psychology, or in aesthetics, or in ethical beliefs, or in sociology, or in languages conceived as storehouses of human experience. In this way the prime requisite, that anyhow there shall be some important application, is secured.

That is to say, starting usually in one such special field of knowledge, certain features are identified, by insight, as likely to be generic; by imaginative generalization these are then constructed into metaphysical general principles. By this method, which Whitehead calls that of 'imaginative rationalization', we are able to discover the constant, invariable necessities which are missed in the employment of the more usual 'method of difference':[1]

the reason for the success of this method of imaginative rationalization is that, when the method of difference fails, factors which are constantly present may yet be observed under the influence of imaginative thought. Such thought supplies the differences which the direct observation lacks. It can even play with inconsistency; and can thus throw light on the consistent, and persistent, elements in experience by comparison with what in imagination is inconsistent with them. The negative judgment is the peak of mentality.

The metaphysical principles arrived at by this imaginative generalization constitute the 'working hypotheses' in terms of which the various items of experience are then to be interpreted. The hypotheses are tested in this process of interpretation, that is, by the extent of their applicability to all experience:[2]

The success of the imaginative experiment is always to be tested by the applicability of its results beyond the restricted locus from which it originated. In default of such extended application, a generalization started from physics, for example, remains merely an alternative expression of notions applicable to physics. The partially successful philosophic generalization will, if derived from physics, find applications in fields of experience beyond physics.

This method of 'imaginative rationalization' is that 'orderly method' by which the 'speculative reason' proceeds. In essence the method consists in direct insight issuing in generalization. This is how Descartes, to give but one example, in fact arrived at his theory of *res extensa* and *res cogitans:* by insight he identified

[1] P R 5–6 [7]. [2] P R 6 [8]. Cf. also S M W 189–90.

'extension' and 'cogitation' respectively as generic features (the former having originated in his work in mathematical physics), and generalized them as the metaphysical features of two kinds of substance or actuality. As we shall see in detail later, Whitehead holds that Descartes' insight was correct, but that his generalization had not been successful: 'cogitation' and 'extension' are not *metaphysical* features of actual entities, though they are indeed features of very wide generality respectively characterizing *some* things.

It should also be noted that this method of 'imaginative generalization' is essentially 'hypothetical'; there can be no indubitable immediate assurance of the correctness of the factor of 'direct insight'. This is why all philosophical, and scientific, investigation is by the method of the 'working hypothesis'. That is to say, the imaginative rationalization has to be taken as an 'hypothesis' and subjected to a careful and elaborate procedure of verification as a most prominent element in the whole process of 'inquiry' or 'investigation'.

In metaphysics, Whitehead holds,

the first requisite is to proceed by the method of generalization so that certainly there is some application; and the test of some success is application beyond the immediate origin. In other words, some synoptic vision has been gained.[1]

The second condition for the success of imaginative construction is unflinching pursuit of the two rationalistic ideals, coherence and logical perfection.[2]

That is to say, the general procedure or method of metaphysical inquiry is precisely the elaboration of a scheme of ideas and the testing of that scheme, internally by the criteria of coherence, logical consistency, and necessity in universality, and externally by its applicability and adequacy. As Whitehead puts it, 'the true method of philosophical construction is to frame a scheme of ideas, the best that one can, and unflinchingly to explore the interpretation of experience in terms of that scheme'.[3] This is the method which has in fact been followed by all the great meta-

[1] P R 6 [8].   [2] P R 7 [8]. Cf. also S M W 34–5, and F R 66–8, 71.   [3] P R X [x].

physicians;[1] each of the great metaphysical schemes has been an attempt to conceive the nature of actuality by constructing a system. Each scheme in the history of philosophy is thus a great 'imaginative experiment' in the endeavour to conceive the ὄντως ὄν.

In the framing or constructing of a metaphysical scheme the procedure to be followed is that of 'imaginative generalization'. What is of particular importance to note, Whitehead points out, are the conditions for the success of the philosophical construction:[2]

In framing a philosophic scheme, each metaphysical notion should be given the widest extension of which it seems capable. It is only in this way that the true adjustment of ideas can be explored. More important even than Occam's doctrine of parsimony—if it be not another aspect of the same—is this doctrine that the scope of a metaphysical principle should not be limited otherwise than by the necessity of its meaning.

By not limiting an idea or principle 'otherwise than by the necessity of its meaning', we not only ensure its complete generality and thus necessity, but also, in an important respect, the coherence of the scheme; for the requirement of coherence is the ground of Occam's maxim *entia non sunt multiplicanda praeter necessitatem*. Thus, for example, Descartes' failure to generalize fully either of his principles of 'extension' or 'cogitation' resulted in his 'multiplying beyond necessity' his first principles, with consequent incoherence.

Whitehead insists that it is only by developing our ideas as to the generic nature of actuality into a system 'that the true adjustment of ideas can be explored', that is, that they can be investigated for their coherence and consistency, thereby establishing their tenability as metaphysical ideas. It is Whitehead's explicit view, therefore, that[3]

---

[1] Cf. P R 22 [24–5]: '. . . empirically the development of self-justifying thoughts has been achieved by the complex process of generalizing from particular topics, of imaginatively schematizing the generalizations, and finally by renewed comparison of the imagined scheme with the direct experience to which it should apply.'

[2] A I 304–5.   [3] P R 10 [12].

philosophy will not regain its proper status until the gradual elaboration of categoreal schemes, definitely stated at each stage of progress, is recognized as its proper objective.

This is accordingly the objective he set himself in his later period, namely, to develop and elaborate a metaphysical scheme, in as much detail as possible, and in terms of this set of ideas to investigate the major philosophical problems. Through this elaboration and discussion the ideas are subjected to the tests of coherence, consistency, universality, and also of applicability and adequacy. The exposition of Whitehead's metaphysical scheme must now be our concern.

PART TWO

WHITEHEAD'S CATEGOREAL SCHEME: THE DOCTRINE OF 'PROCESS'

CHAPTER IV

The Category of Actual Entity

---

§ 7

A PLURALITY OF ACTUAL ENTITIES

In declaring that the final metaphysical problem is 'to conceive a complete fact', Whitehead pointed out that 'we can only form such a conception in terms of fundamental notions concerning the nature of reality'. Among the most important of these 'fundamental notions' in terms of which in metaphysics we have to think or conceive is that of 'being' or 'existence'. We have seen that the 'ontological principle' is the basic assertion about 'being' or 'existence'. Thus the 'ontological principle' is another 'category' or 'fundamental notion'. The affirmation, implicit or explicit, of the ontological principle, we have shown, entails the concept of 'actual entity'—or οὐσία, 'substance', 'monad' (whatever term be used)—as a further metaphysical category.

The term 'actual entity', in its primary sense, signifies the general metaphysical category of '*that* which is'. The same is the case with the cognate terms οὐσία, 'substance', 'monad', etc. Within the context of a particular philosophical theory, however, each of these terms can also bear the secondary connotation of '*what* that is which is', i.e. of a certain conception of the *nature* of 'actual entity' (οὐσία, 'substance', 'monad'). But it is of the utmost importance to be clear that the metaphysical *category* of 'actual entity' (οὐσία, 'substance', etc.) does not logically entail any particular conception of the *nature* of an actual entity. That is to say, the *category* of 'actual entity', etc., cannot validly be treated as a clear and distinct premise from which by deduction to conclude to the nature of an actual entity. If this category be treated as a premise—and it often has been—it means that a particular conception of the nature of actuality is implicitly imported into the premise. In other words, it is not the category as such which is the premise in this case, but the term 'substance', etc., in its secondary sense. This is plainly inadmissible. 'Actual entity' (οὐσία, 'substance', 'monad') is a 'fundamental notion' in terms of which we have to think, but it is precisely the nature of actual entity, of οὐσία, 'substance', which has to be discovered; it is this which is primarily in dispute, as Aristotle clearly saw, and which constitutes the metaphysical problem *par excellence*. The occasions of original metaphysical thinking have been endeavours speculatively to discover the nature of actuality. Our concern here is the conception of the nature of actuality at which Whitehead arrived.

By the ontological principle, Whitehead maintains,[1]

'Actual entities'—also termed 'actual occasions'—are the final real things of which the world is made up. There is no going behind actual entities to find anything more real. They differ among themselves: God is an actual entity, and so is the most trivial puff of existence in far-off empty space. But, though there are gradations of importance, and diversities of function, yet in the principles which actuality exemplifies all are on the same level. The final facts are, all alike, actual entities.

In one respect this passage can be read as an alternative formulation of the ontological principle. In another respect, however, it is evident that it is something more: it is an interpretation of the ontological principle in terms of certain further fundamental notions. For in this passage the conception is accepted not only of a plurality of actual entities, but also that they differ among each other: 'there are gradations of importance, and diversities of function'. But these doctrines are not logically entailed in the

[1] P R 24 [27–8].

ontological principle. We have seen[1] that the ontological principle is the affirmation that *some* entities are 'actual', or that at least *one* entity is 'actual'. The ontological principle is therefore consistent with both pluralism and monism. But neither can be held to be a necessary implication of the ontological principle to the exclusion of the other, as a matter of sheer logical entailment. The decision between monism and pluralism has to made be on other grounds.

The issue between monism and pluralism is part of the general problem of the nature of actuality, of οὐσία: 'For it is this that some assert to be one, others more than one, that some assert to be limited, others unlimited.' The issue between monism and pluralism cannot be settled in separation from, and antecedently to, the problem of the nature of 'that which is'. On the contrary, from Parmenides to McTaggart, monism has clearly always been arrived at as the outcome of the inquiry into the nature of 'that which is', of actuality; that is, investigation of the nature of actuality has led the philosophers in question to the conclusion that actuality must be One, a changeless, self-sufficient, unitary whole. But the case with pluralistic doctrines is not essentially different. In both there is involved the speculative identification of the generic features constituting the nature of actuality.

Whitehead rejects monism on two chief grounds. One is that this doctrine is unable to satisfy the criterion of coherence. Monism is the doctrine that there is only one entity which is 'actual', i.e. existent in the full sense. Not only is this One all there *is*; it is also held that as the sole actually existing entity, its metaphysical nature must exhibit the necessary features of unitariness and changelessness. But it is the requirement of every metaphysical system that it account for the experienced plurality of entities, and for such features as change, disorder, evil, error. A monistic theory is compelled to do so in terms of 'modes' and/or 'appearances' of the one actual entity. In Whitehead's words, 'a multiplicity of modes is a fixed requisite, if the scheme is to retain any direct relevance to the many occasions in the

---

[1] P. 24 above.

experienced world'.[1] But by the introduction of the doctrine of 'modes' or 'appearances' a monistic theory is involved in incoherence. As Whitehead puts it, speaking of Spinoza, 'the gap in the system is the arbitrary introduction of the "modes" '.[2] For if actuality be One, a changeless, self-sufficient, unitary whole, it cannot consistently be regarded as a necessary implication of its nature that it diversify itself into a plurality of modes or appearances. Thus the conception of a plurality of modes is strictly an additional, and separate, principle, not entailed in that of the monistic One. That is to say, there can be no reason in the nature of a *monistic* actuality for it to diversify itself into a plurality of changing modes or appearances. As Whitehead says, 'how can the unchanging unity of fact generate the delusion of change?'[3] And what about disorder, frustration, error, evil? 'It is quite incredible', Whitehead remarks, 'that the Absolute, as conceived by monistic philosophy, should evolve confusion about its own details.'[4] This separate principle of a plurality, brought in to make the scheme applicable to the data of experience, cannot be coherent with the principle of a monistic actuality.

Exhibiting the incoherence of a system, it should be noted, simply means that something is wrong with it. This analysis does not presuppose any alternative theory. Such a theory is, however, involved, in any indication as to where the error lies. In Whitehead's view the error in monism consists in the mistaken identification of certain features as constituting the metaphysical nature of actuality. This mistake is the second ground upon which Whitehead rejects monism. What this feature is which Whitehead holds is mistakenly regarded by monism to exemplify the nature of actuality, we shall discuss in some detail in Chapter VI. We shall then see that Whitehead, in his system, inverts the roles of the 'one' and the 'modes'. The latter are, for him, the *actual* entities.

Adopting pluralism, Whitehead maintains that 'the final facts are, all alike, actual entities'. This is but a formulation of the

[1] P R 8 [10].   [2] P R 8 [10].   [3] M T 73.   [4] M T 70.

The Category of Actual Entity

ontological principle on a pluralistic basis; that is, it is another way of saying that there are many entities which are 'actual'. But does this necessarily imply that all actual entities are *alike*, that they are all of one basic kind, that is to say, that they all exhibit the same generic principles? Many metaphysical systems have held the contrary, namely that there are generically different kinds of actual entities. The doctrine of Descartes is a case in point. According to this there are *res cogitans* and *res extensa*, two kinds of actuality with generic features radically different and mutually exclusive. In addition, in Descartes' system, as in so many others, God is regarded as still another kind of actuality. For, in Whitehead's words, Descartes 'would ascribe to God "existence" in a generically different sense'.[1]

Whitehead rejects theories of two or more different kinds of actual entity on the same two general grounds as he rejected monism, namely, that these theories fail to satisfy the requirement of coherence, and that they are involved in the 'fallacy of misplaced concreteness', i.e. mistakenly identifying as generic features of actuality, ones which are in fact special. This is most readily exemplified by a consideration of Descartes' philosophy. Descartes had regarded 'extension' and 'cogitation' as the mutually exclusive principles or features exhibited by two kinds of actuality. These features of 'extension' and 'cogitation' are what, in his view, are the general features characterizing 'bodies' and 'minds' respectively.

Now in some sense no one doubts but that there are bodies and minds. The only point at issue is the status of such bodies and minds in the scheme of things. Descartes affirmed that they were individual substances, so that each bit of matter is a substance and each mind is a substance.[2]

That is to say, Descartes identified the features which constitute the nature or essence respectively of bodies and minds as *metaphysical* features. We have noted earlier[3] that in this Descartes is properly following the procedure of 'imaginative rationalization'; the question is whether his hypothesis can be accepted.

[1] P R 103 [116]. [2] R M 92. [3] P. 47–8 above.

The first test must be for its coherence, and in this it fails. We have already seen that in Whitehead's view,

in modern philosophy Descartes' two kinds of substance, corporeal and mental, illustrate incoherence. There is, in Descartes' philosophy, no reason why there should not be a one-substance world, only corporeal, or a one-substance world, only mental. According to Descartes, a substantial individual 'requires nothing but itself in order to exist'. Thus this system makes a virtue of incoherence. But, on the other hand, the facts seem connected, while Descartes' system does not; for example, in the treatment of the body-mind problem.[1]

The 'connection between facts' is the crux of the difficulty facing all such systems which maintain two or more types of actual entities. There is quite clearly some connection between the 'facts', i.e. actual entities, respectively constituting the 'body' and the 'mind'. But if these actualities be of generically different kinds, then there can be no connection between them, as we shall show in some detail later.[2] Thus Descartes' system cannot give a philosophical explanation of the mind-body connection, and he is finally driven from his metaphysics to a purely irrational appeal to 'practice'.[3]

The theory Whitehead accordingly adopts is that all actual entities are generically of one kind: 'though there are gradations of importance, and diversities of function, yet in the principles which actuality exemplifies all are on the same level'. That is to say, there is one set of completely universal principles which apply to all actual entities whatever. Not even God can be regarded as an exception to this set if coherence is to be attained. In Whitehead's doctrine 'God's existence is not generically different from that of other actual entities, except that he is 'primordial' in a sense to be gradually explained'.[4] Coherence

---

[1] P R 8 [9–10]. [2] § 22 below.

[3] This is quite clearly stated by Descartes himself in the following interesting passage in one of his letters to Princess Elizabeth (pp. 274–5 in *Descartes' Philosophical Writings*, selected and translated by N. Kemp Smith): 'It is by relying exclusively on the activities and concerns of ordinary life [*en usant seulement de la vie et conversations ordinaires*], and by abstaining from metaphysical meditation . . . that we can learn to apprehend the union of soul and body.' [4] P R 103 [116].

can be secured only if there be one set of metaphysical principles—'in the proper general sense of "metaphysics" '.

§ 8

'BEING' AND 'BECOMING'

The ontological principle is the assertion that the ὄντως ὄν, the 'really real', is an 'actual', i.e. a fully existent, individual entity. Since 'actual entities' 'form the ground from which all other types of existence are derivative or abstracted', it is evident that the category of actual entity assumes a certain basic position among the categories. That is to say, actual entities constitute the primary subject of the metaphysical inquiry; it is their nature which metaphysics seeks to discover. The problem, as Aristotle says, is 'what is οὐσία?' In other words, the problem is to determine those features which are completely generic to that which is, without which it could not *be*.

From the time of Parmenides at least it has been recognized that in order to be, the ὄντως ὄν must be what it is. This involves that in some fundamental sense it must be 'individual', 'unitary', 'self-identical', and 'self-sufficient'. In part it was this requirement which Descartes also was concerned to express in defining 'substance' as 'an existent thing which requires nothing but itself in order to exist'.[1]

It has also been appreciated that if the ὄντως ὄν must be what it is in order to be, this implies that in some sense it must also be 'changeless'; that is, 'changelessness' must in some respect be included as an equally fundamental feature of the ὄντως ὄν.

But with this factor of 'changelessness' difficulties enter. It gives rise to one of the crucial metaphysical problems, for 'changelessness' has somehow to be adjusted to the factor of 'change'. How philosophers have sought a solution to this problem has constituted one of the great 'divides' in philosophical theory.

[1] *Principles of Philosophy*, Part I, 51.

Setting aside the two extreme possibilities of entirely denying either 'change' or 'changelessness', one main tendency has been to conceive the ὄντως ὄν as wholly devoid of change, as 'eternal', and to regard 'change' as a feature of a different 'realm' or 'world', a 'deficiently real' world, a world of 'appearance'. In theories following this line, 'being' is set in sharp antithesis to 'becoming'. The ὄντως ὄν is changeless, eternal 'being', and excludes all 'becoming', which is relegated to an inferior status in another realm.

If, following Plato, the ὄντως ὄν be regarded as eternal 'being', constituting a realm quite distinct from and other than that of the realm of 'becoming', we have a conception which is inimical to the recognition of the ontological principle. It was in fact in opposition to this kind of theory that Aristotle asserted his principle. If one realm alone *is*, it is a contradiction to maintain that another also is or exists; yet this other must be or exist if it constitute a separate and distinct realm. This contradiction is not avoided by maintaining that the other realm 'derives its being' from the 'truly real' realm. If both *are*, then one alone cannot constitute the ὄντως ὄν or actuality. The firm recognition of the ontological principle involves the rejection of the doctrine of 'degrees of being'. This whole theory of a bifurcation of the universe depends for its plausibility upon the ambiguity of the term 'being'. The assertion of the ontological principle is the realization that such a bifurcation cannot coherently be maintained.

This bifurcation is avoided by the doctrine of a monistic ὄντως ὄν, regarded as eternal 'being'. But by excluding 'change' and 'becoming' from the ὄντως ὄν, monism implicitly also violates the ontological principle. For, with the exception of Parmenides, monists do not regard 'becoming' as simply 'non-being', sheer nothingness. For them there *is* 'becoming'; i.e. it exists. But it does not exist as a feature of the monistic ὄντως ὄν, and on this theory there can be no other actuality of which it can be a feature.

On the other side of the 'divide' are the theories which regard the notions of 'being' and 'becoming' as not completely incompatible, and which seek to combine them in the nature of the ὄντως ὄν, the actual entity.

In the philosophical tradition this attempt has in the main followed the line indicated by Aristotle in his statement that 'the most distinctive mark of substance appears to be that, while remaining numerically one and the same, it is capable of admitting contrary qualities'.[1] That is to say, an actual entity is conceived as remaining changeless in its essential nature, whilst undergoing changes of quality and relation. The reconciliation of 'change-lessness' and 'change', of 'being' and 'becoming', is sought in a distinction between 'essential' and 'accidental' features. An actuality must be changeless in its *essential* nature, for unless it remains 'one and the same' it cannot retain its 'individuality' and 'self-identity'. Its 'essential' features are those without which it could not be what it is. If change is to be accommodated, it can only be in other features which are not essential to the entity, features which can alter whilst leaving the individuality and self-identity of the entity unaffected. It is clearly fundamental to this conception of an actual entity that it 'endures' or 'persists'; as Professor Broad has said, 'the notion of a substance involves the persistence of something through a lapse of time'.[2] The entity endures self-identically (i.e. without essential change) throughout a succession of accidental changes.

Now our everyday experience is certainly dominated by enduring things which change, things which remain, for the ordinary purposes of living, 'the same' despite the changes they undergo: it is the same person who yesterday was healthy and today is ill; it is the same tree which during summer is green and in winter is bare and brown, which until this morning was grow-ing erect and now lies felled. The development of language has been determined by mankind's dealings with these enduring things. Traditional Aristotelian logic exhibited the formal structure of this language of everyday usage in the subject-predicate form of proposition.

[1] *Categoriae*, 4ª 10 (transl. E. M. Edghill).
[2] *The Mind and its Place in Nature*, p. 34.

Whitehead has pointed out that the long 'dominance of Aristotelian logic from the late classical period onwards has imposed on metaphysical thought the categories naturally derivative from its phraseology'.[1] These categories are those of 'substance' and its 'predicates' or 'properties'—qualities, relations, etc. The first point Whitehead wishes to bring out is that the notion of an actual entity as an unchanging subject of change is a generalization from the enduring things of everyday experience; that is to say, by imaginative generalization we arrive at the concept of 'something' which is what it is, changeless, and enduring as such throughout adventures of accidental change. This 'something' is the unchanging substratum of changing qualities and relations— hence the term 'substance'. It was this line of thought which led Aristotle to his conclusion that 'the most distinctive mark of substance appears to be that, while remaining numerically one and the same, it is capable of admitting contrary qualities'. This unchanging 'something' is readily conceived as a 'stuff', 'matter', 'material'.

Secondly, the subject-predicate logic, whose relevance is primarily to the things of everyday living, has been taken to be equally relevant to metaphysical thought. Accordingly, as Whitehead has said, it has come to be assumed, tacitly or explicitly, that 'the final metaphysical fact is always to be expressed as a quality inhering in a substance'.[2] That is to say, the 'final metaphysical fact', the actual entity, is conceived as a generalization of the enduring things of everyday life. This conception of an

[1] P R 41 [45].

[2] P R 220 [239]. Cf. also P R 41 [45]: 'Many philosophers, who in their explicit statements criticize the Aristotelian notion of "substance", yet implicitly throughout their discussions presuppose that the "subject-predicate" form of proposition embodies the finally adequate mode of statement about the actual world.' For example, he points out (P R 192 [209]), for Locke 'and also for Hume, in the background and tacitly presupposed in all explanations, there remained the mind with its perceptions. The perceptions, for Hume, are what the mind knows about itself; and tacitly the knowable facts are always treated as qualities of a subject— the subject being the mind. His final criticism of the notion of the "mind" does not alter the plain fact that the whole of the previous discussion has included this presupposition. Hume's final criticism only exposes the metaphysical superficiality of his preceding exposition.'

actual entity, as an enduring, changeless substance undergoing qualitative changes has been accepted as fundamental in metaphysics, especially during the modern period, principally under the influence of traditional Aristotelian logic.[1] As Whitehead has put it, 'the exclusive dominance of the substance-quality metaphysics was enormously promoted by the logical bias of the mediaeval period. It was retarded by the study of Plato and of Aristotle. These authors included the strains of thought which issued in this doctrine, but included them inconsistently mingled with other notions. The substance-quality metaphysics triumphed with exclusive dominance in Descartes' doctrines'.[2]

§ 9

WHITEHEAD'S CRITICISM OF THE CONCEPTION OF AN ACTUAL ENTITY AS 'SELF-IDENTICALLY ENDURING'

Whitehead acknowledges that for most everyday purposes the things with which we are concerned are legitimately and correctly conceived as self-identically enduring entities: 'the simple notion of an enduring substance sustaining persistent qualities, either essentially or accidentally, expresses a useful abstract for many purposes of life'.[3] But it is the concept of an 'abstraction' and not of a concrete actuality. That is to say, though they are 'entities', they are not *actual* entities; though they do exist, their 'existence' is not the 'full' existence of actual entities, but is existence of a 'derivative' kind. In saying that they are 'abstractions' Whitehead means that their existence is of a kind derivative from that of actual entities.

The essential relevance of the subject-predicate logic, as we have seen, is to these enduring entities, and this is why Whitehead

---

[1] Whitehead points out, however, that 'this dominance of his logic does not seem to have been characteristic of Aristotle's own metaphysical speculations' (P R 41 [45]).   [2] P R 192 [209].   [3] P R 109 [122].

63

says that 'the subject-predicate form of proposition is concerned with high abstractions'.[1] That is to say, it is concerned with entities which are not proper *actual* entities. Fundamental difficulties ensue in philosophical thought when actual entities are conceived in terms of *enduring* entities sustaining qualities. For in such a doctrine an actual entity is conceived as a generalization of the features common to entities which are not true actual entities, for example, the feature of self-identical endurance. As Whitehead has put it, 'whenever we try to use it [i.e. the concept of an enduring entity] as a fundamental statement of the nature of things, it proves itself mistaken. . . . In metaphysics the concept is sheer error. The error does not consist in the employment of the word "substance"; but in the employment of the notion of an actual entity which is characterized by essential qualities, and remains numerically one amidst the changes of accidental relations and of accidental qualities'.[2]

We must now examine Whitehead's reasons for rejecting this conception of an actual entity as enduring self-identically amidst change. This conception we have seen to be the outcome of one attempt at reconciling 'changelessness' and 'change'. It is important to appreciate that 'change', in the context of this problem, is the notion of advance, transition, or passage from one set of conditions, state, or mode, to another; in one phrase, it is the notion of 'process'. That is to say, the problem at issue is that raised by our experience of 'things in a process of change'. The world is exhibited in our experience as in a constant flux, in a continuous 'process of change', and it is this which is our concern. The doctrine under criticism, as Whitehead states it with characteristic terse incisiveness, is that this 'process can be analysed into compositions of final realities, themselves devoid of process'.[3] In other words, the process of change is held to be ultimately analysable into the differences between the successive arrangements and/or states of entities which themselves are essentially changeless. These entities are conceived as the 'unchanging subjects of change'.

[1] P R 41 [45].   [2] P R 109–110 [122].   [3] M T 131.

Whitehead maintains that this analysis of process or change is fallacious, and that the error is to be found in the notion that an actual entity or substance can *exist* and *endure* changelessly, i.e. itself entirely devoid of process. Descartes was aware of a difficulty in this; in his view it arises from an inadequate conception of 'duration' or 'endurance'. 'In truth', he wrote,[1] 'it is perfectly clear and evident to all who will attentively consider the nature of duration that the conservation of a substance, in each moment of its duration, requires the same power and act that would be necessary to create it, supposing it were not yet in existence; so that it is manifestly a dictate of the natural light that conservation and creation differ merely in our mode of thinking [and not in reality].'

In Descartes' doctrine, therefore, the *existence* of an actuality is 'instantaneous'; it is thus not only devoid of the transition or process involved in duration, but of all process whatever; it is in the strictest sense 'changeless'. Duration consists in the transition to the successive instantaneous existences of the actualities. As Whitehead has put it, 'the matter of fact was, for him, to be seen in the instant and not in the endurance. For him, endurance was the mere succession of instantaneous facts'.[2] The essential point of Descartes' analysis is that 'duration' is not validly conceived to consist in the self-identical persistence of an actuality; since each instantaneous created entity is numerically distinct from the others in the route of succession, there is accordingly not 'one and the same' entity 'enduring'.

One evident conclusion from this analysis of Descartes' is that in talking about or conceiving an 'enduring entity', we are not dealing with an *actual* entity, for the actual entities are the instantaneous created substances. In conceiving an 'enduring entity' we are conceiving the whole route of succession *as one entity*. An 'enduring entity' is therefore a derivative abstraction from the created substances, and is not itself a substance or actual entity. It should, however, be noted that Descartes, overlooking this implication of his analysis, does nevertheless also treat an 'enduring

[1] *Third Meditation*, tr. J. Veitch.   [2] M T 199.

65

entity' as an actual substance, thereby committing the 'fallacy of misplaced concreteness'.

Another important point of Descartes' analysis is that the instantaneous substances, since they are devoid of process, and accordingly of *activity*, cannot themselves be the reason for, or the cause of, the process consisting in the transition to the successive substances. The process constituting endurance must therefore be the product or outcome of the activity of some other entity with the 'power and act' of creation. Further, also the very *existence* of the instantaneous substances is dependent upon the action of that other entity.

There emerges, therefore, a most important implication of Descartes' analysis, namely, that there cannot be 'existence' at all, in any sense, without *activity*, and thus without 'process'— for action involves transition, which is process. Moreover, the creating being must himself exist by virtue of his own activity; that is, he must be *causa sui*, for unless this be so Descartes will be involved in an infinite regress of creators in order to account for the process of creating activity of each.

Descartes' acknowledgement of God as the only true substance[1] is thus perfectly consistent; God's existence is the only full, 'actual' existence, all other entities being dependent upon God for their existence. Accordingly, in his treatment of other entities —such as the instantaneous *res extensa*—as substances, Descartes has fallen prey to the 'fallacy of misplaced concreteness'. For these entities are *not* 'actual'; their 'existence' is not existence in the full sense of proper 'actual' entities.

The fundamental difficulty involved in the doctrine that 'process can be analysed into compositions of final realities, themselves devoid of process', centres on the problem whether the 'final realities', i.e. actual entities, can *exist* at all devoid of process. Whitehead maintains that 'actual existence', i.e. the existence of an 'actual' entity, cannot be either 'instantaneous' or a 'changeless endurance'. In both these conceptions process or change is entirely excluded from the nature of the individual actuality. But if an actual entity be

---

[1] *Principles of Philosophy,* Part I, 51.

66

in itself devoid of process, then process can be accounted for only by an incoherent appeal to some actuality of a kind generically different from the actualities under consideration. Descartes, as we have seen, does so explicitly. Many others, lacking the philosophical acuity possessed by Descartes, fail to see that there is a problem at all in the notion of an actuality devoid of process, and merely combine, without regard to the inconsistency of doing so, the notion of a changeless individual actuality with that of a process of change.

It is of the utmost importance, Whitehead insists, to realize 'that the erroneous notions of process devoid of individualities, and of individualities devoid of process, can never be adjusted to each other. If you start with either of these falsehoods, you must dismiss the other as meaningless'.[1] That is to say, if it be held that individual actualities be 'changeless', then there is no way of consistently and coherently accounting for process or change. Likewise there cannot be mere process, a mere continuity of becoming, for, as we shall see later,[2] it is then impossible to have any individual actualities.

[1] M T 132.   [2] See below, § 11.

CHAPTER V

The Category of Process

§ 10

THE CATEGORY OF PROCESS

Whitehead thus explicitly rejects the traditional lines of thought in their attempt at adjusting 'changelessness' and 'change'. In all of them an actual entity is regarded as essentially 'changeless'. 'It is fundamental to the metaphysical doctrine of the philosophy of organism', Whitehead says,[1] 'that the notion of an actual entity as the unchanging subject of change is completely abandoned.' His doctrine is that the only way of consistently and coherently achieving a reconciliation of 'changelessness' and 'change', of 'being' and 'becoming', is to conceive 'process' as essential to the nature of an actual entity.

In dealing with this problem it is of the highest importance, bearing the ontological principle in mind, to appreciate that it centres on 'existence', and primarily on 'existence' in the full 'actual' sense, that is, the existence of concrete *actual* entities. The doctrine Whitehead maintains is that the *existence* of an actual entity must involve 'process'. If that be so, then all other senses of 'existence' will accordingly also have reference to process, for, by the ontological principle, all other forms of existence are derivative from 'actual' existence.[2] Whitehead's doctrine, in his own

[1] P R 39 [43].

[2] We shall see later (§ 16 and § 19 below) in precisely what respect entities other than *actual* entities are implicated in process.

The Category of Process

statement, is 'that "existence" (in any of its senses) cannot be abstracted from "process". The notions of "process" and "existence" presuppose each other'.[1]

In saying that the 'notions of "process" and "existence" presuppose each other', Whitehead means that if the notion of 'process' or 'change' be admitted at all, there must be an existing, i.e. 'actual', entity which is 'in process'. For 'admitting' process means acknowledging its 'existence'; but since 'process', as such, is not an actual entity, by the ontological principle its 'existence' must be derivative from the full, 'actual' existence of an actual entity. Thus 'process' presupposes 'existence' in the full sense of the existence of 'actual' entities. And conversely, 'actual existence' presupposes 'process', for unless 'process' be intrinsically involved in the 'existing' of an *actual entity*, it is impossible coherently and consistently to admit process in any form whatever.

In other words, an *actual* entity cannot *exist* as entirely changeless, devoid of process, i.e. as 'eternal'; a 'process of change' is intrinsic to its existing. The concept of 'eternal existence', if applied to an *actual* entity, is strictly a contradiction in terms—we shall see later[2] that it can consistently be applied only to a kind of entity which is *not* 'actual'. Whitehead states this doctrine of his by saying that 'the process itself is the constitution of the actual entity; in Locke's phrase, it is the "real internal constitution" of the actual entity. In the older phraseology employed by Descartes, the process is what the actual entity is in itself, "*formaliter*"'.[3]

This is what Whitehead has called his 'principle of process'. In an alternative formulation, it is the principle that an actual entity's ' "being" is constituted by its "becoming" '.[4] In other words, its 'existing' is constituted by its 'process'.

The terms 'becoming' and 'process' have just been stated as equivalent, but it should be noted that the words are not synonymous. Their equivalence here is, however, justifiable. 'Becoming' means 'coming to be' or 'coming into being', i.e. 'coming into existence'. By the ontological principle, 'becoming' is the 'becoming of *actual* existence'; that is, it is the coming into

[1] M T 131.   [2] § 16 below.   [3] P R 309–10 [335].   [4] P R 31 [34–5].

existence of an actual entity. 'Process', in its fundamental sense, is this 'process of becoming' of an actual entity: *its* 'existence' (i.e. 'being') is constituted by *its* 'process' (i.e. 'becoming'). All other meanings of 'process' are derivative from this root meaning of the process involved in the becoming of an actual entity.

Error in thought is the inevitable result of failure to distinguish this basic sense of 'process' from its derivative senses. In reference to the becoming of an actual entity, the term 'process' must not be understood in some derivative sense. Thus the 'process of becoming' of an actual entity is not a mere 'undergoing of transition', in the sense of a passive 'occurring to' the entity. Any 'transition', as we saw in the previous chapter,[1] ultimately implies some agency effecting that transition. If incoherence is to be avoided, that agency in reference to the 'transition' or 'process' involved in the existence of an actual entity, must be the agency of that actual entity itself. This doctrine, as Whitehead states it, with the ontological principle quite evidently in mind, is 'that there is no agency in abstraction from actual occasions, and that existence involves implication in agency'.[2]

Thus the 'process' constituting the 'becoming', and thereby the 'existence' or 'being', of an actual entity is a 'process of activity', i.e. the 'process' involved in 'acting'. That is to say, *actual* existence involves 'agency', 'acting'. More precisely, actual existence, the existence of actual entities, is *constituted by* their 'acting'.

We can accordingly appreciate Whitehead's choice of the term 'actual' for the precise technical sense in which he employs it. His use is in its strict etymological derivation from the Latin *actus*. Thus an *actual* entity is an *acting* entity; that is to say, it is 'acting', 'agency' which constitutes *existence* in the 'full' sense.

[1] § 9.   [2] A I 379.

The Category of Process

THE ATOMICITY OF BECOMING

Whitehead's rejection of the conception of an actual entity as the unchanging subject of change is thorough and consistent. In his doctrine as he says, 'an actual entity is a process, and is not describable in terms of the morphology of a "stuff" '.[1] That is, an actual entity is not to be conceived as some kind of 'stuff' which *is* or *exists* antecedently to its process. Its 'process of becoming' *constitutes* its 'being', its 'existing'; apart from that process of becoming there can be no 'being', no existence at all. Likewise an actual entity is not to be conceived as 'brought into being' by its process, and thereafter, having 'fully become', capable of existing as a 'completed being'—for this would entail implicitly conceiving an actual entity 'in terms of the morphology of a "stuff" '. On the theory Whitehead advances, an actual entity *is* (i.e. exists) only 'in the becoming'.

At this point a number of questions might be raised about this theory. In conceiving 'process' in this way as fundamental to an actual entity, is Whitehead not logically committed to repudiating the notion of 'changelessness' entirely as a feature of an actuality? And is he not thereby involved in a difficulty analogous to that of the theory he has rejected? That is, by regarding an actual entity as a 'process', is he not unable consistently and coherently to account for the factor of 'changelessness' at all? Further, if the notion of 'changelessness' be abandoned, does not the notion of 'individuality' go also, and with it 'unitariness', 'self-sufficiency', and 'self-identity'? For how can these notions consistently be applied to a continuous process of becoming? And how, indeed, can there be an 'individual' if there be only a continuous 'becoming'; for does not the notion of 'individuality' imply a 'completed unity'? But how can there be a completed unity when an actuality exists only 'in the process', and when, at the termination of that process, there just *is* no existent at all?

[1] PR 55 [65].

Whitehead agrees that these difficulties do result, and these objections are valid, if we attempt to conceive actuality as a 'continuous process', as a kind of Heracleitean flux. This, however, is not his doctrine. Whitehead maintains that a 'continuous process' is strictly a misconception, whether it be a 'continuous process of becoming' or any other sort of continuous transition, as for example, in the widely accepted view of 'time' as a 'continuous flow'. 'There is a prevalent misconception that "becoming" involves the notion of a unique seriality for its advance into novelty. This is the classic notion of "time", which philosophy took over from common sense.'[1] The reason why a 'continuous process' is a misconception is that it involves two notions, namely, 'continuity' and 'process' (or 'becoming') and, as Whitehead expresses it, 'if we attempt to combine the notions of supersession [i.e. 'process'] and continuity we are at once entangled in a vicious regress'.[2]

This becomes clear by the application of Zeno's method. The supposition in question is that becoming is a continuous process, a continuous supersession of one portion or act of becoming by another. Now consider any two portions, A and B, of such a continuous process, such that B supersedes A:

If B supersedes A, then the continuity of B requires that some earlier portion of B has superseded A antecedently to the latter portion of B. This argument can be repeated on that earlier portion of B, however you choose that portion. Thus we are involved in an infinite regress. Also the supersession of A has to commence at what should be the infinite end of the regress. But there is no infinite end. Hence supersession cannot be regarded as the continuous unfolding of a continuum.[3]

That is to say, if becoming be a continuous process, then any portion of it, say B, supersedes an earlier portion, A. But B is itself a continuous process, so that the latter part of B supersedes its earlier part. And the same applies to that earlier part, and so on *ad infinitum*. Thus we can never get to the beginning of B: for

---

[1] P R 48 [52].

[2] 'Time' in *Proc. Sixth Intern. Congress of Philosophy*, p. 63.

[3] *Ibid.* Cf. also P R 94 [106], and S M W 157–160.

The Category of Process

whatever portion of B we indicate presupposes an earlier portion of B which became after the beginning of B and antecedently to that earlier portion.

The point Whitehead is concerned to bring out is that this result of a vicious regress indicates that there is something amiss with the conception of a 'continuity of becoming'. The error, he holds, lies in the combination of the notions of 'continuity' and 'becoming'; they cannot be combined as a 'continuous becoming' or a 'continuity of becoming' without involving this vicious regress. Thus there cannot be a 'continuous becoming'. As he summarily stated this point, 'if we admit that "something becomes", it is easy, by employing Zeno's method, to prove that there can be no continuity of becoming'.[1]

The conclusion Whitehead draws from this is two-fold. The first, which we shall consider now, concerns primarily the problem of 'continuity'; the second, which we shall deal with in the following section, has particular reference to 'becoming', or 'process', in its root meaning.

We have to account for the factor of 'continuity', for in some respect the universe presents itself as an 'extensive continuity'. One important aspect of this is the feature of 'duration' or 'endurance' which came up for consideration in an earlier section. Whitehead points out that 'the extensive continuity of the physical universe has usually been construed to mean that there is a continuity of becoming'.[2] We have seen[3] that Descartes disagrees with this view. In his doctrine the 'extensive continuity' of the universe is constituted by two quite distinct factors, the 'spatial' and the 'temporal'. For him actual entities (or at least one species of them) are *in themselves* spatially extended; these are the *res extensa*, which constitute the universe a spatially extended plenum. Thus 'extensive continuity', in its spatial aspect, is for Descartes an intrinsic feature of physical actuality. But temporal extension or 'endurance' is not such an intrinsic feature; it is analysable into the succession of distinct, instantaneously created, spatially extended, entities. In other words, Descartes holds that spatially

[1] P R 48 [53].   [2] P R 48 [53].   [3] § 9 above.

73

the universe is a continuum, but that temporally it is not. Thus both Descartes and Whitehead agree that 'supersession cannot be regarded as the continuous unfolding of a continuum'. Descartes' doctrine is that there is a supersession of instantaneous spatial continua, each a distinct existent newly created. Temporal continuity, for him, is not a feature of actuality, but of a succession of actualities.

For reasons which were considered earlier, Whitehead holds, in opposition to Descartes, that actuality must in itself involve a 'process of becoming'. Thus the problem for him is whether the 'extensive continuity' of the universe can be constituted by a 'process of becoming', that is, whether the 'process of becoming' can be 'regarded as the continuous unfolding of a continuum'. Whitehead rejects this supposition because a 'continuous unfolding of a continuum' entails a 'continuity of becoming', and this has been shown to be impossible. Therefore, since 'becoming' is a generic metaphysical feature of actuality, 'extensive continuity' must be rejected as also being such a feature. 'Extensive continuity', Whitehead maintains, must be accounted for in the same way as Descartes accounted for temporal extensive continuity or duration, namely, as being constituted by the succession or supersession of individual units of becoming.

The theory Whitehead advances, therefore, conceives actual entities as 'epochal' units of becoming, in each of which the process of becoming is completed; and each epochal unit of becoming as succeeding and being succeeded by other such epochal units. Thus each actuality becomes; it is a unit process of becoming. Each is a process of becoming distinct from the others. That is to say, there is not one continuous process of becoming. 'Continuity' enters with, and is constituted by, the succession of distinct, completed units of becoming. Accordingly, as Whitehead puts it, 'there is a becoming of continuity' (i.e. 'continuity' becomes by the succession of unit becomings), but there is 'no continuity of becoming'[1] (i.e. there is no continuous process of becoming).

[1] PR 48 [53].

The Category of Process

The 'process of becoming' is the becoming of individual actual entities, and their succession results in the 'extensive continuity' of the universe; in Whitehead's words, 'the actual occasions are the creatures which become, and they constitute a continuously extensive world'.[1] It is important to note that the 'continuously extensive world' is not itself an actual entity. 'Continuous extensiveness' is thus not a metaphysical feature of actual entities; it is constituted by the *succession* of actualities. In other words, 'continuous extensiveness' is the feature of an 'abstract' entity.

Accordingly, Whitehead declares, 'the ultimate metaphysical truth is atomism. The creatures are atomic'.[2] That is to say, if we hold the doctrine that actuality is a process of becoming, then since there cannot be a continuously extensive process of becoming, actuality must be 'atomic', consisting in epochal units of becoming, and the extensive continuity of the universe must be constituted by the succession of the atomic actualities.

§ 12

THE EPOCHAL THEORY OF ACTUALITY

We must now consider the second of the conclusions Whitehead draws from the application of Zeno's method to the problem of the 'becoming' of actuality. So far we have concentrated our attention on the factor of 'continuity' in its relation to becoming. Whitehead's argument has been that the application of Zeno's method demonstrates that there can be no continuity of becoming; in other words, becoming cannot constitute a *continuous* process. 'Continuity' is the notion of an unbroken, an uninterrupted sequence. Now, according to this argument, if we select for consideration any particular portion of that sequence, say B, we

[1] P R 48 [53].　　　　[2] P R 48 [53].

can never, as we have seen, get to the beginning of it. Therefore there is no act of becoming to commence B, and thus to supersede A; as Whitehead has put it, 'therefore there is nothing which becomes, so as to effect a transition into the [portion B] in question'.[1]

In the previous section it has been shown that the difficulty presented by the 'extensive continuity' of the universe can be overcome by rejecting 'continuity' as a metaphysical feature of actuality, and by regarding it as constituted by the succession of atomic actualities which themselves are processes of becoming. That is to say, the *succession* is continuous, an uninterrupted sequence. But that succession does not itself constitute the becoming of one actuality; there are many actualities succeeding each other continuously.

But, the question must now be raised, has not Whitehead, by his theory of atomic processes of becoming superseding each other continuously, merely evaded the difficulty raised by the conception of an actuality as an act of becoming instead of solving it? For is not Zeno's argument to be applied with equal force to the processes of becoming constituting the individual actual entities? That is to say, if an actuality is a process of becoming, are we not in that case also faced with the difficulty of a vicious regress? For is it not involved that the latter portion of that process supersedes the earlier portion, with the result again that we cannot get to the beginning, and consequently that 'there is nothing which becomes so as to effect a transition into' the process of becoming?

Whitehead agrees that Zeno's argument must be brought to bear on the individual processes of becoming, and further, that it is fatal if these processes be conceived as themselves each a continuous supersession of act or portion of becoming. As he has put it, 'the argument [from Zeno's paradoxes], so far as it is valid,

---

[1] P R 95 [106]. Whitehead adds that 'the difficulty is not evaded by assuming that something becomes at each non-extensive instant of time. For at the beginning of the [portion of time selected] there is no next instant at which something can become'.

elicits a contradiction from the two premises: (1) that in a becoming something (*res vera*) becomes, and (ii) that every act of becoming is divisible into earlier and later sections which are themselves acts of becoming.[1]'

The contradiction, Whitehead maintains, is only to be avoided by rejecting the second of the two premises. That is to say, if we hold that becoming is the becoming of an actuality—which we must hold, as we have seen in earlier sections, if 'becoming' or 'process' is to be admitted at all—then we cannot validly regard the atomic process of becoming as a continuous supersession.

It is evident that the problem cannot be solved by further atomization. The difficulty, Whitehead points out, arises with the introduction of the notion of 'continuity' into the process of becoming of an individual actual entity. The problem is solved, however, if we hold

that in every act of becoming there is the becoming of something with temporal extension; but that the act itself is not extensive, in the sense that it is divisible into earlier and later acts of becoming which correspond to the extensive divisibility of what has become.[2]

Stated briefly, his doctrine is 'that the creature is extensive, but that its act of becoming is not extensive'.[3] An actual entity is 'extensive' because its 'becoming' carries the implication of an 'extended temporal quantum'; i.e. a 'process of becoming' implies transition, and thus temporal extensiveness. Now 'extensiveness' entails 'divisibility'. But if something is divis*ible*, it does not follow that it is therefore necessarily divid*ed*. That is to say, the act or process can be one undivided whole. Thus an actuality can 'become *as a whole*', and accordingly be 'extensive' (and thus divisible) without being 'divided'. This is Whitehead's meaning when he says that 'extensiveness becomes, but "becoming" is not itself extensive';[4] that is, the atomic actuality is 'extensive' by virtue of its process of becoming, but that process of becoming is itself one 'epochal whole', and is not divid*ed* into earlier and later acts of becoming superseding each other continuously.

[1] P R 94 [106].   [2] P R 96 [107].   [3] P R 96 [107].   [4] P R 48 [53].

77

Whitehead therefore maintains that if we admit process or becoming at all, then this conception of actuality as 'epochal' is a prerequisite for meeting Zeno's difficulty.

§ 13

THE 'BECOMING' AND 'PERISHING' OF ACTUAL ENTITIES. WHITEHEAD'S RECONCILIATION OF 'CHANGE' AND 'CHANGELESSNESS'

We are now in a position to appreciate that this theory of actuality as 'epochal becoming' enables Whitehead consistently and coherently to resolve the problem of 'changelessness' and 'change', of 'being' and 'becoming'. From the earliest times the predominant tendency has been to deny 'change' the status of a fundamental feature of the ὄντως ὄν, the actual entity, because of the difficulty of reconciling it with the notions of 'individuality', 'unitariness', 'self-identity', and 'self-sufficiency'. These demand 'changelessness' as a fundamental feature: for an actual entity to *be*, it must be 'what is is'; to change is to cease to be what is, and thus to become another.[1] In other words, the 'self-identity' of an individual actual entity requires that it be 'changeless', and this necessitates the exclusion of 'change' as a fundamental metaphysical feature of an actual entity.

Whitehead's doctrine can be expressed by saying that if we take into account an ambiguity in the notion of 'change', we will be able to admit 'change' as a metaphysical feature in a form which is necessitated by 'individuality', and which is not incon-

---

[1] Cf. Plato, *Phaedo*, 78. Also Gilson, *op. cit.*, p. 11: 'As Leibniz was fond of saying, it is one and the same to be *a* thing and to be a *thing*. In other words, the "really real" is free from otherness, because what we could ascribe to it as other than what it is would actually be "another being". For the same reason, being as such is free from change. In a doctrine where *to be* is *to be the same*, otherness is the very negation of being. Thus, in virtue of its self-identity, which forbids it to change unless indeed it ceased to be, true being is immutable in its own right.' (Italics in original.)

sistent with 'self-identity' and 'changelessness'. Indeed, if this form of 'change' be admitted as a metaphysical feature, then 'individuality', 'unitariness', 'self-identity', 'self-sufficiency', *and* *changelessness* are necessitated *by it*.

'Change' is the general notion of 'alteration, modification, passing from one state or condition to a different one'. But there will be different *kinds* of change, depending upon what is being referred to. Thus the kind of change involved in an act or process of becoming must be carefully distinguished from the kind of change constituted by a transition from one entity to another. The kind of change which must be admitted as an ultimate metaphysical feature of the ὄντως ὄν, the actual entity, is that of the 'process' constituted by the 'becoming', the 'coming into existence', of an actual entity. Whitehead's doctrine, as we have seen,[1] is that 'the notions of "process" and "existence" presuppose each other'. Also, it has been shown, there cannot be 'process' merely, a 'process devoid of individualities'. The conclusion of the previous section is summarily stated by Whitehead when he says that 'process and individuality require each other'.[2]

Now the individual unit of process, which is the becoming of an actual entity, must be conceived as an 'epochal whole'. The actuality becomes 'as a whole', and *is* or *exists* as a whole of becoming. As 'one indivisible whole' it is an *individual;* 'as a whole' it is what it is, i.e. *self-identical;* 'as a whole' it is *unitary* and *self-sufficient.* Conceived as a unit epochal whole it is therefore *changeless.* That is to say, an actuality *becomes* as an epochal whole— thus 'changing' in the sense of the process involved in its becoming —and at the termination or completion of its process of becoming, its being or existence necessarily ceases: the actual entity 'perishes'.[3] In his doctrine, therefore, Whitehead says, 'actual entities perish, but do not change; they are what they are'.[4]

---

[1] § 10.   [2] M T 133.

[3] Thus his doctrine, Whitehead writes (P R 83 [94]), 'is the attempt to describe the world as a process of generation of individual actual entities, each with its own absolute self-attainment. . . . The "perpetual perishing" (cf. Locke, II, XIV, ?) of individual absoluteness is thus foredoomed'.

[4] P R 48 [52].

The 'change' which is here denied as a metaphysical feature of actuality is 'change' in the other sense mentioned above. 'Change' in this sense is constituted by the difference between actual entities in some order of succession; as Whitehead puts it, 'the fundamental meaning of "change" is "the difference between actual entities comprised in some determinate event" '.[1] This is the kind of change which constitutes 'motion' and 'endurance'. It is change in this sense which is strictly inconsistent with 'individuality' and 'self-identity', and which is accordingly excluded as a metaphysical feature when an actual entity is held to be 'changeless'.

This requirement of 'changelessness' as a metaphysical feature is satisfied by the theory of the epochal becoming and perishing of actualities, through its denial of 'change' in this latter sense. As Whitehead remarks, 'an actual entity never moves: it is where it is, and what it is'.[2] Thus by making a distinction between different senses of 'change' and 'changelessness', Whitehead is able consistently to admit both 'change' and 'changelessness' as ultimate metaphysical features of actuality. In his doctrine an actual entity is 'changeless', but it does not 'endure'; and an actual entity 'changes', in the sense of 'becoming', but it does not 'move'.[3]

[1] P R 101 [114].   [2] P R 101 [113].   [3] Cf. M T 73.

CHAPTER VI

The Category of the Ultimate

§ 14

THE CATEGORY OF THE ULTIMATE: 'CREATIVITY'

For Whitehead 'process', and not the 'changelessness' implied by the notion of a static, enduring 'stuff', is the fundamental metaphysical feature of the ὄντως ὄν, the actual entity. This basic 'process' is that constituted by the 'acts of becoming' of the individual actualities. And, by virtue of the 'perishing' of the individual actualities, there is 'process' also in the derivative sense of the supersession of the epochal acts of becoming. Thus 'there are two species of process, macroscopic process, and microscopic process. The macroscopic process is the transition from attained actuality to actuality in attainment; while the microscopic process'[1] is the act of attaining actuality. Both species of process, as we shall see increasingly, must be taken into account in a full metaphysical description. Since the microscopic process is the fundamental metaphysical feature of actuality, we must, in examining the nature of actuality as process, attend primarily to that species.

The microscopic process is the act of becoming of an actual entity; each actuality becomes by virtue of its own activity. Whitehead's is therefore a doctrine of the self-creation of each actual entity.

Earlier we saw,[2] in discussing Descartes' theory, that only that

[1] P R 304 [326].   [2] § 9 above.

entity which exists by virtue of its own activity, and is thus *causa sui*, can be regarded as a proper *actual* entity. It must be emphasized, however, that this applies not only to Descartes' theory; as Whitehead points out, 'every philosophy recognizes, in some form or other, this factor of self-causation in what it takes to be ultimate actual fact'.[1] In monistic theories this is evident. Most pluralistic theories, either explicitly or by implication, reserve the factor of self-causation to one unique actuality, and then, as we have seen, become involved in incoherence and the fallacy of misplaced concreteness by regarding other entities as also 'actual'. The only way for a pluralistic theory to avoid these difficulties is to ascribe self-causation to each of the many actual entities. This is what Whitehead explicitly does in holding that the 'process' which is a generic metaphysical feature of all actual entities is basically an act of self-creation.

Whitehead therefore conceives a multiplicity of actualities, each being or existing as a 'process of becoming' by virtue of its own activity. Each individual actuality *is* (i.e. exists as) an 'act of becoming', and each act *becomes* an individual actual entity. That is, each individual actuality arises out of a process of activity which is generic to all. Each actuality is thus an individualization of the ultimate generic activity. In other words, each actuality constitutes a particular individual form taken by the generic activity.

In saying this it is implied that there is no 'activity' as such apart from the activity of the individual actualities, in the same sense as, in a materialistic theory, there is no 'matter' apart from the individual actual entities; each material actuality exists as the generic 'matter' in a particular individualization. 'Matter', in this theory, is generic in that all actualities, however they might differ among themselves, have the essential feature of being 'material'. Theories such as that of Aristotle are analogous; in these, however, 'matter' is not the 'hard impenetrable stuff' of the 'materialists', but is conceived as the generalized concept of 'that which is formed'. Aristotle maintained, as against Plato, that 'form' as

[1] P R 209 [228].

such cannot be an actual entity, οὐσία; it can exist only as the 'form of' an actual entity. For him 'matter' is that 'ultimate' which 'is formed'; it is that which takes different forms, thereby giving rise to the individual οὐσίαι. 'Matter' as such is an abstraction; the concrete actual entity, οὐσία, is an individual instance of 'formed matter'. That is, though 'matter' is generic and 'ultimate', its exists only in the concrete individualizations. It is evident that this, like Whitehead's doctrine of a generic 'activity', is required by the ontological principle.

The notion of an 'ultimate' which exists only in its individual instances is, Whitehead insists, of great importance in philosophical theory; tacitly or explicitly philosophical thought has to recognize a metaphysical 'category of the ultimate'.

In all philosophic theory there is an ultimate which is actual in virtue of its accidents. It is only then capable of characterization through its accidental embodiments, and apart from these accidents is devoid of actuality.[1]

There is a certain difficulty, however, in achieving a clear and consistent conception of the 'ultimate'. If we concentrate on the individual actualities, there appear to be only the actualities, with perhaps some discernible common feature. This is especially the case when the 'stuff' modes of thought are dominant; there are 'enduring individuals' which undergo adventures of accidental change: there is accordingly a strong tendency to fail to appreciate explicitly that the individuals constitute individualizations of an 'ultimate'. But this 'ultimate' is nevertheless implicitly recognized in, for example, the conception of a 'material world': for then tacitly the actualities composing the universe are conceived as individual instances of 'material'.

If, on the other hand, we concentrate on the 'ultimate', there is a strong tendency to conceive it as itself 'actual', as somehow 'more real' than the individual embodiments, the outcome being the adoption of a monistic theory. But this theory is arrived at by the fallacy of misplaced concreteness: an 'abstraction' is

[1] P R 9 [10–11].

83

regarded as an *actual* entity. In Whitehead's words, 'in such monistic schemes, the ultimate is illegitimately allowed a final, "eminent" reality, beyond that ascribed to any of its accidents'.[1]

A monistic philosophy like Spinoza's, which conceives the individualities as 'modes' of the one true substance, corrects the widespread tendency of pluralistic theories to fail to recognize the 'ultimate'; but it does so at the cost of denying actuality to the individual embodiments. What is requisite, Whitehead maintains, is to recognize the 'ultimate' without denying actuality to the individualizations of the ultimate. In his doctrine the 'ultimate' is not conceived as itself an *actual* entity: it is the basic activity of self-creation generic to all individual actual entities. That is to say, it is the generic activity conceived in abstraction from the individual instantiations of that activity. This 'ultimate', this generic activity of self-creation, Whitehead terms 'creativity'. Accordingly, as he puts it,[2]

'Creativity' is another rendering of the Aristotelian 'matter', and of the modern 'neutral stuff'. But it is divested of the notion of passive receptivity, either of 'form' or of external relations; it is the pure notion of the [generic] activity conditioned by . . . the actual world. . . . Creativity is without a character of its own in exactly the same sense in which the Aristotelian 'matter' is without a character of its own. It is that notion of the highest generality at the base of actuality. It cannot be characterized, because all characters are more special than itself. But creativity is always found under conditions, and described as conditioned.

In Whitehead's philosophy 'creativity' replaces Aristotle's 'matter' as the 'ultimate'; but although there are certain similarities, there are also important differences between the two conceptions. They are similar in that both are that which takes different forms, that which exists only in its individualizations. But Whitehead conceives the 'ultimate' as *activity*, creative activity, and in doing so is specifically maintaining that *to the 'ultimate'*, and to no other element in an actuality, is to be ascribed the *efficacy* whereby the ultimate takes different forms. As he says, he conceives the 'ultimate' as ' "creativity", in the dictionary sense of the verb *creare*, "to bring forth, beget, produce" '.[1] In Aristotle's doctrine, on the other hand, the 'efficacy', the 'act' whereby the ultimate, 'matter', takes different forms is not to be ascribed to the 'ultimate' itself, but to 'form'. As Professor Gilson has expressed this point:[2]

Obviously, if there is in a substance anything that is act, it is not the matter, it is the form. The form then is the very act whereby a substance is what it is, and, if a being is primarily or, as Aristotle himself says, almost exclusively *what* it is, each being is primarily and almost exclusively its form. This, which is true of the doctrine of Aristotle, will remain equally true of the doctrine of his disciples, otherwise they would not be his disciples. The distinctive character of a truly Aristotelian metaphysics of being—and one might be tempted to call it its specific form—lies in the fact that it knows no act superior to the form, not even existence. There is nothing above being; in being there is nothing above the form, and this means that the form of a given being is an act of which there is no act.

Whitehead rejects this doctrine. Whitehead and Aristotle are in agreement in holding that 'act', 'acting', is a generic feature of actuality.[3] But if the act whereby an actuality is what it is be 'form', then 'form' is tacitly being regarded as the 'ultimate'. 'Form', however, cannot fulfil the requirements of an 'ultimate', as Aristotle well knew when he considered the notion of 'form' whilst refraining from identifying 'form' and 'being'. Whitehead draws the logical conclusion that the 'act' whereby actuality is what it is, is itself the 'ultimate'. That is, the 'ultimate' is not something else which includes the factor of 'activity'; *acting* as *such* is sufficient to fulfil the requirements of an 'ultimate', i.e. a 'that' 'which is actual by virtue of its accidents', a 'that' of which the many actual entities are individualizations. For in Whitehead's theory, as we have seen, an actual entity *is* an act of becoming; the 'being' of an actual entity is its 'becoming'. Thus whereas

---

[1] PR 302 [324]. [2] Gilson, *op. cit.*, p. 47.
[3] For Aristotle, cf. Gilson, *op. cit.*, pp. 43–4, and Owens, *op. cit.*, Chapter 14.

Aristotle identifies 'being' and 'form', Whitehead identifies 'being' and 'acting'; an *actual* entity is an *acting* entity.

Thus in Whitehead's doctrine the universe is made up of actual entities which are unit processes of acting. Apart from these individual acting entities there is nothing whatever which is 'actual'. Therefore ultimately the universe, as Whitehead conceives it, is constituted by a 'process of creative activity', analogously to the materialist conception of the universe as ultimately constituted by enduring 'matter'. This 'creative activity' or 'creativity' is universal and ultimate in the same sense as the materialists' 'matter' is universal and ultimate, viz., it is the universal generic feature of all actual entities.

'Creativity' is therefore 'ultimate' in the sense, first, that it constitutes the generic metaphysical character of all actualities; and secondly it is the 'ultimate' in the sense that the actualities are individualizations of it. That is to say, 'creative activity' or 'creativity' is not merely a common feature of the individual actual entities, any more than 'matter' is merely a common feature of 'material things'; creativity is an 'ultimate' instantiated in individual actualities, and of which the individual actualities are instances.

It should be noted that this conception of an 'ultimate' 'which is actual by virtue of its accidents' is necessary as a prerequisite in the conception of a 'universe', for the individual actualities, viewed in their separate individuality, are contingent and accidental—in Whitehead's or any other conception—and can thus provide no 'ground' either for there being a *universe*, or for the universe being what it is. It is this requirement of a 'ground' which led, for example, to Aristotle's conception of an 'unmoved mover', and in some other philosophies to a God conceived as a transcendent creator, or to a monistic 'Absolute'. Whitehead rejects all theories of a wholly transcendent 'ground' as involving incoherence. The line indicated by the monistic theory is the only tenable one if coherence in a metaphysical system is to be achieved, namely, that the 'ground' of the universe must be ascribed to the 'ultimate'. But this requires that the 'ultimate be so conceived as coherently and consistently to constitute that 'ground'.

Whitehead achieves this by conceiving the 'ultimate' as 'creativity', a universal process of creative activity which, while transcending each *individual* actual creature, is not itself actual, but is instantiated in the individual actualities.[1] Thus is secured the conception of a connected 'universe'. And thus is secured the character of the universe to be perpetually 'going on': for its 'ultimate' character is that of self-creating activity. The individual actual entities are the 'creatures' of this universal 'creativity'. They are not creatures of creativity in the sense that creativity is a 'creator', i.e. in the sense that 'creativity' is itself a transcendent actuality creating them; but in the sense that the 'ultimate', creativity, individualizes itself in the individual creatures. In this conception, as will be seen in more detail later,[2] God is not a transcendent creator, but is the primordial creature of creativity; that is, God is the primordial instantiation of creativity.

This conception secures too the *existence* of the universe without the need of a transcendent creator to account for its existence. In this system creativity is the ultimate 'ground' for the existence of the universe, in that the universe *exists* by virtue of its ultimate character as creativity, as creating activity.[3] For, as we have seen, 'being' or 'existence' consists in the 'activity of becoming'; thus the 'existence' of the universe is constituted by its ultimate nature as a perpetual self-creating activity.

'Creativity', Whitehead points out, is not to be conceived as an 'entity in the sense in which [actual] occasions and eternal objects [i.e. 'forms'] are entities'.[4] He does not list creativity, the 'category of the ultimate', among his 'categories of existence'. Creativity, he wrote,[5] 'is the general metaphysical character which underlies all occasions, in a particular mode for each occasion. There is nothing with which to compare it: it is Spinoza's one infinite substance', but not conceived as an 'actual entity'.

[1] This, as we shall see later (§ 38), does not obviate the need for a unique primordial instance of creativity, namely, God.   [2] § 39 below.
[3] This requires being complemented by the discussion in Chapter XVI below.
[4] S M W 220.   [5] S M W 220.

§ 15

THE 'CONCRESCENCE' OF ACTUAL ENTITIES

Whitehead's doctrine, in summary, is therefore 'that the actual world is a process, and that the process is the becoming of actual entities. Thus actual entities are creatures'[1] of Creativity. 'The word Creativity', he points out,[2] 'expresses the notion that each [actual entity] is a process issuing in novelty.' This is the 'microscopic' process, the act of becoming of an actual entity. There is also the 'macroscopic' process, which is 'the transition from attained actuality to actuality in attainment'.

Hitherto this macroscopic process has been treated in its aspect as the mere supersession of the individual perishing actualities. But the actual entities must not be conceived as individually wholly independent and separate, merely superseding each other. Each is a creature of the creativity which proceeds perpetually to new creations. Whitehead expressed this by saying that

there is a rhythm of process whereby creation produces natural pulsation, each pulsation forming a natural unit of historic fact. In this way amid the infinitude of the connected universe, we can discern vaguely finite units of fact.[3]

There is a rhythm in the universal creative process: the process of attaining actuality, of becoming, passes into the process of transition from the attained actuality to another in attainment. Thus this process of transition, 'in Locke's language, is the "perpetually perishing" which is one aspect of the notion of time'.[4] But since actual entities, in this doctrine, are conceived as successive individualizations of the universal creativity, this process of transition is, in another aspect, the *passing* of attained actuality *into* actuality in attainment. As Whitehead has put it,[5] 'in another aspect the transition is the origination of the present in conformity with the "power" of the past'.

That is to say, the present actuality, which is in the process of

[1] PR 30 [33].   [2] AI 303.   [3] MT 120.   [4] PR 298 [320].   [5] PR 298 [320].

origination, in the process of becoming, is a novel creation out of 'components' constituted by antecedent actualities. Whitehead uses the word 'conformity' advisedly, for the present actuality in becoming is a *new* creature, self-created; it is not an antecedent actuality in a new 'state'. But the novel creature cannot be an origination 'out of nothing'—that would constitute a violation of the ontological principle; it has to have 'data'. The primary data for an actuality in becoming are the antecedent actualities which have become. That is, the antecedent actualities constitute the data for, and the 'components' of, the new actuality in becoming. The new actual entity is a novel origination, but it 'conforms' to the past in the sense that its components are derivative from antecedent actualities.

The actuality in becoming is a 'growing together' of the antecedent data into a novel unity. Whitehead uses the word 'concrescence' to signify this process of becoming which constitutes the new actual entity. He explains that 'the word Concrescence is a derivative from the familiar Latin verb, meaning "growing together" ',[1] and adds that the use of this word 'also has the advantage that the participle "concrete" is familiarly used for the notion of a complete physical reality'.

Thus, Whitehead says, each actual entity, 'viewed in its separate individuality, is a passage between two ideal termini, namely, its components in their ideal disjunctive diversity passing into these same components in their concrete togetherness'.[2] By 'disjunctive diversity' he means that the antecedent actualities, in themselves, are individual—diverse individuals in disjunction. As data for a subsequent new actuality, they become (i.e. pass into being) components of a 'concrete togetherness' which *is* the new actuality. The new creature is 'concrete' (i.e. actual) by virtue of its 'concrescence', its process of 'growing together'; in other words, its 'concreteness' or 'actuality' is constituted by its act of achieving a novel unity. The rhythm of the universal creative process therefore distinguishes itself into two phases, which are the two species of process.

[1] A I 303.   [2] A I 303.

One kind is the fluency [process] inherent in the constitution of the particular existent. This kind I have called 'concrescence'. The other kind is the fluency whereby the perishing of the process, on the completion of the particular existent, constitutes that existent as an original element in the constitutions of other particular existents elicited by repetitions of process. This kind I have called 'transition'.[1]

[1] P R 298 [320].

CHAPTER VII

The Category of Eternal Object

§ 16

ETERNAL OBJECTS OR FORMS OF DEFINITENESS

In this universal, two-phase process constituting the universe, the *actual* entities are the individual 'pulsations', the individual 'concrescences'. No other entities are 'actual'; all other entities exist only as 'components' of the individual concrescences, or as abstract derivations from the individual actual entities. This is an alternative statement of the ontological principle in terms of the category of process. As Whitehead has put it:[1]

The nature of any type of existence [entity] can only be explained by reference to its implication in creative activity, essentially involving three factors: namely, data, process with its form relevant to these data, and issue into datum for further process—data, process, issue.

'The alternative', he adds, 'is the reduction of the universe to a barren tautological absolute.'

The 'data' for any one actuality in the process of concrescence, we have seen, as required by the ontological principle, must be the antecedent actualities which have become. However, before we can understand how the antecedent data can 'grow together' to constitute a new actuality, we must first examine another kind of entity not so far discussed.

[1] M T 126-7.

91

Each actual entity is an individualization of the creativity; that is to say, the individuality of each actual entity is constituted by the ultimate creativity taking a particular form. The analogy with Aristotle's doctrine is exact. Just as for Aristotle there is no 'matter' purely as such, so for Whitehead there is no 'activity' purely as such; the concept of activity as such is an abstraction. There are only the concrete individual acts, which are the concrete individual actual entities.

But an individual act (and thus an actual entity) is of a particular form or character, as in Aristotle's doctrine each individual οὐσία has a particular form. An act, in order to be an act, must have some determinate form, some definite character. That is to say, it is by virtue of its form that it is a definite act; without a form of definiteness there could be no individual act, and thus no actual entity. A 'form of definiteness' is therefore a fundamental, necessary ingredient of an actuality. Alternatively expressed, for there to be an individual actuality, its activity must take a definite form. Its 'being' as an *actual* entity requires its definiteness being determined by a particular kind of 'entity', namely, its 'form'.

For 'forms of definiteness' are 'entities': they exist. But they do not exist as themselves 'actual', but only as the forms of definiteness *of* actual entities. Their mode of existence is that of 'components' of *actual* entities.

In Whitehead's philosophy, as in Aristotle's, despite their status as 'ingredients' in actual entities, the forms of definiteness must be distinguished as among the most fundamental types of entities. Although they *exist* only as determinants of the definiteness of actual entities, the forms are not merely the forms of *particular* individual actualities, determining the definiteness of those alone and having no relation to others. For example, different actual entities can have the same form. Forms have universality; they are capable of 'informing' various different actualities. It is evident that in the forms we have to recognize a unique kind of entity which, in certain respects, stands in an extreme contrast to 'actual' entities.

The Category of Eternal Object

We must admit that in some sense or other, we inevitably presuppose this realm of forms, in abstraction from passage, loss, and gain. For example, the multiplication table up to 'twelve-times-twelve' is a humble member of it. In all our thoughts of what has happened and can happen, we presuppose the multiplication table as essentially qualifying the course of history, whenever it is relevant. It is always at hand, and there is no escape.[1]

Whitehead has made it clear that 'these forms of definiteness are the Platonic forms, the Platonic ideas, the medieval universals'.[2] But because his conception of them differs somewhat from that of antecedent thought, he has termed them 'eternal objects'.[3] His reasons for the choice of this term as an alternative for 'forms of definiteness' will be elucidated in the rest of this chapter.

We can appreciate that these entities are 'eternal' by contrasting their 'being' with that of actual entities. We have seen that the 'being' of actual entities *is constituted by* their process of becoming—their 'being', both in the sense of their 'existing' (i.e. the 'fact of' their existing), and in the sense of the 'nature of' their existing (i.e. the mode in which they exist): their 'existing' is their 'acting', and the nature of their existence is that of 'acting'. 'Acting' is the very constitution of their 'being'. Their 'being' (in both senses) thus essentially involves 'change', i.e. the transition implicit in 'becoming'. Actual entities thus *come into existence* in the sense of being *novel creations*.

Forms, on the other hand, are *not* novel creations; their 'being', in the sense of the *nature of* their existing, does not consist in a process of becoming. Becoming, process, transition, are essentially

[1] M T 93.   [2] F R 26.

[3] Cf. P R 60 [69–70]: 'The term "Platonic form" has here been used as the briefest way of indicating the entities in question. But these lectures are not an exegesis of Plato's writings; the entitie.. in question are not necessarily restricted to those which he would recognize as "forms". Also the term "idea" has a subjective suggestion in modern philosophy, which is very misleading for my present purposes; and in any case it has been used in many senses and has become ambiguous. The term "essence", as used by the Critical Realists, also suggests their use of it, which diverges from what I intend. Accordingly, by way of employing a term devoid of misleading suggestions, I use the phrase "eternal object" for what in the preceding paragraph of this section I have termed a "Platonic form".'

irrelevant to their nature, to their 'being' in this sense. This is what is meant by saying that they are 'eternal'.

But their 'being', in the sense of the *fact of* their existing, does involve process, since they are the determinants of the definiteness of the process of acting of actual entities. That is to say, they 'come into existence' in the sense of 'informing' the actualities in the process of becoming, but not in the sense that they themselves are new creatures. Thus the definiteness of an *actual entity* becomes, but the definiteness of a *form* does not become: it is what it is, eternal, a form of that particular definiteness and no other.

Whitehead uses the term 'ingression' for expressing this 'coming into existence' in the sense of 'informing' or determining the definiteness of actualities. The forms have 'ingression' in the novel actual entities, thereby determining their definiteness. Thus, Whitehead writes,[1]

in such a philosophy the actualities constituting the process of the world are conceived as exemplifying the ingression (or 'participation') of other things [entities] which constitute the potentialities of definiteness for any actual existence. The things which are temporal arise by their participation in the things which are eternal.

This 'ingression' of the forms implies that in some sense they are antecedent to the actualities in which they have ingression. The precise sense of their 'antecedence' must be carefully noted. It would be quite inadmissible to suppose that forms are 'antecedent' by virtue of their 'eternity', for this would imply tacitly treating 'eternally existing' forms as some kind of actuality. By the ontological principle, this 'antecedence' cannot consist in the forms themselves being 'actualities', existing in some kind of Platonic 'world of forms'. They can exist only as 'ingredients' in actual entities. Accordingly it must be from the past actualities that the forms have ingression into present actualities, namely those which are in the process of becoming. In other words, forms are 'given', and thus become 'objects', only by virtue of their existence in antecedent actual entities.

[1] P R 54 [63].

It must be emphasized that eternal forms exist only as ingredients in some or other actual entity; by their nature they must have ingression in *some* actuality. But there is nothing in their nature to determine *which* actuality they will have ingression into. On the contrary, *in themselves* they are neutral as to the particular actual entities into which they have ingression. Eternal objects are those ingredients in actual entities whereby the definiteness of those actualities is determined; and, as we shall see in more detail as we proceed, 'any entity whose conceptual recognition does not involve a necessary reference to any definite actual entities of the temporal world is . . . an "eternal object" '.[1]

In these words Whitehead gives a precise definition of 'eternal object'.

The forms, in their very nature, are 'timeless' or 'eternal', and 'given'. They are 'given to' the actualities in question (namely, those in becoming), and are thus 'objects' for those actualities as subjects. It is because they are essentially and always 'given' as 'objects' for an actuality in becoming, and because in their nature they are 'eternal', that Whitehead has termed them 'eternal objects'.

§ 17

ACTUALITY AND POTENTIALITY

The relationship of eternal objects to actual entities, as entailed in this factor of 'givenness', is complex, and must be examined in some detail. We have seen that in their nature eternal objects are neutral in regard to their ingression into particular actualities. This can be expressed by saying that in themselves the eternal forms are merely *potential* for the determination of the definiteness of some or other actualities; in themselves the eternal objects are 'pure potentials' for the determination of actuality. As Whitehead points out,[2] their nature as 'potentialities' is entailed in their 'givenness':

[1] P R 60 [70].   [2] P R 60 [70].

An eternal object is always a potentiality for actual entities; but in itself . . . it is neutral as to the fact of its . . . ingression' in any particular actual entity of the temporal world. 'Potentiality' is the correlative of 'givenness'. The meaning of 'givenness' is, that what *is* 'given' might not have been 'given'; and that what *is not* 'given' *might have been* 'given'.

The philosophical tradition early recognized the concept of 'potentiality' as standing in contrast to 'actuality', and the need for defining its metaphysical status. Whitehead, like Aristotle, insists that 'potentiality' must be regarded as an important metaphysical notion:

The notion of potentiality is fundamental for the understanding of existence, as soon as the notion of process is admitted. If the universe be interpreted in terms of static actuality, then potentiality vanishes. Everything is just what it is. Succession is mere appearance, rising from the limitation of perception. But if we start with process as fundamental, then the actualities of the present are deriving their characters from the process, and are bestowing their characters upon the future. Immediacy is the realization of the potentialities of the past, and is the storehouse of the potentialities of the future.[1]

That is to say, the conception of a universe in which there is process, change, growth, development, implies the notion of 'potentiality'. For a universe in which there is change, etc., entails that tomorrow there will be something different from what is the case today, something which today is *not* 'actual'. It will be actual tomorrow, but today it is only 'potential'. In other words,[2]

apart from 'potentiality' and 'givenness', there can be no nexus of actual things in process of supersession by novel actual things. The alternative is a static monistic universe, without unrealized potentialities; since 'potentiality' is then a meaningless term.

But the notions of 'potentiality' and 'givenness' are abstract notions, and must therefore refer to actualities for their meaning. Thus, what is 'potential' is *potential for* something 'actual'.

[1] M T 136.   [2] P R 62 [72].

Moreover, there is no 'potentiality' purely as such: it is always an *entity* which is 'potential' for an *actual entity*. This, as Whitehead points out, and as we shall see in more detail as we proceed, is the very meaning of 'entity', namely, that it is a potential for actuality. The elucidation of this will take us through the following chapter; here we will deal with only one aspect of it.

This is that involved in the previous quotation. It links 'potentiality' with the factor of 'novelty'. There cannot be anything 'novel', that is, different from what is already 'actual', unless there be 'entities' which are 'potential'. As Whitehead has put it,[1]

it is evident that [the notions of] 'givenness' and 'potentiality' are meaningless apart from a multiplicity of potential entities. These potentialities are the 'eternal objects'.

The point is that, by the ontological principle, something 'novel' cannot come into existence 'out of nowhere'; it must be 'given' as an 'unrealized potentiality'. This 'unrealized potentiality' must be constituted by 'entities', the word 'unrealized' simply underlines the contrast of 'potentiality' with 'actuality'. Thus the notion of 'novelty' can have no meaning unless there be entities which are '*pure potentials*'. These are the eternal objects.

The notion of 'potentiality', we have said, stands in contrast to that of 'actuality'. Thus, Whitehead maintains, there are two types of contrasting entity, actual entities and eternal objects, respectively constituting the type of 'actuality' and the type of 'pure potentiality'. But though they constitute two contrasting types of entity, it does not follow that they *exist* as distinct and separate. 'Actuality and Potentiality require each other in the reciprocal roles of example and character';[2] that is to say, 'Actuality is the exemplification of Potentiality, and Potentiality is the characterization of Actuality'.[3] Thus, Whitehead writes, 'in order to understand Actuality, we must ask, What is character, and What is it that has character?'[4] His answer is that it is actuality which has character, or rather more strictly, that it is Creativity which has character, thereby constituting the actual entities. And

[1] P R 62 [72].   [2] M T 97.   [3] M T 96.   [4] M T 97.

character, considered in abstraction from actual entities, is constituted by certain entities, the eternal objects, the pure potentials,
the forms which determine the definiteness of actualities.

Thus Whitehead does not accept the doctrine of 'Platonic
realism' in the sense that eternal objects are a kind of actuality,
existing independently from actual entities; he is fully in accord
with Aristotle's rejection of this doctrine. But to admit eternal
forms as a type of entity contrasting with actuality, while not
existing separately from actuality, makes it necessary to specify
more elaborately what precisely is the relationship between these
two types of entity.

We can begin to do this by considering the nature of eternal
objects as 'pure potentials'. Potentiality, we have seen, is 'potentiality for' actuality. Thus in their nature as 'potentials', eternal
objects must be 'given' to actual entities. That is, 'potentiality'
implies 'givenness'; or more strictly 'capacity for givenness', for
there is an important element of indeterminateness in 'potentiality'.
But potentialities must *be given* to actualities in order to exist
at all. It is 'as given', 'as data', that they are 'objects' for particular
actualities. Now 'as objects' the potentialities have lost that
element of 'capacity for' givenness, since 'as objects' they *are
received* by the actualities in question. Thus, just as 'potentiality'
involves 'givenness', so 'givenness' involves 'reception'. As
Whitehead has put it,[1]

the notion of 'givenness' carries with it a reference beyond the mere
data in question. It refers to a 'decision' whereby what is 'given' is
separated off from what for that occasion is 'not given'. This element
of 'givenness' in things implies some activity procuring limitation.

But, it must be clear, while the eternal forms, by virtue of
their nature as 'potential', possess the feature of 'givenness', to
them must not be ascribed the 'activity procuring limitation'
which is the correlative of 'givenness'. In themselves the forms
are *pure* potentials; in themselves they are indifferent as to the
particular actualities into which they have ingression. Their
'givenness' implies that they *must have* ingression into *some* or

[1] P R 58 [68].

other actuality, but not *which* actuality that is to be. In other words, the 'decision' as to which actualities the eternal forms will have ingression into does not, and cannot, lie with the forms themselves. It cannot, for 'decision' is an *act*, and by the onto-logical principle, only *actual* entities are capable of acting.[1] This 'decision', this 'activity procuring limitation', lies with the actual entities in question, namely those in the process of concrescence, those receiving the forms.

Eternal objects and actual entities are therefore necessary to each other. The activity constituting the existence of an actual entity must be an 'activity procuring limitation', for otherwise it could not be that particular actual entity which it is rather than another; in fact, there must be limitation if an actual entity is to *be* at all. Thus an actuality, in order to be, to exist, must 'decide', it must select from among potentialities, which must accordingly be 'given'. Properly to understand the relation of actuality and potentiality it is essential to be clear, as Whitehead puts it,[2] that ' "decision" cannot be construed as a casual adjunct of an actual entity. It constitutes the very meaning of actuality'. That is to say, 'decision' constitutes the essential nature of the act whereby actuality 'becomes'. Since this 'decision' is basically one as to the ingression of eternal objects, it means that ' "actuality" is the decision amid "potentiality" '.[3] Thus, White-head says,[4] 'just as "potentiality for process" is the meaning of the more general term "entity" or "thing"; so "decision" is the additional meaning imported by the word "actual" into the phrase "actual entity" '.

It will be noted that in this passage 'potentiality' is *not* restricted to eternal entities; *all* entities are potentials. In other words, there are potentials other than 'pure potentials' or eternal objects, and these must be investigated in order to achieve an adequate understanding of the relation of potentiality and actuality.

---

[1] In Whitehead's statement (P R 58 [68]): 'The ontological principle declares that every decision is referable to one or more actual entities, because in separa-tion from actual entities there is nothing, merely nonentity—"The rest is silence".'

[2] P R 58 [68]. [3] P R 59 [68]. [4] P R 58–9 [68].

CHAPTER VIII

The Category of Relativity

§ 18

THE CATEGORY OF RELATIVITY

The ontological principle states that actual entities are the only fully existent entities. All other entities exist only in the derivative sense of being implicated in the existence of actual entities. As Whitehead has put it[1] in a passage already quoted,[2]

The nature of any type of existence can only be explained by reference to its implication in creative activity.

In a conception of the universe as involving process, change, development, the *actual* entities are *acting* entities. To 'be' is to 'be something'; existing implies limitation. So the 'acting' is that of 'deciding'. 'Decision' implies 'data', something 'given'. This 'something' which is 'given', and 'received'—thereby limiting the actuality to that particular character and not another—we have seen to be entities which are 'potentials'. They are 'potentials' in contrast to the 'actuals', which are those entities in the process of becoming, in the process of acting.

In the previous chapter we discussed one such type of 'potential entity', namely the 'pure potentials' or eternal objects. But we saw there that although these pure potentials are 'eternal' in their essential nature, by the ontological principle they cannot 'exist'

[1] M T 126. [2] § 16 above.

100

except as implicated in particular actual entities. They have no independent existence in some 'Platonic realm of forms'. Thus from the point of view of an actual entity in the process of concrescence, the 'givenness' of the eternal objects is that of their implication in the antecedent actualities; that is, eternal objects are 'given' to an actual entity in becoming in their capacity as determining the definiteness of antedecent actualities. Whitehead speaks of these antecedent actual entities as being 'in the universe' or 'in the actual world' of the concrescing actual entity in question.

Thus what is in fact 'given' to a concrescing actual entity is not 'pure potentials' as such, but antecedent actualities as formed or determined by certain eternal objects. That is, the antedecent actual entities are 'given' *through the mediation of* eternal objects,[1] and the eternal objects are 'given' as implicated in the antecedent actual entities. The 'data' for any actual entity are therefore complex. It is of importance that this complexity be carefully analysed.

The antecedent actualities are 'data' for an actual entity in the process of becoming. Being 'data' means that they are 'given', and we have seen that the correlative of 'giveness' is 'potentiality'. Thus antecedent actualities, as well as eternal objects, stand to present concrescing actualities as 'potentials' to 'actuals'. Only concrescing, i.e. 'acting' entities are *actual* in the full, proper sense. The acting of antecedent actualities is completed; as such they are, in the strict sense, no longer 'actual'. As completed they are 'data' for succeeding actual entities, and are thus 'potentials' in relation to the succeeding 'actuals'.

It will be observed that 'actuality' and 'potentiality' are therefore relative: an entity which is now 'actual' will subsequently, when its activity is complete, become 'potential' for a new 'actuality'. It must be carefully noted that, by the ontological principle, *actuality* always constitutes the point of reference for the definition of 'potentiality'. 'Potentiality' always means an entity which is 'potential for' an entity which is 'actual'; and an 'actual' entity is one which is *in the process* of acting.

[1] 'How' this mediation is effected is the main topic of the next Part.

This conception of 'actuality' and 'potentiality' is a direct implication of the ontological principle interpreted in terms of the Category of Process. Whitehead sees this implication as an important general metaphysical principle or category, and has termed it the 'principle of relativity'. Stated in its full generality it is the principle[1]

that the potentiality for being an element in a real concrescence of many entities into one actuality, is the one general metaphysical character attaching to all entities, actual and non-actual; and that every item in its universe is involved in each concrescence. In other words, it belongs to the nature of a 'being' that it is a potential for every 'becoming'.

In this statement the category of relativity makes two assertions: the first is the basic one, and the second is an implication of it.

The first assertion is that it is a general metaphysical feature of every 'entity' that it is a 'potential'; in Whitehead's words, 'it belongs to the nature of a "being" [in any sense] that it is a potential for a "becoming" ', i.e. for an actuality. The reason is that, by the ontological principle, an 'entity' can exist only *either* as itself 'actual' (i.e. acting), *or* as implicated in the activity of some actuality. It thus follows that the latter class of entities must have the 'potentiality' for implication; they must be 'potentials' for 'actuals' as a condition of their 'being', their 'existing'. 'Potentiality', as Whitehead points out,[2] is strictly the meaning of 'entity'. And with this general statement we include the former class of entities, viz. 'actual' entities, in the scope of the category of relativity. For all 'actual' entities in turn become 'potentials' upon the completion of their process of self-creative activity.

We now come to the second assertion. Since 'it belongs to the nature of a "being" that it is a potential for a "becoming" ', that is, since every 'entity' is a 'potential' for an actuality, it follows that every actuality must *receive* those potentials 'in its universe', namely those which are 'given'. 'Potentiality' involves 'givenness', and 'givenness' involves 'reception'. It would be an invalid objection to this to say that 'givenness' does not necessarily involve 'reception', that there can be 'giving' without 'receiving'. For if there be 'non-receptions' it means *either* 'rejection', *or* just no relationship at all. If the former, it nevertheless implies 'reception' of some kind; for there must be some form of 'reception' in order to have 'rejection'; there must be some form of 'reception' to render it possible for 'decision', and thus 'rejection', to be effected. If the latter be the case, then the entity in question is not 'in the universe' of that particular actuality. The second assertion thus implies that[1]

the data for any one pulsation of actuality consist of the full content of the antecedent universe as it exists in relevance to that pulsation. They are this universe conceived in its multiplicity of details. These multiplicities are antecedent pulsations, and also, there are the variety of forms harboured in the nature of things, either as realized form or as potentialities for realization. Thus the data consist in what has been, what might have been, and what may be. And in all these phrases the verb 'to be' means some mode of relevance to historic actualities.

§ 19

'ABSTRACT' AND 'REAL' POTENTIALITY

It will be noted that Whitehead speaks, in the foregoing passage, of 'the variety of forms harboured in the nature of things, either as realized form or as potentialities for realization'. This distinction between 'realized form' and 'potentialities for realization' might appear to contradict what has been said above about the 'givenness' of eternal objects being that of their implication in antecedent actual entities. However, when the nature of eternal forms is studied in further detail, it becomes clear that this is not the case.

Implicit in the discussion of potentiality in the previous two sections is a distinction which must now be made fully explicit. This distinction is that between pure abstract or 'general' potentiality, and what can be called 'conditioned' potentiality.

[1] M T 121.

The notion of 'potentiality' is in one respect ambiguous. Potentiality can have a purely abstract, general sense, meaning just all and every possibility, without regard to the particular conditions actually obtaining. Now this pure abstract potentiality must be 'something'; it must be constituted by some kind of 'entity'. This pure abstract or general potentiality 'is the bundle of possibilities, mutually consistent or alternative, provided by the multiplicity of eternal objects'.[1] That is to say, these entities are the eternal forms, *but as considered in complete abstraction from, and without relevance to, their particular ingression into actualities.* When so considered, Whitehead points out,[2] it follows

that an eternal object can be described only in terms of its potentiality for 'ingression' into the becoming of actual entities; and that its analysis only discloses other eternal objects. It is a pure potential. The term 'ingression' refers to the particular mode in which the potentiality of an eternal object is realized in a particular actual entity, contributing to the definiteness of that actual entity.

The potentiality of an eternal object, considered just in itself, is a pure abstract, general 'potentiality for ingression'. As Whitehead stresses in this passage, 'ingression' 'refers to the particular *mode* in which the potentiality of an eternal object is realized in a particular actual entity'. It *must* have ingression to exist; thus it must be realized in some mode. But it might be realized in alternative different modes. To elucidate this more fully we must deal with the other meaning of potentiality.

The potentiality which constitutes the primary 'data' for a particular actuality in becoming is not a purely abstract potentiality, but is a 'conditioned' potentiality. That is, the potentiality for the achievement of a particular definiteness by the actuality in question is 'conditioned' by what is 'given' to it. What is 'given' are the antecedent actualities, and they have effected a certain 'decision amid potentiality', thereby 'realizing' a selection of eternal objects. Thus in contrast with the 'general' potentiality constituted by the pure abstract eternal objects, this 'conditioned' potentiality is the *real* potentiality for the actuality in question

[1] P R 90 [102].   [2] P R 31 [34].

It is the 'real' potentiality because it is constituted by those eternal objects as 'realized' by the antecedent actualities; that is, those eternal objects are the ones 'really', i.e. in fact, 'given'.

This two-fold aspect of the notion of potentiality can be expressed in another way. 'Potentiality' implies 'indetermination'; that is, a 'potential' entity is indeterminate as to its implication in a particular actuality. 'Determination' is effected by the act of decision of an *actual* entity. This indeterminateness as to implication is the very essence of 'potentiality' in its contrast with 'actuality'. Whitehead summarizes his doctrine in the following terse, somewhat elliptical passage:[1]

that mode of implication is only rendered fully determinate by that concrescence, though it is conditioned by the correlate universe. This indetermination, rendered determinate in the real concrescence, is the meaning of 'potentiality'. It is a *conditioned* indetermination, and is therefore called a *'real* potentiality'.

'Potentiality' means 'indetermination, rendered determinate in the real concrescence' because concretely or 'really', 'potentiality' does not *exist* separately from actuality. This is only to state in another way what was said earlier, namely that 'potentiality' involves 'givenness', and 'givenness' involves 'reception'. When we consider 'concrete fact', potentiality *exists* as implicated in actualities; and it is 'given' as implicated in antecedent actualities. Thereby the 'indetermination' of potentiality is 'conditioned'. It is only in abstraction that the indetermination of potentiality is 'pure'.

We have insisted that 'potentiality' is strictly 'potential entity'. Thus this dual aspect of 'potentiality' is exemplified in the dual aspect of the nature of eternal objects: as 'pure' or 'general' potentials, and as 'conditioned' or 'real' potentials. In any instance of its existing, an eternal object is always 'conditioned'; that is, it 'exists' through being implicated in the definiteness of an actual entity. But that particular mode of implication does not exhaust its possibilities; it might have been implicated in that actuality in some other mode. In other words,

[1] P R 30–1 [34].

Whitehead's Metaphysics

each entity in the universe of a given concrescence *can*, so far as its own nature [as a 'potentiality'] is concerned, be implicated in that concrescence in one or other of many modes; but in fact it is implicated in only *one* mode.[1]

For example, after a meal the smell of steamed fish is implicated in me in a different mode from what it was before the meal. The 'mode of implication' consists, in a final analysis, in the particular combination of the eternal objects in question with other eternal objects. But we cannot enter further into this analysis here.

   The point I am concerned to bring out is that although in any instance of existing, an eternal object is always 'conditioned', its essential nature is not thereby restricted. Even in that conditioned mode, its alternatives are not wholly forfeit; for the eternal object still retains an aspect of 'might have been'. To put this in another way, to consider an eternal object in its essential nature, we cannot confine it to any particular mode of its ingression; it must be considered in abstraction from all modes of ingression. Thus, Whitehead points out,[2]

general potentiality is absolute, and real potentiality is relative to some actual entity, taken as a standpoint whereby the actual world is defined.

General potentiality is absolute because it is abstract. As concrete or 'real', potentiality is always relative to some actuality. An eternal object is both a 'pure' and a 'conditioned' potentiality: it 'exists' as conditioned, but in its nature it is nevertheless pure or general.

   Eternal objects alone among all entities exhibit the full twofold character of 'potentiality'. This is part of the reason why Whitehead sees eternal objects as a type of entity standing in extreme contrast to *actual* entities. Further, other entities are 'potential' by virtue of the implication of eternal objects. Ante-

---

[1] P R 30. Whitehead points out (P R 90 [102]) that 'it must be remembered that the phrase "actual world" is like "yesterday" and "tomorrow", in that it alters its meaning according to standpoint. The actual world must always mean the community of all actual entities, including the primordial actual entity called "God" and the temporal actual entities'.   [2] P R 90 [102].

cedent actualities provide an illustration of this which is very much to the point here.

An actuality a, in the process of acting, is *actual*. But with the completion of its process, its 'creative activity', that which essentially constitutes its 'actuality', ceases. a is then no longer 'actual'. But it is not simply 'nothing'; it is 'something', some 'entity'. As such it is 'potential' for a succeeding actuality β. a is a 'real' potential, for in its 'actual' existence a had effected a 'realization' (or 'actualization') of certain 'pure' potentials. In fact, when we consider a in its capacity as a datum for β, a *is* (i.e. exists as) nothing but those 'conditioned' (as opposed to 'pure') eternal objects. Accordingly Whitehead speaks indifferently (according to the emphasis required for the discussion) of the antecedent actualities and the 'conditioned' eternal objects as the 'real' potentials.

Further justification of this doctrine must take the form of showing in more detail how and why antecedent actualities *are* 'conditioned' eternal objects. This will be done in § 31 below. Here I only want to add that this relationship of 'actuality' and 'potentiality' cannot be understood in terms of static modes of thought. Things must be conceived as 'in the process'. We have discussed above[1] the two-fold rhythm of the universal creative process:

'the fluency inherent in the constitution of the particular existent', and 'the fluency whereby the perishing of the process, on the completion of the particular existent, constitutes that existent as an original element in the constitutions of other particular existents elicited by repetitions of process'.[2]

We can now see that the category of process, the category of relativity, and the category which Whitehead has called the ontological principle, 'state different aspects of one and the same general metaphysical truth':[3]

The first category states the doctrine in a general way: that every ultimate actuality embodies in its own essence what Alexander terms 'a principle of unrest', namely, its becoming. [The category of relativity] applies this doctrine to the very notion of 'entity'. It asserts that the notion of an 'entity' means 'an element contributory to the process of becoming'. We have in this category the utmost generalization of the notion of 'relativity'. The [ontological principle] asserts that the obligations imposed on the becoming of any particular actual entity arise from the constitutions of other actual entities.

§ 20

THE 'OBJECTIFICATION' OF ACTUAL ENTITIES

The 'obligations' referred to in the preceding quotation, are imposed on the concrescing actuality by virtue of the antecedent actualities being 'data' for the actual entity in becoming. Since they are 'data', the antecedent actualities are 'objects for' the concrescing actualities receiving them. Whitehead accordingly speaks of the antecedent actualities being 'objectified for' the concrescing actuality in question.

An actual entity in the process of concrescence is a 'subject', creating itself out of 'data', its 'objects'. As we have seen, only those which are *in the process of becoming* are properly 'actual' entities. They are the 'acting' entities, subjects acting, and thereby enjoying what Whitehead terms 'subjective immediacy':[1]

This self-functioning is the real internal constitution of an actual entity. It is the 'immediacy' of the actual entity. An actual entity is called the 'subject' of its own immediacy.

But when the process of self-creative activity terminates, the actual entity 'perishes'; it thereby ceases to be a 'subject' acting, and instead is then an 'object' for the superseding actualities:[2]

Actuality in perishing acquires objectivity, while it loses subjective immediacy. It loses the final causation which is its internal principle of unrest, and it acquires efficient causation whereby it is a ground of obligation characterizing creativity.

[1] P R 34 [38].   [2] P R 40 [44].

The Category of Relativity

It must be emphasized that it is only when the process of becoming has terminated and when accordingly there is a *completed* actual entity, that this actuality can become 'objectified'; while it is in the concrescent process it is a 'subject', a subject creating itself, and as such it is incomplete and thus unable to be an 'object' for another. An actuality cannot be a 'subject' and an 'object' at one and the same time; an actuality can be 'objectified for' another only when it is completed and has thereby lost its 'subjective immediacy'.

§ 21

THE 'OBJECTIVE IMMORTALITY' OF ACTUAL ENTITIES

'Actual entities "perpetually perish" subjectively.'[1] But although they cease thereby to exist in the full sense of 'exist', and are then no longer properly 'actual', they do not become sheer 'nothingness'. They remain 'entities', which means that they 'exist' in another, a 'dependent' way: upon perishing they become 'objectified for' superseding *actual* entities, and 'exist' then as 'elements' in the concrescing actualities. Therefore although actualities perish subjectively, they are 'immortal objectively'.[2] As Whitehead has summarized his doctrine:[3]

Thus we should balance Aristotle's—or, more rightly, Plato's— doctrine of becoming by a doctrine of perishing. When they perish, occasions pass from the immediacy of being into the non-being of immediacy. But that does not mean that they are nothing. They remain 'stubborn fact': Pereunt et imputantur.

'Stubborn fact' is the settled past; it is constituted by 'objectified' actualities. For, in accordance with the ontological principle, 'the objectifications of other actual occasions form the given data from which an actual occasion originates'.[4] Thus, Whitehead points out,[5] 'the term "objectification" refers to the particular

[1] P R 40 [44]. [2] P R 40 [44]. [3] A I 305. [4] P R 105 [117–18]. [5] P R 31 [34].

mode in which the potentiality of one actual entity is realized in another actual entity'. In other words, the antecedent actuality, in that particular objectification (which is dependent upon the 'decision' of the present concrescing actuality), is the 'real' potentiality for that concrescing actuality. Whitehead expresses this point by saying that[1]

the functioning of one actual entity in the self-creation of another actual entity is the 'objectification' of the former for the latter actual entity.

The 'functioning' of antecedent, i.e. settled past, actualities in present concrescing actualities is constituted by their 'objectification'. By contrast, Whitehead speaks of the 'functioning of eternal objects' as their 'ingression' in actual entities:[2]

the functioning of an eternal object in the self-creation of an actual entity is the 'ingression' of the eternal object in the actual entity.

It should be noted that the term 'functioning' in neither case implies 'agency' on the part of the entity functioning. This should be stressed because the contrary supposition might arise from Whitehead's statement above that upon objectification an actual entity 'acquires efficient causation whereby it is a ground of obligation characterizing creativity'.

In his doctrine an 'efficient cause' is a past actuality, as objectified. An efficient cause cannot 'act'; it is an 'efficient cause' by virtue of its 'pastness'. The past does not 'act' in the present, for, as past, its activity is over; it merely 'functions' in the present by being a 'ground of obligation' conditioning the activity of present *actual* entities. The objectified actualities 'characterize creativity' because, as data, they condition the character of creative activity beyond themselves. Accordingly, Whitehead remarks, 'this functioning of creatures, that they constitute the shifting character of creativity, is here termed the "objective immortality" of actual entities'.[3]

Thus the nature of an actual entity too, like that of an eternal object, has a two-fold aspect, also brought out respectively by the

[1] P R 34 [38].   [2] P R 34–5 [38].   [3] P R 43 [47].

two words making up the term Whitehead uses, viz. 'actual' and 'entity'. The former word stresses its 'activity', and thus its 'subjective immediacy', while the latter stresses its 'potentiality' as involved in its role as 'objectified' or 'objectively immortal'. Whitehead has expressed this by saying[1]

that two descriptions are required for an actual entity: (a) one which is analytical of its potentiality for 'objectification' in the becoming of other actual entities, and (b) another which is analytical of the process which constitutes its own becoming.

In other words,

to be actual must mean that all actual things are alike objects, enjoying objective immortality in fashioning creative actions; and that all actual things are subjects, each prehending the universe from which it arises.[2]

It is because of this essential two-fold aspect of the nature of the ὄντως ὄν, the actual entity, that Whitehead retains the word 'actual' even for the actualities as objectified, and this as no longer strictly 'actual' in the sense of 'acting'.

Once again it must be emphasized that this involves conceiving things 'in the process', 'dynamically' and not 'statically'. Whitehead insists that his theory implies

the abandonment of the subject-predicate form of thought, so far as concerns the presupposition that this form is a direct embodiment of the most ultimate characterization of fact. The result is that the 'substance-quality' concept is avoided; and that morphological description is replaced by description of dynamic process.[3]

On this theory, he explains further,[4]

also Spinoza's 'modes' now become the sheer actualities; so that, though analysis of them increases our understanding, it does not lead us to the discovery of any higher grade of actuality. The coherence, which the system seeks to preserve, is the discovery that the process, or concrescence, of any one actual entity involves the other actual

---

[1] P R 31 [34].
[2] P R 78 [89]. The term 'prehension' is explained in Chapter XII below.
[3] P R 8 [10].   [4] P R 8-9 [10].

entities among its components. In this way the obvious solidarity of the world receives its explanation.

This involvement by an actual entity of other actual entities among its components is rendered possible by the two-fold nature of actual entities. In the dynamic creative process constituting the universe, these two aspects of actuality are relative. Thus, Whitehead points out,[1]

the principle [category] of universal relativity directly traverses Aristotle's dictum, '(A substance) is not present in a subject'. On the contrary, according to this principle an actual entity *is* present in other actual entities. In fact if we allow for degrees of relevance, and for negligible relevance, we must say that every actual entity is present in every other actual entity. The philosophy of organism is mainly devoted to the task of making clear the notion of 'being present in another entity'. This phrase is here borrowed from Aristotle: it is not a fortunate phrase, and in subsequent discussion it will be replaced by the term 'objectification'. The Aristotelian phrase suggests the crude notion that one actual entity is added to another *simpliciter*. This is not what is meant.

The concern of the next Part is to make clear *how* one actual entity can be 'present in' another.

[1] P R 69 [79–80].

PART THREE

WHITEHEAD'S CATEGOREAL SCHEME:
THE DOCTRINE OF 'EXPERIENCE'

CHAPTER IX

The 'Reformed' Subjectivist Principle

§ 22

RELATEDNESS: INTERNAL AND EXTERNAL

Whitehead's fundamental divergence from the philosophical tradition, we have seen, lies in his thoroughgoing acceptance of 'process' as a basic metaphysical feature of actuality. Antecedent attempts to give due weight to the factors of 'process', 'change', 'becoming', fail to make them proper metaphysical features of actuality; in one way or another they are relegated to a subordinate ontological status. This is so even in the case of Aristotle: for him 'becoming' is a stage in the achievement of 'actuality'; 'actuality' as such, ἐντελέχεια, is the outcome of the process, and excludes δύναμις. For Whitehead the 'process', the 'becoming', *is* the 'being', the 'existence', of an actual entity. It is in this that the essential novelty and importance of Whitehead's philosophy consists. His metaphysical scheme is the detailed elaboration of this conception of actuality, and the writings of his later period as a whole are investigations of the implications of this conception. His metaphysical doctrine, we have so far seen, is that

Process for its intelligibility involves the notion of a creative activity belonging to the very essence of each occasion. It is the process of eliciting into actual being factors in the universe which antecedently to that process exist only in the mode of unrealized potentialities. The process of self-creation is the transformation of the potential into the actual, and the fact of such transformation includes the immediacy of self-enjoyment.[1]

This transformation is enabled by the 'inclusion' of antecedent actualities in the actualities in the process of self-creation. In order to understand how this 'inclusion' is effected, how it is possible for one actuality to be 'present in' another, it is necessary to investigate much further the nature, the 'what', of an actual entity. How are we to conceive an actual entity such that it is capable of 'including' other actualities? What must be the nature of this 'including'?

It should be noted that this problem of 'inclusion' is not one peculiar to Whitehead's theory; we have here a general metaphysical problem which all theories have to face. It is the problem of 'relatedness', of how one actuality is 'related' to another. It appears in a special form in epistemology in the problem of perception: the problem of how 'external' entities, which are the 'objects' of percipient subjects, can be 'immanent in' those experiences. For unless those objects be in some respect immanent in the percipients, there can be no *experience of* those objects, and we would thus be involved in the solipsist dilemma. Whitehead has expressed this by saying that

there can only be evidence of a world of actual entities, if the immediate actual entity discloses them as essential to its own composition. Descartes' notion of an unessential experience of the external world is entirely alien to the organic philosophy. This is the root point of divergence; and is the reason why the organic philosophy has to abandon any approach to the substance-quality notion of actuality.[2]

To put this in other words, there can only be evidence of an external world if the actualities composing that world be 'internal' or 'internally related' to the percipient actuality. Being 'internally related to' means 'making a difference to', which involves being in some respect 'included' or 'immanent' in the percipient actuality. Whitehead's point is that unless the object be internally related to the percipient—and thereby 'making a difference to',

[1] M T 206–7.   [2] P R 201 [219–20].

and thus being 'essential to the composition' of the percipient—the experience of the percipient cannot be an experience *of* the actual entity external to the percipient. A consistent substance-quality conception must hold, with Leibniz, that other actualities are entirely 'externally related' to the percipient, so that in fact there is no actual experience *of* those actualities. This is what Whitehead means by his phrase 'an unessential experience of the external world'; in this conception the external world is not internally related to the percipient. It is evident that this substance-quality doctrine of actuality is inconsistent with the conception of an experience or perception *of* external things. If, on the other hand, we do maintain that perception is of external things, then, Whitehead holds, it is essential to recognize that

the perceptive constitution of an actual entity presents the problem, How can the other actual entities, each with its own formal existence, also enter objectively into the perceptive constitution of the actual entity in question?[1]

Whitehead points out, as will be shown in more detail, that

the classical doctrines of universals and particulars, of subject and predicate, of individual substances not present in other individual substances, of the externality of relations, alike render this problem incapable of solution.[2]

This problem is presented not only by the fact of perception, but also, Whitehead maintains, by all relatedness in which one entity has an effect on another, i.e. 'makes a difference' to another. His point is that such relatedness is *internal* relatedness. *External* relatedness is, from the point of view of the actualities in question, no relatedness at all; they, as it were, know nothing whatever of each other. That there is between them any [external] relatedness at all (such as 'distance between', 'to the north of', etc.) is only significant from the standpoint of a third actuality observing them.

Whitehead rejects as completely erroneous the presupposition that actualities conceived as, for example, Newtonian or Democritian particles of matter, or Cartesian *res extensa*, despite their purely external relatedness to each other, are nevertheless able to affect each other by *impact*. This is a sheer muddle in thought. For in these doctrines—which exhibit the essential substance-quality conception of actuality—each actuality is conceived as completely self-contained and unaffected in its nature by anything that happens. As Whitehead puts it, 'each substantial thing is thus conceived as complete in itself, without any reference to any other substantial thing'.[1] This is the conception of purely external relations. But, as Leibniz saw, *any* change, even that of acceleration through impact, implies that in some respect a 'difference' has been made to the actualities in question, and thus that the relation of impact is an internal one.[2]

Thus we have *either*, retaining the substance-quality conception of actuality, to deny with Leibniz all internal relationship between actualities, *or* to admit interrelationship between actualities by rejecting the substance-quality conception. For on the basis of the substance-quality conception of actuality no coherent philosophical explanation is possible of the interconnectedness of things evident in all experience.

Such an account of the ultimate atoms, or of the ultimate monads, or of the ultimate subjects enjoying experience, renders an interconnected world of real individuals unintelligible. The universe is shivered into a multitude of disconnected substantial things, each thing in its own way exemplifying its private bundle of abstract characters which have found a common home in its own substantial individuality. But substantial thing cannot call unto substantial thing. A substantial thing can acquire a quality, a credit—but real landed estate, never.[3]

Any attempt, like that of Leibniz, to explain the interconnectedness of things by an appeal to a transcendent agency, that of God or of any other, must necessarily involve incoherence. A coherent philosophical explanation of the interconnectedness of things is

[1] A I 169.
[2] It is of significance that twentieth-century physics has abandoned the notion that no internal difference is made to the particles; all interaction between them involves the gain or loss of 'energy', conceived as an internal ingredient of the particles.   [3] A I 169–70.

possible only in terms of a doctrine of internal relations. This brings us back to the problem of how one actuality can be 'internal to' another, how one actuality can enter into the constitution of another. What must be the nature of actuality for this to be possible?

§ 23

THE 'REFORMED' SUBJECTIVIST PRINCIPLE

In dealing with this problem Whitehead explicitly raises the question of the procedure to be followed. What, he asks, are the primary data for philosophy, the data from which philosophical generalization can proceed? In other words, what are we to take as examples of actual entities, whose generic nature we can discover by the method of imaginative rationalization?

Whitehead points out that one prominent, if not predominant, tendency in the philosophical tradition has been to take the macroscopic objects of experience as instances of actual entities, and to generalize from these. It is to these entities, as we saw above,[1] that the traditional Aristotelian logic is primarily applicable. Hence has arisen the philosophical generalization that 'the final metaphysical fact is always to be expressed as a quality inhering in a substance'.[2] This is the doctrine which Whitehead rejects as making interrelationship impossible.

Descartes, Whitehead maintains, made a most important philosophical advance when he

laid down the principle, that those substances which are the subjects enjoying conscious experiences, provide the primary data for philosophy, namely, themselves as in the enjoyment of such experience. This is the famous subjectivist bias which entered into modern philosophy through Descartes. In this doctrine Descartes undoubtedly made the greatest philosophical discovery since the age of Plato and Aristotle. For his doctrine directly traverses the notion that the proposition,

[1] § 8.   [2] P R 220 [239].

'This stone is grey', expresses a primary form of known fact from which metaphysics can start its generalizations. If we go back to the subjective enjoyment of experience, the type of primary starting-point is 'my experience of this stone as grey'.[1]

That is to say, if the subjectivist principle be accepted that the primary datum is 'the subject experiencing its objects as . . .', then the substance-quality categories must be rejected; 'if the enjoyment of experience be the constitutive subjective fact, those categories have lost all claim to any fundamental character in metaphysics'.[2] For 'the subject experiencing its objects as . . .' cannot validly be analysed in terms of those categories; the attempt to do so cannot but result in error and confusion, for neither the objects nor their characters can be 'qualities' of the experiencing subject.[3] Thus, Whitehead summarizes his point,[4]

with the advent of Cartesian subjectivism, the substance-quality category has lost all claim to metaphysical primacy; and, with the deposition of substance-quality, we can reject the notion of individual substances, each with its private world of qualities and sensations.

Yet, in spite of his subjectivist principle, Descartes did not abandon the substance-quality categories, but continued to conceive experiencing subjects as 'individual substances, each with its private world of qualities and sensations'. In other words,

[1] P R 222 [241].   [2] P R 222 [241].
[3] But, as Whitehead points out, this confused analysis is precisely what did take place. Cf. P R 222–3 [241–2]: 'But like Columbus who never visited America, Descartes missed the full sweep of his own discovery, and he and his successors, Locke and Hume, continued to construe the functionings of the subjective enjoyment of experience according to the substance-quality categories. . . . Hume—to proceed at once to the consistent exponent of the method—looked for a universal quality to function as qualifying the mind, by way of explanation of its perceptive enjoyment. Now if we scan "my perception of this stone as grey" in order to find a universal, the only available candidate is "greyness". Accordingly for Hume "greyness", functioning as a sensation qualifying the mind, is a fundamental type of fact for metaphysical generalization. The result is Hume's simple impressions of sensation, which form the starting-point of his philosophy. But this is an entire muddle, for the perceiving mind is not grey, and so grey is now made to perform a new role. From the original fact "my perception of this stone as grey", Hume extracts "Awareness of sensation of greyness"; and puts it forward as the ultimate datum in this element of experience.'   [4] P R 224 [243].

The 'Reformed' Subjectivist Principle

Descartes conceived 'cogitations'—i.e. sensations, thoughts, volitions, etc.—as in fact purely subjectively existing 'qualities' of the mind. A representative theory of perception followed logically. Whitehead points out that 'it is only by the introduction of covert inconsistencies into the subjectivist principle, as here stated [i.e. as interpreted by Descartes and the British empiricists, in substance-quality terms], that there can be any escape from what Santayana calls, "solipsism of the present moment" '.[1]

Accepting the subjectivist principle, we inevitably become involved in the solipsist difficulty unless we admit that the 'content' of experience is not a purely private qualification of the mind, but is constituted by the immanence of external things; 'if experience be not based upon an objective content, there can be no escape from a solipsist subjectivism'.[2] Thus, Whitehead maintains,

Descartes' discovery on the side of subjectivism requires balancing by an 'objectivist' principle as to the datum for experience.[3]

This is what Whitehead calls the 'reformed' subjectivist principle. That is to say, the subjectivist principle as held by Descartes and his successors, is 'reformed' by the recognition of an 'objectivist principle as to the datum for experience'.

This reformed subjectivist principle entails the recognition that the 'objects' of experience are external things which are in some respect immanent in that subjective occasion of experiencing. Unless that be so, there cannot even be a valid inference to a world of external things. This principle makes it clear that the term 'object' is always correlative to that of 'experiencing subject'; 'object' is not simply a synonym for 'thing', or 'external thing', or 'external entity', but is always that entity *as immanent in* the experiencing subject. Secondly, this principle makes it clear that these 'objects' are entities which in themselves are other than the occasion of experiencing. This is but an implication of the ontological principle, namely, that 'objects' cannot be some-

[1] P R 220 [240].   [2] P R 212 [230-1].   [3] P R 224 [243].

thing originated by the process of experiencing, 'out of nothing'. As Whitehead expresses this:[1]

Two conditions must be fulfilled in order that an entity may function as an object in a process of experiencing: (1) the entity must be *antecedent*, and (2) the entity must be experienced in virtue of its antecedence; it must be *given*. Thus an object must be a thing received, and must not be either a *mode* of reception or a thing *generated* in that occasion. Thus the process of experiencing is constituted by the reception of objects into the unity of that complex occasion which is the process itself. The process creates itself, but it does not create the objects which it receives as factors into its own nature.

Whitehead's doctrine is accordingly that experiencing is basically an *activity* of 'receiving' or 'including' entities as objects. Furthermore,

the objects are the factors in experience which function so as to express that that occasion originates by including a transcendent universe of other things. Thus it belongs to the essence of each occasion of experience that it is concerned with an otherness transcending itself. The occasion is one among others, and including the others which it is among.[2]

We can see, therefore, that the reformed subjectivist principle is not only in accord with the ontological principle, but is required by the other main categories of Whitehead's system, discussed in the previous Part. It can be viewed as a formulation of these categories from the point of view of procedure with regard to the further discovery of the nature of actuality. In Whitehead's words,[3]

the reformed subjectivist principle adopted by the philosophy of organism is merely an alternative statement of the principle of relativity. This principle states that it belongs to the nature of a 'being' that it is a potentiality for every 'becoming'. Thus all things are to be conceived as qualifications of actual occasions. According to the [category of process], *how* an actual entity becomes constitutes *what* that actual entity is. This principle states that the *being* of a *res vera* is constituted by its 'becoming'. The way in which an actual entity is

[1] A I 229.   [2] A I 231.   [3] P R 233 [252–3].

qualified by other actual entities is the 'experience' of the actual world enjoyed by that actual entity, as subject. The subjectivist principle is that the whole universe consists of elements disclosed in the analysis of the experiences of subjects. Process is the becoming of experience. It follows that the philosophy of organism entirely accepts the subjectivist bias of modern philosophy. It also accepts Hume's doctrine that nothing is to be received into the philosophical system which is not discoverable as an element in subjective experience. This is the ontological principle.

CHAPTER X

'Experience' as a Metaphysical Category

§ 24

WHITEHEAD'S REJECTION OF THE CONCEPT OF 'VACUOUS ACTUALITY'

Post-Cartesian philosophy has derived its distinctive character from the introduction of the 'subjectivist principle'. This principle underlies Descartes' method of doubt, and the subjectivist sensationalism which Descartes shares with the British empiricists and Kant, as well as being basic to the Kantian 'Copernican revolution' and modern idealism. The special significance of this principle is that it indicates what is to be taken as the datum fundamentally relevant to the discovery of the nature of actuality. This datum is oneself, experiencing. Whitehead accepts this subjectivist principle, but he purges it of conceptions incoherent with it, such as the substance-quality categories. He insists on the recognition that experiencing is the experiencing of 'objects'; that is, that one's experiencing is constituted by the 'objective inclusion' of an 'otherness transcending oneself'. By his reformed version of the subjectivist principle, the other actualities whose nature we are seeking to discover are 'immanent', as 'objects', in our experiencing. We must examine the implications of this for the discovery of the nature of actuality.

'Experience' as a Metaphysical Category

Whitehead agrees with Descartes that according to this principle, what is to be explicitly taken as an instance of an actual entity is oneself. Secondly, he is at one with Descartes in holding that the factor of 'experiencing' is of primary significance in this context; that is to say, we ourselves must be regarded as essentially 'experiencing entities'. As far as this characterization of ourselves is concerned there is an overwhelming consensus in the philosophical tradition, despite the considerable disagreement as to the precise analysis of 'experience'. In Whitehead's view, as shown in the previous Part, when considering oneself as an actual entity, one must conceive oneself, metaphysically, as an activity of becoming; and when we examine ourselves to find what that generic activity is, we are impelled to the conclusion that it must be 'experiencing'. Apart from other considerations, this is a clear requirement of the reformed subjectivist principle, since it is by virtue of 'experiencing' that other actualities enter into communication with us and thus make it possible for us to discover their nature—for 'what does not so communicate is unknowable, and the unknowable is unknown'.[1]

This brings us to the third implication of the reformed subjectivist principle. This is that since experiencing involves the 'inclusion' of other actualities, those actualities, in order to be capable of being 'included' or 'immanent' in the experiencing actuality, cannot themselves be of a metaphysical nature utterly different from that of the experiencing actuality. We ourselves are indubitably 'experiencing entities', and therefore other actualities which are objects of our experience, cannot be essentially 'non-experiencing entities'. That is to say, they cannot be what Whitehead terms 'vacuous': 'here the term "vacuous" means "devoid of any individual enjoyment arising from the mere fact of realization in that context" '.[2]

It is evident that this rejection of the notion of 'vacuous actuality' is the repudiation, from another point of view, of the doctrine of metaphysical dualism. According to the dualistic

[1] P R 4 [5–6].   [2] A I 281.

doctrine, the actualities comprising the extended 'physical' world are 'dead', without any element of 'feeling' or of anything which is characteristic of 'experience'. Whitehead's argument is that if the 'physical' actualities be 'vacuous' and thus of a generically different metaphysical nature from that of experiencing actualities, then any interrelationship between them must be impossible. This is, stated in a general form, the familiar argument brought against the Cartesian dualism, namely that 'extended' actualities are unable to affect 'cogitating' actualities which, by definition, have no location in space. Whitehead's more general argument is that 'interrelationship' is *internal* relationship, and this implies one entity's being 'immanent' or 'included' in another. But a 'vacuous' actuality, which by definition excludes everything characteristic of 'experience', cannot become any kind of component of 'experience'. Thus a 'vacuous actuality' could never be internally related to an experiencing actuality, and could in no way be 'known'.

According to the reformed subjectivist principle, the nature of other actualities is only to be discovered as 'disclosed in the analysis of the experiences of subjects'. Now when we examine an occasion of experience we find a 'togetherness' of the objectified data. That is, we find the objects as 'together', or 'grown together' into a 'unity of experience'. It must be emphasized that it is this 'experiential unity of objects' which we directly know, of which we have the most intimate acquaintance. For that which we refer to as 'our experience', that which is our 'lived subjective immediacy', that of which each individual experiencer alone can know the 'subjective feel of', is just that 'concrescence' constituting our own particular self as experiencing. As Whitehead expresses it,[1]

there is a togetherness of the component elements in individual experience. This 'togetherness' has that special peculiar meaning of 'togetherness in experience'. It is a togetherness of its own kind, explicable by reference to nothing else.

[1] P R 268 [288].

'Experience' as a Metaphysical Category

This kind of 'experiential togetherness of objects' is the kind of togetherness which we immediately and intimately know. Whitehead now asks whether it is possible for there to be any other kind of togetherness:[1]

The consideration of experiential togetherness raises the final metaphysical question: whether there is any other meaning of 'togetherness'. The denial of any alternative meaning, that is to say, of any meaning not abstracted from the experiential meaning, is the 'subjectivist' doctrine. This reformed version of the subjectivist doctrine is the doctrine of the philosophy of organism.

The contrary doctrine, that there is a 'togetherness' not derivative from experiential togetherness, leads to the disjunction of the components of subjective experience from the community of the external world. This disjunction creates the insurmountable difficulty for epistemology. For intuitive judgment is concerned with togetherness in experience, and there is no bridge between togetherness in experience, and togetherness of the non-experiential sort.

The core of Whitehead's argument is that all meanings of 'togetherness' must be 'derivative or abstracted from experiential togetherness'. By the word 'togetherness' he wishes to connote the converse of a disjunctive diversity, of mere external relatedness. For actualities to be 'together' implies their being *internally related*. Now the only way one actuality can be internally related to another is by its being immanent in the experience of that other. That is to say, internal relationship implies 'experiential togetherness'. Thus the only 'togetherness' possible for actual entities is 'experiential togetherness'. All other meanings of 'togetherness' are derivative, as we shall see, from the experiential togetherness of *actual* entities.

In Whitehead's view 'the contrary doctrine, that there is a "togetherness" not derivative from experiential togetherness', is based on the notion of 'vacuous actuality'. And this notion must be rejected as completely erroneous. It is the outcome, Whitehead maintains, of a mistaken philosophical generalization; that is to say, it is a generalization from entities which are not *actual*

[1] PR 268 [288-9].

127

entities. These entities are the macroscopic objects presented to us in sense perception, the 'physical bodies' of common sense.

The notion of 'vacuous actuality' is very closely allied to the notion of the 'inherence of quality in substance'. Both notions—in their misapplication as fundamental metaphysical categories—find their chief support in a misunderstanding of the true analysis of 'presentational immediacy' [sense perception].[1]

Whitehead's analysis of sense perception will be given later.[2] The relevant point here is that the 'physical bodies' of sense perception are conceived, in the doctrine he is criticizing, as *actual* entities. Descartes' theory of *res extensa* is a particularly clear example of this.

It must be emphasized that Whitehead is not denying a distinction between 'extended bodies' and 'minds'. He writes that 'Descartes is obviously right, in some sense or other, when he says that we have bodies and that we have minds, and that they can be studied in some disconnection. It is what we do daily in practical life'.[3] He insists that 'both matter and mind have to be fitted into the metaphysical scheme'.[4] It is quite beyond question that there are entities, 'bodies', which exhibit the character of vacuous extension; this is certainly the general feature of physical things as displayed to the sense of sight, and to a less prominent extent to the sense of touch. But the important question is whether these vacuous, extended bodies are *actual* entities.

Whitehead rejects the view that they are *actual* entities; they are, he holds, entities constituted by *multiplicities* of actual entities. Now for practical everyday purposes we habitually treat a multiplicity as one single thing; and for practical purposes this is perfectly legitimate. The trouble is, however, that because of this habitual treatment, we are very apt to overlook the fact that the single entity constituted by a multiplicity is an *abstract* entity. A multiplicity treated as one entity is 'abstract' because, although as a composite whole it is a single entity, it is not a 'concrete'

[1] P R 39 [43].   [2] § 27.   [3] F R 71.   [4] R M 95.

entity in the sense in which its components are concrete. It is derived from them and is thus 'abstract' in relation to them as 'concrete'.[1] Philosophically error is inevitable if we treat such an *abstract* entity as an *actual* entity. In particular, Whitehead maintains, 'whenever a vicious dualism appears, it is by reason of mistaking an abstraction for a final concrete fact'.[2] Metaphysical dualism, in other words, is based on the fallacy of misplaced concreteness. Thus we can reject the notion that 'vacuousness' is a metaphysical feature of actual entities.

But we must be clear that the rejection of the notion of 'vacuous *actuality*' does not imply that there are no entities with the characteristic of 'vacuousness'. On the contrary, 'vacuousness' is one of the most prominent features of the macroscopic objects of sense perception. But we shall have to enter into much further analysis before we are able to make properly intelligible Whitehead's philosophical explanation of how and why a multiplicity of *active* entities comes to display to sense perception the character of a single passive, vacuous extension.

Of immediate concern is, first, that an abstract entity (constituted by a multiplicity) displays features which belong to it as a composite whole and not to the individual components as such. 'Vacuousness' is an example of such a feature. Secondly, any such features displayed by a composite whole are 'abstract' features. To say that they are 'abstract' means that they are derived or 'abstracted' from something or some things; and here the relevant 'things' are the component actual entities. Thus abstract features such as that of 'vacuousness' must be derivative from the generic features of *actual* entities. Details of how this derivation or abstraction is effected can only be given when our analysis of the nature of an actual entity has proceeded much further. Here we are only concerned with the general

[1] Every composite whole is 'abstract' in relation to its components, but the components might themselves be composite wholes and thus abstract. Accordingly there can be hierarchies of abstract entities. Only when we come to components which are *actual* entities do we have entities which are 'concrete' in the metaphysical sense; other components of composite wholes are only relatively concrete.

[2] A I 245.

principle that the features of abstract entities must be derivative from the generic features of the component actualities.

We can now see what Whitehead means by saying that all meanings of 'togetherness' are derivative from the root meaning of 'experiential togetherness'. Vacuous physical bodies do not display the feature of 'experiential togetherness'; their togetherness is of a non-experiential kind, such as 'impact' in the usual non-philosophical conception of it. But, as we have seen, for bodies to affect each other by 'impact', there must be internal relationship, and internal relationship is possible only as 'experiential togetherness'. And actualities which are the constituents of the composite abstract entities *are* internally related in this way, and thereby is effected the relationship between the derivative abstract entities, the relationship which, when the abstract entities only are taken into account, appears as a 'non-experiential impact'.

§ 25

THE CATEGORY OF 'EXPERIENCE'

At a particular stage of his discussion in *Process and Reality* Whitehead wrote that 'in describing the capacities, realized or unrealized, of an actual occasion, we have, with Locke, tacitly taken human experience as an example upon which to found the generalized description required for metaphysics'.[1] In the previous chapter we have seen that the basis for this procedure is Whitehead's reformed subjectivist principle. This whole line of thought is of such crucial importance that it merits our giving a brief review of another argument presented by Whitehead in support of this procedure of generalization from human experience.

He starts by pointing to the evident fact, presupposed in all our life and actions, of the interconnectedness of things.

[1] P R 158 [172].

'Experience' as a Metaphysical Category

The world beyond is so intimately entwined in our own natures that unconsciously we identify our more vivid perspectives of it with ourselves. For example, our bodies lie beyond our own individual existence. And yet they are part of it. We think of ourselves as so intimately entwined in bodily life that a man is a complex unity—body and mind. But the body is part of the external world, continuous with it. In fact, it is just as much part of nature as anything else there—a river, or a mountain, or a cloud. Also, if we are fussily exact, we cannot define where a body begins and where external nature ends.[1]

The relevant point is that this intimate interconnectedness of human experience and external nature demands the recognition that human experience is not separate and disjoined from external things.

Ordinary language, and the sciences of physiology and psychology, supply the evidence. This evidence is three-fold: namely, the body is part of nature, the body supplies the basis of emotional and sensory activities, and the agitations of human experience pass into subsequent bodily functionings.[2]

Therefore, Whitehead concludes, we must hold that 'an occasion of experience which includes a human mentality is an extreme instance, at one end of the scale, of those happenings which constitute nature'.[3] Accordingly,

any doctrine which refuses to place human experience outside nature, must find in descriptions of human experience factors which also enter into the descriptions of less specialized natural occurrences. If there be no such factors, then the doctrine of human experience as a fact within nature is mere bluff, founded upon vague phrases whose sole merit is a comforting familiarity.[4]

We have therefore to acknowledge, first, that the generic features of all actuality are to be found exhibited in human experience. Secondly,

the body is that portion of nature with which each moment of human experience intimately cooperates. There is an inflow and outflow of factors between the bodily actuality and the human experience, so

[1] M T 29–30.   [2] M T 157.   [3] A I 237.   [4] A I 237.

that each shares in the existence of the other. The human body provides our closest experience of the interplay of actualities in nature.[1]

Therefore, thirdly, the kind of activity exhibited by the body must be generically the same as that of human experiencing. As Whitehead has put it, 'analogous notions of activity, and of forms of transition, apply to human experience and to the human body. Thus bodily activities and forms of experience can be construed in terms of each other'.[2] Fourthly, the body is part of nature. Thus, Whitehead says, 'we finally construe the world in terms of the types of activities disclosed in our intimate experience'.[3]

It is evident that what we have here is the application of the reformed subjectivist principle. The reason for construing other actualities 'in terms of the type of activities disclosed in our intimate experience' is that oneself, as experiencing, provides the primary instance of an actuality which we intimately know, and that the metaphysical features displayed by this actuality, oneself, must be those generic to all actualities. Therefore,

the direct evidence as to the connectedness of one's immediate present occasion of experience with one's immediately past occasions, can be validly used to suggest categories applying to the connectedness of all occasions in nature.[4]

We can now draw together the conclusions so far reached in our discussion. First, when we examine ourselves, we find ourselves 'experiencing'; that is, we find ourselves in a process of experiencing. Secondly, this experiencing is the experiencing of 'objects'. In Whitehead's words,[5]

the process of experiencing is constituted by the reception of entities, whose being is antecedent to that process, into the complex fact which is that process itself. These antecedent entities, thus received as factors into the process of experiencing, are termed 'objects' for that experiential occasion. Thus primarily the term 'object' expresses the relation of the entity, thus denoted, to one or more occasions of experiencing.

Thirdly, as we have shown in the previous Part, *actual* entities

[1] M T 157.   [2] M T 157–8.   [3] M T 158.   [4] A I 284.   [5] A I 229.

132

are *acting* entities; that is, the metaphysical nature of all actualities is that of 'acting'. We have now seen that this generic 'acting' is 'experiencing'. And further, 'experiencing' is an activity of 'receiving' or 'including' other entities as objects.

Thus Whitehead's doctrine is that the generic 'process of becoming' which constitutes the 'being', the 'existence', of an actuality is the 'process of experiencing': 'process is the becoming of experience'.[1] This process of becoming is the active process of receiving objects and integrating them into one definite unity. Whitehead uses the term 'concrescence' for this process:[2]

'Concrescence' is the name for the process in which the universe of many things acquires an individual unity in a determinate relegation of the 'many' to its subordination in the constitution of the novel 'one'.

It will be noted that accordingly

the most general term 'thing'—or, equivalently, 'entity'—means nothing else than to be one of the 'many' which find their niches in each instance of concrescence.[3]

For each 'entity', whatever it be, as required by the category of relativity,[4] is potentially an 'object' for some occasion of experience.

This doctrine of an actual entity as a process of experiencing means that

an actual occasion is nothing but the unity to be ascribed to a particular instance of concrescence. This concrescence is nothing else than the 'real internal constitution' of the actual occasion in question.[5]

That is to say,

each instance of concrescence *is itself* the novel individual 'thing' in question. There is not 'the concrescence' *and* 'the novel thing': when we analyse the novel thing we find nothing but the concrescence. 'Actuality' means nothing else than this ultimate entry into the concrete, in abstraction from which there is mere nonentity. In other words, abstraction from the notion of 'entry into the concrete' is a self-contradictory notion, since it asks us to conceive a thing as not a thing.[6]

[1] P R 233 [255].   [2] P R 299 [321].   [3] P R 299 [321].
[4] Cf. § 18 above.   [5] P R 300 [323].   [6] P R 299 [321].

Whitehead's Metaphysics

That an actual entity must be conceived as an activity of con-
crescence we have seen in the previous Part to be required by
Whitehead's category of process. What is here added is that this
activity of concrescing is nothing but the activity of experiencing.
The acceptance of the reformed subjectivist principle thus leads
Whitehead to the view that

the actualities of the universe are processes of experience, each process
an individual fact. The whole universe is the advancing assemblage of
these processes. The Aristotelian doctrine, that all agency is confined
to actuality, is accepted. So also is the Platonic dictum that the very
meaning of existence is 'to be a factor in agency', or in other words,
'to make a difference'. Thus, 'to be something' is to be discoverable
as a factor in the analysis of some actuality.[1]

This statement displays the complete coherence of the subjectivist principle in Whitehead's reformed version with the other
principles of his system.

It is particularly to be noted that other entities 'make a difference' to the actuality in the process of concrescence through
their being 'experienced' by this actuality. This experiencing
constitutes the process by which they become internally related
to the concrescing actuality. This point is of special significance
with regard to those entities which are *actual* entities when they
become 'objects' for a concrescing subject. To be 'objects', as we
have seen, they must be 'antecedent' to the process of the concrescing subject, and this means that their own process of concrescence must have been completed; their own subjective
immediacy is then over, and they have 'perished' as *actual*. That
is, they no longer exist in the full sense. They can 'exist' at all
only through being a 'factor in agency', the agency constituting
the becoming of the concrescing subject. And they can become
such a 'factor in agency' only through being experientially
included in the concrescing actuality. The fact of being so included
constitutes the 'objective immortality' of the antecedent actualities.
In other words, antecedent actualities 'exist' only in the sense of
'objects' in the experience of concrescing subjects. Their existence

[1] A I 253–4.

134

as objects is effected by their internal relationship to an experiencing actuality. Therefore, Whitehead insists,[1]

such relatedness is wholly concerned with the appropriation of the dead by the living—that is to say, with 'objective immortality' whereby what is divested of its own living immediacy becomes a real component in other living immediacies of becoming. This is the doctrine that the creative advance of the world is the becoming, the perishing, and the objective immortalities of those things which jointly constitute *stubborn fact*.

We are now a stage further in our investigation of how one actuality can be 'present in' another.

[1] P R viii–ix [ix].

CHAPTER XI

The Analysis of 'Experience'

§ 26

THEORIES OF 'EXPERIENCE'

The fundamental problem, which is the particular concern of this Part, namely, *how* one actuality can be 'present in' another actuality, is answered by Whitehead in terms of a general metaphysical theory of the nature of actuality as 'experiencing activity'. According to this doctrine, actual entities in the process of becoming 'experience' others, thereby including them as 'objects'. Thus 'the discussion of how the actual particular occasions become original elements for a new creation is ... the theory of objectification'.[1]

But for its adequate elucidation, this answer to the question 'how?' must be more fully investigated. In the first place, the term 'experience' has a wide connotation, and its precise meaning in Whitehead's theory can only be clarified by a more detailed analysis. Secondly, to hold that one actuality is 'present in' another through 'experiential inclusion' or through 'objectification' is not sufficient; it still has to be explained in precisely what way that 'inclusion' or 'objectification' is effected.

We have seen that Whitehead, in accordance with the requirements of the reformed subjectivist principle, arrived at the conception of the generic nature of all actualities as 'experiencing

[1] P R 298 [320–1].

The Analysis of 'Experience'

activity' by generalizing from 'human experience'. But what is to be taken as constituting 'human experience'? The term 'experience' has so far been used in a fairly general sense, without precise specification of the conception of it Whitehead holds. Since there are various conceptions as to what constitutes 'experience', we must now clarify Whitehead's specific meaning.

In asking the question as to what *constitutes* 'experience', we are asking the question as to the *generic nature* of 'experience'. It is therefore this which has to be determined. Modern thought on this topic, having its origin with Descartes, has, explicitly or implicitly, been dominated by the presupposition of a metaphysical dualism. Accordingly 'experience'—which is taken to mean specifically 'human experience'—has predominantly had the connotation of 'mentality' and 'consciousness'; 'unconscious experience' has tended to be dismissed as a contradiction in terms.

The analysis of conscious mental experience has traditionally produced two divergent schools of thought. One, typified by Descartes and his 'rationalist' followers, has regarded 'cogitation' or 'thinking' as constituting the generic nature of conscious mental experience; 'perception', in this doctrine, is conceived as essentially a species of 'thought'.[1] The other school, that of Locke and his 'empiricist' followers, regarded 'perception' as basic; 'thinking' is conceived as a secondary, derivative activity, manipulating or arranging the 'ideas' originating in perception. The difference in connotation of the term 'idea' as held by these two schools respectively brings out their divergence as to the generic nature of conscious mental experience. For Descartes an 'idea' is primarily an 'intellectual thought'; for Locke an 'idea' is primarily a 'sensory impression', an 'idea of sensation'. Kant attempted a synthesis of these two doctrines by insisting on both sensory impressions and intellectual concepts (in the form of 'categories of the understanding') as essential to the constitution of 'experience'. But the balance is on the side of 'thought'. As Whitehead remarks,[2]

[1] Cf. Descartes, *Principles of Philosophy*, Part I, 53: '. . . thought constitutes the nature of thinking substance', and 'everything that we find in a mind is so many diverse forms of thinking'. [2] P R 158 [172].

in any metaphysical scheme founded upon the Kantian or Hegelian traditions, experience is the product of operations which lie among the higher of the human modes of functioning. For such schemes, ordered experience is the result of schematizations of modes of *thought*, concerning causation, substance, quality, quantity.

Whitehead maintains that the Lockean 'perception' is much nearer than the Cartesian 'thinking' to being a satisfactory conception of the generic nature of 'experience'. Thinking can legitimately be regarded as constituting the peak of human experience, or as the distinguishing feature of 'humanity'—that which makes us characteristically 'human'; but it does not constitute the generic nature of our 'existence'. Thinking is spasmodic: sometimes it is completely in abeyance —during sleep, or when we are 'knocked unconscious'—yet we 'exist'. Descartes' conclusion, '*cogito, ergo sum*', is valid; but only as a conclusion from the *fact of* 'thinking' to the *fact of* 'existing'. It is invalid to conclude from the *fact of* our thinking, that 'thinking' constitutes the *nature of* our existing.

Secondly, 'thinking *about*' external things is not 'perception *of*' those things. Whitehead agrees, in this respect, with the essential 'empiricist' argument against 'rationalism'; he accepts Hume's dictum that all 'reflection' is derivative from 'sensation'[1]—this is in accordance with the ontological principle.

But although Whitehead is in agreement with the doctrine that 'perception' must be regarded as fundamental, he firmly rejects the widely held 'sensationalist' theory of perception, the theory which identifies 'perception' with 'sense-perception'. Whitehead has stated this sensationalist theory as follows:[2]

(1) that all perception is by the mediation of our bodily sense-organs, such as eyes, palates, noses, ears, and the diffused bodily organization furnishing touches, aches, and other bodily sensations; (2) that all percepta are bare sensa, in patterned connections, given in the immediate present; (3) that our experience of a social world is an interpretative reaction wholly derivative from this perception; (4) that our emotional and purposive experience is a reflective reaction derived

[1] See below, § 35. [2] A I 228.

from the original perception, and intertwined with the interpretative reaction and partly shaping it. Thus the two reactions are different aspects of one process, involving interpretative, emotional, and purposive factors.

In brief, this theory holds that it is the conscious entertainment of definite, clear-cut 'sensa' which essentially constitutes 'perception'; that is, it is these sensa which are the fundamental elements in experience, all else being derivative from them:

The other factors in experience are therefore to be construed as derivative, in the sense of owing their origin to these sensa. Emotions, aspirations, hopes, fears, love, and hate, intentions, and recollections are merely concerned with sensa. Apart from sensa, they would be non-existent.[1]

Now Whitehead agrees that 'undoubtedly there are these sensa, such as sensations of colour, sound, and so on'.[2] But he rejects the assumption 'that because they are definite, therefore they are fundamental'.[3] He has attacked this theory in considerable detail in his various writings; here I shall give only some of the main points of his argument.

It must be clearly borne in mind that what we are concerned to determine is the generic nature of 'perception'. The theory under criticism regards this as consisting in the conscious entertainment of clear-cut, definite sensa.

But when we examine our experience, Whitehead says,[4]

the first point to notice is that these distinct sensa are the most variable elements in our lives. We can shut our eyes, or be permanently blind. None-the-less we are alive. We can be deaf. And yet we are alive. We can shift and transmute these details of experience almost at will.

Further, in the course of a day our experience varies with respect to its entertainment of sensa. We are wide awake, we doze, we meditate, we sleep. There is nothing basic in the clarity of our entertainment of sensa. Also in the course of our lives, we start in the womb, in the cradle, and we gradually acquire the art of correlating our fundamental experience to the clarity of newly-acquired sensa.

The sensationalist theory of the generic nature of human experience, Whitehead maintains, is therefore to be rejected as mistaking the most variable elements for the universal necessities:[1]

> Human nature has been described in terms of its vivid accidents, and not of its existential essence. The description of its essence must apply to the unborn child, to the baby in its cradle, to the state of sleep, and to that vast background of feeling hardly touched by consciousness. Clear, conscious discrimination is an accident of human existence. It makes us human. But it does not make us exist. It is of the essence of our humanity. But it is an accident of our existence.

§ 27

TWO MODES OF PERCEPTION

Whitehead points out that if the clear, conscious sensory discrimination—which he terms 'presentational immediacy'—be not fundamental, then it must be based upon, and derived from, a more elemental form of 'experience'. That there is a more primitive form of 'perception', which is not of the kind of clear-cut sensory presentation, is in accordance with all the evidence. For example, when we consider the more primitive kinds of animal life which have no developed sense organs such as eyes and ears, and which are thus unlikely to have clear sensory discrimination, we find them nevertheless reacting to their environment. As Whitehead says, 'there is reason to suspect a certain dimness of such experience in living things with low types of bodily organization. And yet they react to the external world. In other words, reaction to the environment is not in proportion to clarity of sensory experience'.[2] On the contrary, he points out,[3]

> as we descend the scale, it seems that we find in the lower types a dim unconscious drowse, of undiscriminated feeling. For the lower types, experience loses its illustration of forms [sensa], and its illumina-

___
[1] M T 158.   [2] M T 154.   [3] F R 63–4.

tion by consciousness, and its discrimination of purpose. It seems finally to end in a massive unconscious urge derived from undiscriminated feeling, this feeling being itself a derivation from the immediate past.

By contrast with clear, conscious sensory discrimination, these creatures seem to exhibit a vague, unconscious, 'causal' reaction. This 'reaction does not depend upon sense-experience for its initiation',[1] since this 'causal' reaction is there even when clear sense-perception is in abeyance, or completely absent. This, Whitehead holds, points to the existence of a more elemental kind of perception, a 'causal efficacy', vague as to definition, essentially unconscious.

In human experience this perception 'in the mode of causal efficacy', Whitehead maintains, is most evidently exhibited by what he calls the 'withness of the body'. We have already noted[2] the relevance for philosophical theory of the mind-body unity. Whitehead points out that in most antecedent philosophy this factor of the 'withness of the body' in perceptual experience has not been accorded the attention which its importance merits. In fact, it is only tacitly acknowledged in the phraseology used by various philosophers, while their explicit theories, which hold sensory perception to be the only kind of perception, can give no coherent place to this factor. For example, he writes,[3] we have but to

refer to Descartes in *Meditation I*, 'These hands and this body are *mine*'; also to Hume in his many assertions of the type, we see *with our eyes*. Such statements witness to direct knowledge of the antecedent functioning of the body in sense-perception. Both agree—though Hume more explicitly—that sense-perception of the contemporary world is accompanied by perception of the 'withness' of the body. . . . [But] Hume and Descartes in their theory of direct perceptive knowledge dropped out this withness of the body; and thus confined perception to presentational immediacy. Santayana, in his doctrine of 'animal faith', practically agrees with Hume and Descartes as to this withness of the actual world, including the body. . . . Descartes calls it a certain

[1] M T 154.   [2] § 25.   [3] P R 112 [125].

kind of 'understanding'; Santayana calls it 'animal faith' provoked by 'shock'; and Hume calls it 'practice'.

But this kind of acknowledgement of the withness of the body and the external world is strictly incoherent with the theories of perception adopted by these thinkers; in the latter two it amounts to a form of irrationalism.

This factor of the 'withness of the body', Whitehead insists, must coherently be taken into account, and this can only be if it be integral to a theory of perception; it cannot be tacitly dismissed as irrelevant to perception, as is done in so many doctrines, merely because the particular theory of perception adopted cannot accommodate it. This factor, on the contrary, is of direct relevance in the construction of a theory of perception, for we see *with our eyes*, hear *with our ears*, and so on. Accordingly, Whitehead points out, 'it is this witness that makes the body the starting-point for our knowledge of the circumambient world'.[1] That is, our perceptual knowledge derives in the first place from the bodily sense organs, which in turn are in contact with the wider environment.

But in clear conscious presentational perception we are not normally conscious of this 'withness'. It requires a special direction of attention to become consciously aware of the bodily functioning in sensory perception. Yet it is there, for the clear conscious presentational perception is derived from the bodily sense organs. The essential point to notice is that 'derivation' is itself *unconscious*, and does not enter as a conscious factor into the presentational immediacy: we see *with* our eyes, but on doing so we do not *see* our eyes. Accordingly, Whitehead maintains that it is primarily here, in this 'withness', in this unconscious derivation from the bodily sense organs, that 'we find ... our direct knowledge of "causal efficacy"'.[2]

Further, Whitehead points out,[3]

these conclusions are confirmed if we descend to the scale of organic being. It does not seem to be the sense of causal awareness that the

---

[1] P R 112 [125].   [2] P R 112 [125].   [3] P R 248-9 [268].

lower living things lack, so much as variety of sense-presentation, and then vivid distinctness of presentational immediacy. But animals, and even vegetables, in low forms of organism exhibit modes of behaviour directed toward self-preservation. There is every indication of a vague feeling of causal relationship with the external world, of some intensity, vaguely defined as to quality, and with some vague definition as to locality. A jellyfish advances and withdraws, and in so doing exhibits some perception of causal relationship with the world beyond itself; a plant grows downwards to the damp earth, and upwards towards the light. There is thus some direct reason for attributing dim, slow feelings of causal nexus, although we have no reason for any ascription of presentational immediacy.

It must be emphasized that this causal reaction is a form of 'perception'. That is, it is a form of awareness of entities beyond.

CHAPTER XII

The Category of Prehension

§ 28

THE CATEGORY OF PREHENSION

Whitehead maintains that we have to admit an unconscious 'causal' form of perception as distinct from conscious 'presentational' perception. Further, this unconscious perception 'in the mode of causal efficacy' is more fundamental. For, in the first place, it is not, like conscious presentational perception and thought (or reflection), a special characteristic of only certain high-grade experients; it is a form of perception which is general, being also exhibited by the high-grade percipients, as we have seen. Secondly, the more specialized presentational perception can be displayed as derivative from the basic causal perception.[1]

It is therefore this unconscious perception 'in the mode of causal efficacy', Whitehead holds, which must be regarded as exhibiting the essential features of 'experience'. Accordingly he generalizes *it* as constitutive of the generic nature of all actualities. That is, he conceives the generic acting of an actuality to be an act of unconscious perception of data, an act of perceptually 'grasping' and 'including' them as its 'objccts'.

This is clearly an exceedingly important categoreal concept in Whitehead's metaphysical scheme, and a general neutral term,

[1] Only the general principles of this derivation are given in this book, since epistemology is beyond its scope. See §§ 34–6 below.

which is free from association with doctrines he rejects, is necessary. The terms 'awareness' and 'perception' which we have so far used—even if qualified by the adjective 'unconscious'—are not at all satisfactory. Whitehead noted, as he says,[1] that Leibniz had

employed the terms 'perception' and 'apperception' for the lower and higher ways in which one monad can take account of another, namely for ways of awareness. But these terms are too closely allied to the notion of consciousness which in my doctrine is not a necessary accompaniment. Also they are all entangled in the notion of representative perception which I reject. But there is the term 'apprehension' with the meaning of 'thorough understanding'. Accordingly, on the Leibnizian model, I use the term 'prehension' for the general way in which the occasion of experience can include, as part of its own essence, any other entity, whether another occasion of experience or an entity of another type.

The word 'prehension' has the literal meaning of 'grasping', 'seizing'—from this the word 'apprehension' has been derived with the meaning of 'grasp by the intellect or senses'. Accordingly, Whitehead says, 'I have adopted the term "prehension", to express the activity whereby an actual entity effects its own concretion of other things';[2] for the generic activity constituting an actual entity is an act of 'grasping', of 'appropriating' other entities so as to be the components of its concrescence.

Thus Whitehead's answer to the problem, 'How can other actual entities, each with its own formal existence, also enter objectively into the perceptive constitution of the actual entity in question?' is that the other actual entities are 'prehended' by the concrescing actual entity as subject. That is to say, the *way in which* other entities can be included in the constitution of a particular actuality is by those entities being 'prehended' by the actuality in question.

In order adequately to appreciate *how* the other actualities can be 'included in', or be 'present in' the actual entity in question through being 'prehended' by it, it should be noted that Whitehead speaks, in the previous quotation, of those other actualities

[1] A I 300. [2] P R 71 [81].

each having their own 'formal' existence, and that they are included 'objectively'. By the *formal* existence' of an actual entity Whitehead means the existence of the actuality 'as it is in itself, subjectively', in contrast with what that actuality is 'objectively', i.e. as an 'object' for another. He is here using the terminology of *'formaliter'* and *'objective'* in the same sense in which Descartes used it.

Descartes had pointed to the distinction between the 'formal' existence of things and their 'objective' existence. For example, he wrote,[1]

Hence the idea of the sun will be the sun itself existing in the mind, not indeed formally, as it exists in the sky, but objectively, i.e. in the way in which objects are wont to exist in the mind; and this mode of being is truly much less perfect than that in which things exist outside the mind, but it is not on that account mere nothing, as I have said.

But Descartes is committed, by his metaphysical dualism, to a representative theory of perception, and, as Whitehead remarks, '"representative perception" can never, within its own metaphysical doctrines, produce the title deeds to guarantee the validity of the representation of fact by idea'.[2] Still less can Descartes, on his bases, explain how the *sun itself* can be in the mind. The use of the term 'objectively' does not constitute a solution; it only states more precisely the essential problem. For the problem, it is important to appreciate, is to explain, in terms of the ultimate nature of actuality, the distinction between the 'formal' existence and the 'objective' existence of an entity, thereby displaying both as a form of existence *of that entity*.

In Whitehead's doctrine an actuality, in its ultimate nature, is an activity of becoming. This means, to express it in his words already quoted,[3] that

the process itself is the constitution of the actual entity; in Locke's phrase, it is the 'real internal constitution' of the actual entity. In the older phraseology employed by Descartes, the process is what the actual entity is in itself, *'formaliter'*.[4]

[1] Descartes, *Reply to Objections I.*   [2] P R 74 [85].
[3] § 10.   [4] P R 309–10 [335].

The Category of Prehension

We have seen that this process is an activity of experiencing, or to use his more precise technical term, an activity of 'prehending'. Thus, considered 'formally', an actual entity is a process of prehension; that is,

the experience enjoyed by an actual entity is that entity *formaliter*. By this I mean that the entity, when considered 'formally', is being described in respect to those forms of its constitution whereby it is that individual entity with its own measure of absolute self-realization.[1]

That is to say, the 'formal' description or analysis of an actual entity displays it as a concrescence of prehensions. When the actual entity is analysed it is found to consist of nothing but prehensions of various kinds and degrees of complexity, for, as Whitehead says, 'in Cartesian language, the essence of an actual entity consists solely in the fact that it is a prehending thing (i.e. a substance whose whole essence or nature is to prehend)'.[2] As he has put this summarily,[3]

the first analysis of an actual entity, into its most concrete elements, discloses it to be a concrescence of prehensions, which have originated in its process of becoming. All further analysis is an analysis of prehensions.

Thus 'formally' an actual entity is constituted by an activity of prehending. Its 'formal' existence *is* this process of prehending activity. And when that process has achieved a determinate conclusion, its activity is completed, and consequently its 'formal' existence is at an end. It can exist then only 'objectively', i.e. as an 'object' in the constitution of a superseding actuality. Thus to consider an actual entity 'objectively' is to consider it in its completion, as it presents itself at the completion of its process of becoming. Whitehead has stated the distinction between the 'formal' and the 'objective' existence of an actual entity as follows:[4]

The 'formal' constitution of an actual entity is a process of transition from indetermination towards terminal determination. . . . The 'objective' constitution of an actual entity is its terminal determination,

---

[1] PR 71 [81].   [2] PR 56 [65].   [3] PR 31 [35].   [4] PR 62 [72].

considered as a complex of component determinates by reason of which the actual entity is a datum for the creative advance.

But to understand *how* an actual entity can exist 'objectively' in another involves making an analysis, in some detail, of the activity of prehension.

§ 29

PREHENSION AS 'FEELING'

In Whitehead's doctrine 'each actual entity is conceived as an act of experience arising out of data'.[1] That is to say, an actual entity is exhibited as appropriating, for the foundation of its own existence, the various elements of the universe out of which it arises. Each process of appropriation of a particular element is termed a prehension. The ultimate elements of the universe, thus appropriated, are the already constituted actual entities, and the eternal objects.[2]

Partly because the term 'prehension' is unfamiliar, and partly because Whitehead wishes to have it clearly before the reader what he takes to be the generic nature of 'experiencing', he uses the more suggestive word 'feeling' synonymously—although, as we shall see presently,[3] with a slightly more restricted connotation. So employed, he points out, 'the word "feeling" is a mere technical term; but it has been chosen to suggest that functioning through which the concrescent actuality appropriates the datum so as to make it its own'.[4] That is, the activity of 'prehending' is an activity of 'feeling'; the concrescing actuality 'feels' its data.

It is important to be clear as to what precisely Whitehead means by this term. In the first place, he explains,[5]

this use of the term 'feeling' has a close analogy to Alexander's use of the term 'enjoyment'; and has also some kinship with Bergson's use of the term 'intuition'. A near analogy is Locke's use of the term 'idea'

[1] P R 55 [65].   [2] P R 309 [335].   [3] Pp. 151–2 below.
[4] P R 229–30 [249].   [5] P R 55–6 [65].

including 'ideas of particular things' (cf. his *Essay* III, III, 2, 6, and 7). But the word 'feeling', as used in these lectures, is even more reminiscent of Descartes. For example: 'Let it be so; still it is at least quite certain that it seems to me that I see light, that I hear noise and that I feel heat. That cannot be false; properly speaking it is what is in me called feeling (*sentire*); and used in this precise sense that is no other thing than thinking.[1]

That is to say, 'feeling' is essentially an act of 'experiencing', and more particularly, experiencing other things, 'objects'. But in addition—and this is the second point—by the use of the term 'feeling' Whitehead wishes to stress 'that the basis of experience is emotional. Stated more generally, the basic fact is the rise of an affective tone originating from things whose relevance is given'.[2] The word 'feeling' has the essential connotation of an 'affective tone', but few thinkers in employing the word feeling hold that this affective tone arises *from the data*.

In maintaining this doctrine Whitehead is explicitly rejecting the sensationalist theory of perception. According to this theory, as we have seen,[3] 'our emotional and purposive experience is a reflective reaction derived from the original [sensory] perception'. That is, experience is held by this theory to originate with bare sensa, and emotion and affective tone are regarded as a response arising purely subjectively; as Whitehead remarks, our 'emotional and purposeful experience has been made to follow upon Hume's impressions of sensation'.[4]

Whitehead maintains that the error in this doctrine consists in the disjunction of emotional experience from presentational experience, of affective tone from sensa. He holds, on the contrary, that 'the separation of the emotional experience from the presentational experience is a high abstraction of thought';[5] that is, this separation is the product of mental activity, and does not exist as an original element in experience.[6] We have seen that

---

[1] Descartes, *Meditation II*.   [2] A I 226.   [3] § 26.   [4] P R 227 [246].   [5] P R 227 [247].
[6] Cf. R. G. Collingwood, *The Principles of Art*, pp. 162–3, where a very similar doctrine is maintained. Collingwood speaks of the intellectual 'sterilization of sensa'.

Whitehead's fundamental ground for rejecting the sensationalist theory is that it has fastened on the products of highly developed mentality, and has regarded these as constituting the primary generic features of experience. He claims, as opposed to this, that if we examine our experience without the presupposition of the sensationalist theory, we will recognize in ourselves the existence of the more elemental form of perception 'in the mode of causal efficacy', and that this

mode produces percepta which are vague, not to be controlled, heavy with emotion: it produces the sense of derivation from an immediate past, and of passage to an immediate future; a sense of emotional feeling, belonging to oneself in the past, passing into oneself in the present, and passing from oneself in the present towards oneself in the future; a sense of influx of influence from other vaguer presences in the past, localized and yet evading local definition, such influence modifying, enhancing, inhibiting, diverting, the stream of feeling which we are receiving, unifying, enjoying, and transmitting. This is our general sense of existence, as one item among others, in an efficacious actual world.[1]

The sensationalist theory and the substance-quality habits of thought are, however, deeply ingrained. As Whitehead says, 'we are so used to considering the high abstraction, "the stone as green", that we have difficulty in eliciting into consciousness the notion of "green" as the qualifying character of an emotion'.[2] Yet, he points out, 'the aesthetic feelings, whereby there is pictorial art, are nothing else than products of the contrasts latent in a variety of colours qualifying emotion, contrasts which are made possible by their patterned relevance to each other'.[3] Pictorial art is impossible unless emotion is basic. Accordingly, Whitehead maintains,[4]

the confinement of our prehensions of other actual entities to the mediation of private sensations is pure myth. The converse doctrine is nearer the truth: the more primitive mode of objectification is via emotional tone, and only in exceptional organisms does objectification, via sensation, supervene with any effectiveness.

[1] P R 251 [271].   [2] P R 227 [246].   [3] P R 227 [246–7].   [4] P R 197 [214].

The Category of Prehension

Rejecting the sensationalist theory, Whitehead therefore holds that 'the primitive experience is emotional feeling, felt in its relevance to a world beyond'.[1] In this primitive experience consciousness is absent; as Whitehead says, 'the feeling is blind and the relevance is vague'.[2] In his doctrine,

perception, in this primary sense, is perception of the settled world in the past as constituted by its feeling-tones, and as efficacious by reason of those feeling-tones. Perception, in this sense of the term, will be called 'perception in the mode of causal efficacy'.[3]

It is evident that this doctrine 'attributes "feeling" throughout the actual world'[4] as constitutive of the generic nature of all actual entities. Whitehead explains[5] that he

bases this doctrine upon the directly observed fact that 'feeling' survives as a known element constitutive of the 'formal' existence of such actual entities as we can best observe. Also when we observe the causal nexus, devoid of interplay with sense-presentation, the influx of feeling with vague qualitative and 'vector' definition is what we find.

That is to say, finding that 'feeling' is a basic factor in our own experience, verified also by observation of such other experiencers as we are able to examine, by applying the reformed subjectivist principle, Whitehead generalizes 'feeling' as generic to all actuality.

This 'feeling' is the generic act of 'prehending'. Thus in Whitehead's doctrine, an actual entity

is a process of 'feeling' the many data, so as to absorb them into the unity of one individual 'satisfaction'.[6]

The term 'satisfaction' is consonant with the term 'feeling'; it means the conclusion, the terminal culmination and outcome of the feeling or prehension. For, as Whitehead explains,[7]

an actual entity is a process in the course of which many operations with incomplete subjective unity terminate in a completed unity of operation, termed the 'satisfaction'. The 'satisfaction' is the contentment of the creative urge by the fulfilment of its categoreal demands.

[1] P R 227 [247].   [2] P R 227 [247].   [3] P R 169 [184].
[4] P R 249 [268].   [5] P R 249 [268].   [6] P R 55 [65].   [7] P R 309 [335].

For the moment, however, our particular concern is the notion of 'feeling'. An actual entity, in Whitehead's doctrine, is a 'process of feeling'. That is to say, the analysis of an actual entity

discloses operations transforming entities which are individually alien, into components of a complex which is concretely one. The term 'feeling' will be used as the generic description of such operations. We thus say that an actual occasion is a concrescence effected by a process of feelings.[1]

It is evident that the term 'feeling' is used synonymously with 'prehension'. More precisely, it is a 'positive prehension', for it is the positive inclusion or absorption of an item in the 'universe of the percipient subject', whether that item be an antecedent actuality or an eternal object. As Whitehead says,[2]

a positive prehension is the definite inclusion of that item into positive contribution to the subject's own real internal constitution. This positive inclusion is called its 'feeling' of that item.

This distinction is important, for there is also a definite act of *exclusion* from contribution. This act of exclusion is termed by Whitehead a 'negative prehension':

A negative prehension is the definite exclusion of that item from positive contribution to the subject's own real internal constitution.[3]

In other words, negative prehensions 'eliminate from feeling'.[4] We shall see the significance of negative prehensions later. Here the relevant point is that 'an actual entity has a perfectly definite bond with each item in the universe',[5] as is required by the category of relativity. 'This determinate bond is its prehension of that item.'[6] As Whitehead explains, 'this doctrine involves the position that a negative prehension expresses a bond'.[7] Thus 'prehension' is the generic act of an actual entity, of which there are two species, namely 'positive prehensions' and 'negative prehensions'. The positive prehensions are the positive inclusion of items through 'feeling' them; thus 'these positive prehensions are termed "feelings" '.[8]

[1] P R 300 [322].   [2] P R 56 [66].   [3] P R 56 [66].   [4] P R 32 [35].
[5] P R 56 [66].   [6] P R 56 [66].   [7] P R 56 [66].   [8] P R 311 [337].

CHAPTER XIII

Prehension and Objectification

---

§ 30

THE ACT OF PREHENDING

In the general analysis of the act of prehension, into which we shall now enter in this chapter, we shall ignore the negative prehensions. That is, we shall consider the act of prehension in so far as it involves the positive inclusion of entities. Whitehead states his doctrine as follows:[1]

An occasion of experience is an activity, analysable into modes of functioning which jointly constitute its process of becoming. Each mode is analysable into the total experience as active subject, and into the thing or object with which the special activity is concerned. This thing is a datum, that is to say, it is describable without reference to its entertainment in that occasion. An object is anything performing this function of a datum provoking some special activity of the occasion in question. Thus subject and object are relative terms. An occasion is a subject in respect to its special activity concerning an object; and anything is an object in respect to its provocation of some special activity within a subject. Such a mode of activity is termed a prehension'.

It is important to appreciate that a 'prehension' is a transaction of relating an experiencing subject to a datum as its object. The datum, apart from that prehending transaction, is independently

[1] A I 226–7.

Whitehead's Metaphysics

existent (i.e. if it be an actuality; and if it be an eternal object, it is also 'describable without reference to its entertainment in that occasion'); but as an 'object' it is not.[1] As an 'object' it is integral to the concrete transaction which is the 'subject prehending the object'; the term 'object' has no meaning except as reciprocal to 'subject prehending'. Thus any separate consideration of any element of that concrete act—whether the 'subject', the 'activity', the 'object', or any other—is the consideration of an abstraction.

Now this act of positive prehension is an act of 'feeling'. As Whitehead says,[2]

here 'feeling' is used for the basic generic operation of passing from the objectivity of the data to the subjectivity of the actual entity in question. Feelings are variously specialized operations, effecting a transition into subjectivity.

Also, this act of feeling is in its essence 'emotional':

the primitive form of physical[3] experience is emotional—blind emotion —received as felt elsewhere in another occasion and conformally appropriated as a subjective passion. In the language appropriate to the higher stages of experience, the primitive element is *sympathy*, that is, feeling the feeling *in* another and feeling conformally *with* another.[4]

The point is that 'formally' every actual entity—not only the actual entity which is the prehending subject, but also that which is the prehended datum—is constituted by an activity of prehending, i.e. by an activity of feeling. That feeling is 'emotional'.

Thus when an actuality in the process of concrescence prehends (feels) an antecedent actuality which is its datum, it 'feels' conformally with the 'feeling' of that datum. That is, the 'subjective form' of the feeling of the concrescing actuality conforms to the 'subjective form' of the feeling of the datum; the concrescing actuality 'feels' now what the past actuality 'felt' when it was possessed of 'subjective immediacy'. What Whitehead terms 'subjective form' is the '*how*' of the feeling; it is the particula

---

[1] See discussion in § 19 above.   [2] P R 55 [65].
[3] For an explanation of the term 'physical' see below § 31.   [4] P R 227 [246].

154

'affective tone' qualifying the feeling. This doctrine can be stated alternatively by saying that the 'character' (i.e. 'emotional character') of the prehending subject conforms to the 'character' of the feeling of the datum. To 'feel' a datum as object is to 'feel' (to 'have a feeling') conforming to the feeling of the datum.

Accordingly, Whitehead points out,[1] in its concrete consideration

a prehension involves three factors. There is the occasion of experience within which a prehension is a detail of activity; there is the datum whose relevance provokes the origination of this prehension; this datum is the prehended object; there is the subjective form, which is the affective tone determining the effectiveness of that prehension in that occasion of experience.

Or, stated more briefly,[2]

every prehension consists of three factors: (a) the 'subject' which is prehending, namely, the actual entity in which that prehension is a concrete element; (b) the 'datum' which is prehended; (c) the 'subjective form' which is *how* that subject prehends that datum.

All three factors are essential to the consideration of a prehension in its concreteness, as we shall appreciate more fully in the following section. Any one of them, separately conceived, is an abstraction. The prehension is the whole concrete act of the subject feeling the datum with that subjective form.

This is clearly brought out in a definition Whitehead has given of prehension:[3]

The 'prehension' of one actual entity by another actual entity is the complete transaction, analysable into the objectification of the former entity as one of the data for the latter, and into the fully clothed feeling whereby the datum is absorbed into the subjective satisfaction— 'clothed' with the various elements of its 'subjective form'. But this definition can be more generally stated so as to include the case of the prehension of an eternal object by an actual entity; namely, the 'positive prehension' of an entity by an actual entity is the complete transaction analysable into the ingression, or objectification, of that

---

[1] A I 227.   [2] P R 31 [35].   [3] P R 71 [82].

entity as a datum for feeling, and into this feeling whereby the datum is absorbed into the subjective satisfaction.

It should be noted that the 'fully clothed feeling' is not apart from the 'objectification'. On the contrary, the 'objectification' *is effected by* the feeling; the feeling is that act 'whereby the datum is absorbed into the subjective satisfaction'. This 'absorption' *constitutes* the 'objectification'. That is, the datum becomes an 'object' through being felt; it is then the 'object' of the 'subject feeling'. The actual entity which is the datum, in so far as it is describable without reference to a subject prehending it, is only *potentially* an object. It *is* an object only when it is felt by some concrescing subject. That 'being felt' as an object constitutes its 'absorption', its 'inclusion', in the prehending subject. We shall now examine in some detail how this 'objectification' is effected.

§ 31

THE PROCESS OF OBJECTIFICATION

For this purpose, and in order to avoid complexity of exposition, we shall consider the simplest case of prehension, namely that in which one single actual entity prehends another single actual entity as datum. Whitehead terms such a prehension a 'simple physical feeling'. A feeling is 'physical' when the datum is an actual entity; when the datum is an eternal object Whitehead calls the prehension of feeling 'conceptual'. 'Conceptual feelings' will be discussed subsequently and will be omitted from consideration here. A physical feeling is 'simple' when a single actual entity is the datum. Accordingly,

a 'simple physical feeling' entertained in one subject is a feeling for which the initial datum is another single actual entity. . . . Thus in a simple physical feeling there are two actual entities concerned. One of them is the subject of that feeling, and the other is the *initial* datum of that feeling.[1]

Whitehead points out that 'owing to the vagueness of our conscious analysis of complex feelings, perhaps we never consciously discriminate one simple physical feeling in isolation'.[2] But it is a logical requirement that all the more complex types are built up out of simples. Accordingly, Whitehead says, 'all our physical relationships are made up of such simple physical feelings, as their atomic bricks'.[3]

Further, these physical relationships are what constitute the 'causal' relationships of nature:

A simple physical feeling is an act of causation. The actual entity which is the initial datum is the 'cause', the simple physical feeling is the 'effect', and the subject entertaining the simple physical feeling is the actual entity 'conditioned' by the effect. This 'conditioned' actual entity will also be called the 'effect'. All complex causal action can be reduced to a complex of such primary components. Therefore simple physical feelings will also be called 'causal feelings'.[4]

But in holding that they are 'causal', it must not be forgotten that these simple physical feelings are essentially 'perceptual'; as Whitehead puts it, 'it is equally true to say that a simple physical feeling is the most primitive type of an act of perception, devoid of consciousness'.[5]

Now the two actual entities involved in a simple physical feeling are each constituted by acts of prehension or feeling. Thus when the prehending actuality feels another actuality as datum, it feels the feeling of the datum. This means that 'a simple physical feeling is one feeling which feels another feeling';[6] it feels conformally with that other feeling. But a simple physical feeling has a subject, namely the prehending actuality; and 'the feeling felt has a subject diverse from the subject of the feeling which feels it'.[7] Thus there are two subjects. The antecedent actuality which is the cause, when it was in its process of concrescence, 'enacted'

[1] P R 334 [361].   [2] P R 335 [362].   [3] P R 335 [362].
[4] P R 334 [361].   [5] P R 334 [361].   [6] P R 335 [362].   [7] P R 335 [362].

its feeling; the prehending actuality, the effect, then feels the feeling of the cause by 're-enacting' or 'reproducing' that feeling.

It is to be noted that the feeling of the prehender is not simply an enaction of *a* feeling; it is a *re*-enaction of *the feeling of the datum*. That is, 'the cause passes on its feeling to be reproduced by the new subject as its own, and yet as inseparable from the cause'.[1] This is a vital point. The feeling of the prehender is its own, by virtue of its being the subject of that acting; but its feeling is a 're-enaction' or 'reproduction' of the cause's feeling. Thus the re-enacted feeling is not only the prehender's feeling; it is also the cause's feeling.

But the re-enacted feeling is not the cause's feeling 'formally'. The cause 'formally' is the antecedent actuality, as subject, enacting its feeling. The feeling *re-enacted* by the prehender is the cause's feeling 'objectively', while it is the prehender's feeling 'formally' and 'subjectively'. In this way, through the re-enaction of its feeling, the cause is 'objectively' in the effect. It is important to be clear that

the cause is objectively in the constitution of the effect in virtue of being the feeler of the feeling reproduced in the effect.[2]

The essential point is that the feeling conformally reproduced by the effect is a re-enaction of the cause's feeling. That feeling cannot be separated from its subject, for there cannot be a feeling without a subject; the concept of 'a particular feeling divorced from its subject is nonsense'.[3] Thus,

the reason why the cause is objectively in the effect, is that the cause's feeling cannot, as a feeling, be abstracted from its subject which is the cause.[4]

---

[1] P R 335 [362–3]. It should be noted that Whitehead's use here of the active verb 'passes on' (or in other passages, 'transmits') is not to be understood as implying that in this transaction the 'cause' is the agent, and the 'effect' a mere passive recipient; the cause 'passes on' its feeling by virtue of being the datum, and thus the object, of the feeling-activity of the prehender. The cause is in the past, and its activity is thus over; the prehender, the effect, is the agent acting.
[2] P R 335 [363].   [3] P R 326 [353].   [4] P R 336 [363].

In other words, there is not simply 'a feeling', but 'an actuality feeling'.

This re-enaction or reproduction, and thus 'objectification', of the cause 'can be more accurately explained in terms of the eternal objects involved'. Whitehead's statement of it is as follows:

There are eternal objects determinant of the definiteness of the objective datum which is the 'cause', and eternal objects determinant of the definiteness of the subjective form belonging to the 'effect'. When there is re-enaction there is one eternal object with two-way functioning, namely, as partial determinant of the objective datum, and as partial determinant of the subjective form. In this two-way role, the eternal object is functioning relationally between the initial data on the one hand and the concrescent subject on the other.[1]

That is to say, the definiteness of the feeling of the cause is determined by the ingression of a particular eternal object (to consider the simplest case). In other words, that feeling is defined as being what it is by that eternal object; the eternal object is the 'form' of the feeling. When that feeling is re-enacted, the same eternal object is determinant of the definiteness of the feeling as re-enacted.

The eternal object is here functioning 'relationally'; that is, it is 'relating' object to subject. It is not merely the case that there are two subjects feeling, with no more connections between them than that both feelings happen to be defined by the same eternal form. For the form of the effect's feeling, by the ontological principle, is derived from the cause. That is to say, the form of the effect's feeling, i.e. the eternal object determining that feeling, since it is derived from the cause, is not a pure abstract potential, but is a *real* potential.[2] Thus it is the eternal object *as determining* the cause.

Further, it is only *conceptually* that an eternal object can be held in separation from the actuality whose definiteness it is determining;[3] *concretely* an eternal object is not apart from the feeling, any

---

[1] P R 337 [364]. Whitehead makes a distinction between 'initial datum' and 'objective datum', but for the purposes of this introductory book this distinction can be ignored and both taken simply as 'the datum'.

[2] See § 19 above.   [3] This will be explained in detail in § 35 below.

more than the feeling can be apart from its subject—the eternal object is the form *of* the feeling *of* the actuality. Accordingly the eternal object determining the feeling of the percipient effect is not a pure abstract eternal object, but is that eternal object which is the form of the cause. This, therefore, is the nature of the two-way functioning of the eternal object whereby the cause is included objectively in the effect.[1] In this way, as Whitehead expresses it,[2]

in 'causal objectification' what is felt *subjectively* by the objectified actual entity is transmitted *objectively* to the concrescent actualities which supersede it. . . . In this type of objectification the eternal objects, relational between object and subject, express the formal constitution of the objectified actual entity.

We now have Whitehead's detailed answer to the problem: 'How can other actual entities, each with its own formal existence, also enter objectively into the actual entity in question?' We have seen[3] that this problem necessitates explaining, in terms of the ultimate nature of actuality, the distinction between the 'formal' and the 'objective' existence of an actual entity, displaying them both as forms of existence of that actuality. In Whitehead's doctrine the ultimate nature of actuality is an activity of feeling, that is, an activity of 'transforming entities which are individually alien, into components of a complex which is concretely one'.[4] Whitehead's solution of this problem is that the cause's feeling, enacted by the cause as subject, is the cause 'formally'; and that feeling, re-enacted by the effect, is the cause 'objectively'. For, as has been shown, 'a simple physical feeling has the dual character of being the cause's feeling re-enacted for the effect as subject'.[5] As Whitehead has expressed this alternatively,[6]

in a simple physical feeling there is a double particularity in reference to the actual world, the particular cause and the particular effect. In

[1] Cf. R M 80–1: 'In the concretion the creatures are qualified by the ideal forms, and conversely the ideal forms are qualified by the creatures. Thus the epochal occasion, which is thus emergent, has in its own nature the other creatures under the aspect of these forms, and analogously it includes the forms under the aspect of these creatures.'   [2] P R 80 [91].

[3] § 28 above.   [4] P R 300 [322].   [5] P R 336 [363].   [6] P R 336 [363].

Prehension and Objectification

Locke's language (III, III, 6), and with his limitation of thought, a simple feeling is an idea in one mind 'determined to this or that particular existent'.

But it is to be noted that in Whitehead's theory the representative theory of perception is avoided. For in Whitehead's doctrine the objectification of the cause in the effect, i.e. in the percipient, is not a 'representation' of the cause or perceived actuality. The effect 'reproduces' or 're-enacts' the cause. Thus the objectification of the cause constitutes a partial identification of cause and effect. In Whitehead's words,[1]

this transference of feeling effects a partial identification of cause with effect, and not a mere representation of the cause. It is the cumulation of the universe and not a stage-play about it.

Objectification constitutes a 'transference of feeling' because, as Whitehead explains,[2]

by reason of this duplicity in a simple physical feeling there is a vector character which transfers the cause into the effect. It is a feeling *from* the cause which acquires the subjectivity of the new effect without loss of its original subjectivity in the cause.

That is to say, the 'transference of the cause into the effect' does not involve the cause 'formally' being in the effect. The cause 'formally' retains its original subjectivity (i.e. as in its process of acting), but the cause 'acquires the subjectivity of a new effect' through being the 'object' of the feeling of that new effect as subject. Thus one and the same cause can be 'objectively' existent in a number of effects.

Because objectification is the inclusion or transference of the cause or past actuality into the new actuality or effect,

simple physical feelings embody the reproductive character of nature, and also the objective immortality of the past. In virtue of these feelings time is the conformation of the immediate present to the past. Such feelings are 'conformal' feelings.[3]

---

[1] P R 336 [363].   [2] P R 336 [363–4].   [3] P R 336 [364].

That is, the past exists objectively in the present through simple physical feelings reproducing the past. But not only is the present 'reproductive' of the past; it is also 'cumulative' of the past. For the cause 'formally' itself embodied a re-enaction of an antecedent feeling—that is, the cause's feeling had its own datum. Thus, as Whitehead says, 'this antecedent initial datum has now entered into the datum of the effect's feeling at second-hand through the mediation of the cause'.[1] Accordingly, 'this passage of the cause into the effect is the cumulative character of time'.[2] Also, Whitehead points out, 'the irreversibility of time depends on this character'.[3]

[1] P R 336 [363].   [2] P R 336 [363].   [3] P R 336 [363].

PART FOUR

THE NATURE OF ACTUALITY:
A METAPHYSICAL DESCRIPTION

CHAPTER XIV

The Genetic Analysis of an Actual Entity

---

§ 32

AN ACTUAL ENTITY AS 'SUBJECT–SUPERJECT'

We have now expounded Whitehead's main metaphysical categories, and have shown that they constitute an interrelated scheme in terms of which to understand the nature of the ὄντως ὄν, of 'complete fact'. But in our discussion so far there is much which still requires explanation. Of course the elucidation of a great deal of this lies beyond the scope of this book, since it requires the detailed *application* of the metaphysical ideas to cosmological, epistemological, and other problems. But there are a good many purely metaphysical problems which still require clarification. For example, on the basis of the theory as it has been presented up to this point, it is not evident for what reasons (i.e. on what principles) actualities differ from each other in character. For if the data for each actual entity in becoming be 'the full content of the antecedent universe',[1] and we are accordingly led to the conclusion that 'every actual entity is present in every other actual entity',[2] how are we to explain the manifest variety in the universe? Why are not all actualities identical, as appears to be the implication of this conception?

[1] M T 121.   [2] P R 69 [79].

That is to say, when pushed to their strict metaphysical generality, do not Whitehead's categories lead to insuperable difficulties of this kind? Is he not then inevitably driven to incoherence in accounting for the differences between things, in that he is compelled, in order to explain them, to introduce principles which are in arbitrary disconnection from the other categories? For example, does not the distinction made in the previous chapter between 'physical' and 'conceptual' prehension, already involve the covert introduction of such an arbitrarily disconnected principle? For, granted that his basic principles necessitate 'physical' prehension as being the 'objective' inclusion of one actuality in another, do these principles equally necessitate 'conceptual' prehension? Or is the latter an arbitrarily introduced notion in order to cover items which his main categories leave inexplicable?

In order to deal with problems such as these, Whitehead has had to pursue his analysis of the nature of actuality in very much greater detail than we have so far indicated. We are accordingly compelled to follow him in some of this detail, although it must be pointed out that since this book is intended to be only introductory, we shall not enter into the full complexity of Whitehead's analysis—an analysis which surpasses in the extent of its detail and meticulous rigour anything which has so far been achieved in the entire history of philosophy. The coherence of Whitehead's system can be properly and adequately investigated only by entering into the full complexity of his analysis, for his categories do in fact entail that complexity, as our subsequent discussion will indicate.

Such a detailed investigation cannot be undertaken here, however. Our purpose, being the more restricted one of 'introducing' Whitehead's concepts, requires a procedure or treatment in which those ideas are successively expounded. But because of the essential interconnectedness of principles, this procedure results in a certain degree of simplification, especially when in the earlier stages of the discussion we do not take into account notions to be expounded later. This is an inevitable limitation of this order of exposition. A full examination must adopt a rather different procedure, one more like that of *Process and Reality*; that is to say, it must presuppose an exposition such as we are making here.

Our attempt now must be progressively to rectify the earlier simplification in order to gain a more adequate understanding of Whitehead's metaphysical doctrine. In the previous section we had a clear instance of such a simplification. In discussing the process of objectification we took two actual entities as being concerned in this transaction. Now it is perfectly legitimate to do so provided that we are aware of having simplified in order to facilitate exposition. There was in fact a two-fold simplification, and it is important that this be corrected.

In the first place, no actual entity can have only one single actuality as datum; each has an indefinite number of data. Indeed, by the category of relativity, the data for any one actuality 'consist of the full content of the antecedent universe as it exists in relevance for that pulsation' of actuality. The second simplification in our discussion is that we implicitly treated the actuality in becoming as being fully constituted 'formally' by the one simple physical feeling. The constitution of an actual entity is, however, vastly complex, as we shall now demonstrate.

Since 'a "simple physical feeling" entertained in one subject is a feeling for which the initial datum is another single actual entity',[1] and since any single actual entity has as data a large number of antecedent actualities, it follows that an actual entity must have a large number of simple physical feelings. It should be noted that a doctrine of 'simple' physical feelings is necessitated by any theory maintaining that experience is 'complex' and 'analysis-able'. A complex whole can be constructed out of 'simples'; and unless there be 'simples' as components, a whole cannot be 'complex', and analysable. Likewise, there can be no 'integration', and thus growth and development, unless there be 'elements' or 'simples' to be integrated.

In Whitehead's doctrine, an actual entity is 'formally' a pro-cess of concrescence, of the 'growing together' of the objects

---

[1] P R 334 [361]. Cf. § 31 above.

prehended into an integral unity. Thus the initial phase of many simple physical feelings must be succeeded by phases of activity integrating those diverse simple physical feelings into one completed unitary feeling which is the 'satisfaction' of that actual entity. The 'satisfaction', we have seen,[1] is the terminal culmination and outcome of the whole process of feeling; it is 'the contentment of the creative urge'.[2] The phase of integrating activity must itself be complex, for one reason because of the diversity of the data in the first phase: there are many items given which, by virtue of their mutual incompatibility, are incapable of conjoint realization in the new actuality, and accordingly there must be a complex of activity to deal with this situation.

Our task in this Part must be to analyse the complex constitution of an actual entity, at least in its main features. In doing so we shall necessarily have to take full account of the interrelationships of actualities, for, as has been made clear,[3] 'the analysis of an actual entity, into its most concrete elements, discloses it to be a concrescence of prehensions',[4] and a 'prehension' is an act of including an otherness transcending itself.

It must be very carefully borne in mind that in order properly to understand this complexity constituting an actual entity, an actuality must be conceived as *in the process* of activity. As Whitehead says,[5]

each actual entity is a cell with atomic unity. But in analysis it can only be understood as a process; it can only be felt as a process, that is to say, as in passage.

In this chapter we see more fully why it can only be understood as a process. As a unitary process an actual entity is undivided. But it is nevertheless divisible, in the sense that the various factors constituting its complex unity can be distinguished. Now in making these distinctions we are abstracting from the concrete whole; it is therefore vital that these abstractions be constantly referred back to that whole of activity, or we are liable to incur

[1] § 29.   [2] P R 309 [335].   [3] § 28.   [4] P R 31 [35].   [5] P R 321 [347].

168

falsification through implicitly falling into static modes of thinking.

We are concerned to analyse an actuality in its complex process of becoming. In this analysis an 'actual entity is seen as a process; there is a growth from phase to phase; there are processes of integration and of reintegration'.[1] But, we must be clear, all the many prehensions or feelings involved are the feelings of that one actual entity; that is, though the feelings be many, they have *one* subject. Thus when we are conceiving the feelings individually, we are conceiving the subject under some one aspect, constituted by the feeling in question.

This factor of the 'subject' must be carefully considered, for the very term is liable to be misleading owing to its associations with the static modes of thought. Thus, while the prehensions must have a 'subject', the 'subject' must not be conceived as 'in being' antecedently to the process of prehending activity, as a *terminus a quo*; for there can be a 'subject' only when there is a process or activity of prehending. But on the other hand, by the category of process, the 'being' of an actual entity is constituted by its 'becoming'. Thus the subject 'becomes'; it is emergent from the process of activity. It is not emergent, however, in the sense of being wholly subsequent to the acts of feeling, as a *terminus ad quem*, for then there would have been feelings without a subject, without a 'feel*er*'. It is important to appreciate that the subject must be *with* the actings. Whitehead explains that[2]

the term 'subject' has been retained because in this sense it is familiar in philosophy. But it is misleading. The term 'superject' would be better.

Whitehead accordingly uses the combined term 'subject-super-ject', for, in his words,[3]

an actual entity is at once the subject experiencing and the superject of its experiences. It is subject-superject, and neither half of this de-cription can for a moment be lost sight of. The term 'subject' will be mostly employed when the actual entity is considered in respect to its own real internal constitution. But 'subject' is always to be construed as an abbreviation of 'subject-superject'.

An actual entity as 'subject-superject' must be conceived as one 'epochal whole' of activity. As we have seen earlier,[1] an actual entity becomes 'as a whole', and exists as a whole of becoming. The *whole* is the *subject* experiencing. But that experiencing is the activity of self-creation of the actuality as *superject*. Thus the actual entity is at once subject of its experiences, and the outcome or superject of its experiences. However, the superject is not other than the subject; it is the subject as conceived in its completion. The subject, on the other hand, is the whole, including the superject, conceived as *in the process* of its activity. It must be emphasized that the subject-superject must essentially be thought of as an epochal whole of activity of which conceptually we distinguish various aspects. And in this distinguishing it is the whole which is considered under a particular aspect.

§ 33

SELF-CAUSATION AND SUBJECTIVE AIM

Since the experiencing of an actual entity is its activity of self-creation, it follows that the subject-superject is the end which the activity aims to achieve. As Whitehead puts it,[2]

the subject-superject is the purpose of the process originating the feelings. The feelings are inseparable from the end at which they aim; and this end is the feeler. The feelings aim at the feeler, as their final cause. The feelings are what they are in order that their subject may be what it is.

The feelings originate as feelings of objects, of antecedent data, but that origination implies 'purpose' or 'aim'. There can be no

[1] § 12.   [2] P R 313 [339].

activity without some aim, purpose, direction; and 'feeling' is an 'activity', not a mere 'passivity'. The fundamental purpose motivating the activity of an actual entity is its own self-creation. Purpose implies aim, and aim implies end. This end is the actuality as superject. Thus the superject is the *final cause* operating in the becoming of an actual entity. The *efficient cause*, as we have seen,[1] is constituted by the objectified data.

It will be noted that in accordance with the ontological principle, both causes are factors within the constitution of an *actual* entity, that is, one which is in the process of becoming. But both, also by the ontological principle, are derivative from other actual entities. We shall come to the derivation of the final cause later;[2] the efficient cause is the antecedent data as objectified. Thus

according to this account, efficient causation expresses the transition from actual entity to actual entity; and final causation expresses the internal process whereby the actual entity becomes itself. There is the becoming of the datum, which is to be found in the past of the world; and there is the becoming of the immediate self from the datum. This latter becoming is the immediate actual process. An actual entity is at once the product of the efficient past, and is also, in Spinoza's phrase, *causa sui*.[3]

A vital point in this is that since an actual entity is a process of self-creation, it must have its final cause as an inherent element within it. This can be expressed by saying that it is an activity of self-*causation*. As we have seen earlier,[4] Whitehead points out that 'every philosophy recognizes, in some form or other, this factor of self-causation in what it takes to be ultimate actual fact'.[5] The problem is to maintain this consistently and coherently. Descartes, for example, failed to do so; for him God alone was *causa sui*. Spinoza achieved coherence with his doctrine of the monistic substance as *causa sui*. Whitehead holds a doctrine of a plurality of actual entities, each an activity of self-causation. 'In this way an actual entity satisfies Spinoza's notion of substance: it is *causa sui*. The creativity is not an external agency with its own ulterior

---

[1] § 21. [2] § 38. [3] P R 209 [228]. [4] § 14. [5] P R 209 [228].

purposes';[1] for the creativity is not an *actuality*. The coherence of the doctrine is exemplified in that according to it

all actual entities share with God this characteristic of self-causation. For this reason every actual entity also shares with God the character-istic of transcending all other actual entities, including God. The universe is thus a creative advance into novelty. The alternative to this doctrine is a static morphological universe.[2]

The self-causation of an actual entity implies that it embodies its own 'decision' as to what it is to be. This factor of 'decision' was discussed previously in connection with the distinction between 'actuality' and 'potentiality';[3] now some further aspects and implications of it must be brought out.

This 'decision' which actuality involves in its very nature as 'acting', implies that an actual entity also possesses as a necessary inherent element the correlative factor of 'freedom'. Now 'free-dom' entails 'responsibility'. Metaphysically, this responsibility is two-fold. Primarily, because an actual entity necessarily embodies its own 'decision' as to what it is to be, it must be 'responsible' for what, by virtue of its prehensions, it becomes. For, according to the category of process, '*how* an actual entity *becomes* constitutes *what* that actual entity *is*; so that the two descriptions of an actual entity are not independent'.[4] Thus the primary, and ultimate, responsibility of an actual entity is for becoming that actual entity which it does become, or in other words, for being what it is. And because it is a metaphysical necessity that it is subsequently objectively immortal in other actual entities, it is derivatively responsible also for its effects on others. Whitehead observes that

in our own relatively high grade of human existence, this doctrine of feelings and their subject is best illustrated by our notion of moral responsibility. The subject is responsible for being what it is in virtue of its feelings. It is also derivatively responsible for the consequences of its existence because they flow from its feelings.[5]

[1] P R 313–14 [339].   [2] P R 314 [339–40].   [3] § 17.
[4] P R 31 [34].   [5] P R 313 [339]. Cf. also P R 64 [74–5].

The Genetic Analysis of an Actual Entity

It is evident that this doctrine of feelings and their subject, of feelings aiming at their subject, cannot be understood in terms of static subject-predicate modes of thought. As Whitehead puts it,[1]

if the subject-predicate form of statement be taken to be metaphysically ultimate, it is then impossible to express this doctrine of feelings and their superject. It is better to say that the feelings *aim at* their subject, than to say that they *are aimed at* their subject. For the latter mode of expression removes the subject from the scope of the feeling and assigns it to an external agency. Thus the feeling would be wrongly abstracted from its own final cause. This final cause is an inherent element in the feeling, constituting the unity of that feeling. An actual entity feels as it does in order to be the actual entity which it is.

We can properly understand this doctrine only if it be constantly borne in mind that we are conceiving a unitary whole of activity, in the process of its acting, and that the whole *is* the actual entity. The distinguishable elements are thus partial aspects of that whole. The feelings comprising the actual entity are many, and could not possess a unity and an internal consistency were it not that the superject, as final cause, is an inherent element in the entire process of feeling. Clearly this can only be conceived by thinking of the actual entity as one epochal whole, in fact undivided.

Before going on to further analysis, it is useful to pause to note that this doctrine of Whitehead's of the subject-superject is importantly divergent from traditional philosophy. This is brought out by considering the contrast, for example, with Kant's philosophy. Whitehead has stated it as follows:[2]

The philosophy of organism is the inversion of Kant's philosophy. *The Critique of Pure Reason* describes the process by which subjective data pass into the appearance of an objective world. The philosophy of organism seeks to describe how objective data pass into subjective satisfaction, and how order in the objective data provides intensity in the subjective satisfaction. For Kant, the world emerges from the subject; for the philosophy of organism, the subject emerges from the world—a 'superject' rather than a 'subject'.

[1] P R 313 [339].   [2] P R 123 [135–6].

173

He goes on to explain that[1]

the word 'object' thus means an entity which is a potentiality for being a component in feeling; and the word 'subject' means the entity constituted by the process of feeling, and including this process. The feeler is the unity emergent from its own feelings; and the feelings are the details of the process intermediary between this unity and its many data. The data are the potentials for feeling; that is to say, they are objects. The process is the elimination of indeterminateness of feeling from the unity of one subjective experience.

It will be noted that Kant retains the presupposition of the subject as the self-identical, changeless substance undergoing accidental changes. It is in this notion that we have a root point of divergence of Whitehead's philosophy from antecedent thought, which is typified, for example, by Descartes. As Whitehead has expressed it,[2]

Descartes in his own philosophy conceives the thinker as creating the occasional thought. The philosophy of organism inverts the order, and conceives the thought as a constituent operation in the creation of the occasional thinker. The thinker is the final end whereby there is the thought. In this inversion we have the final contrast between a philosophy of substance and a philosophy of organism. The operations of an organism are directed towards the organism as a 'superject', and are not directed from the organism as a 'subject'. The operations are directed *from* antecedent organisms and *to* the immediate organisms. They are 'vectors', in that they convey the many things into the constitution of the single superject. The creative process is rhythmic: it swings from the publicity of many things to the individual privacy; and it swings back from the private individual to the publicity of the objectified individual. The former swing is dominated by the final cause, which is the ideal; and the latter swing is dominated by the efficient cause which is actual.

[1] P R 123 [136].   [2] P R 210 [228–9].

CHAPTER XV

The Analysis of Prehension

---

§ 34

PHYSICAL AND CONCEPTUAL PREHENSION

Whitehead's answer to the general metaphysical problem of the nature of the ὄντως ὄν, the problem as to 'what' an actual entity is, is that 'the essence of an actual entity consists solely in the fact that it is a prehending thing (i.e. a substance whose whole essence or nature is to prehend)'.[1] We have seen in the last few chapters that the primary prehension must be 'physical' prehension, that is, prehension for which the data are actual entities.[2] In the preceding chapter it was shown that the process of prehension constituting an actual entity must be complex. This complex of prehending activity is directed to the achievement of a concrescent unity which *is* the actual entity. Thus an actual entity is the 'superject' of its own activity of self-creation.

The superject, as final cause, is therefore the end to which the activity of an actual entity is directed. It is accordingly, as Whitehead says in the passage quoted at the end of the previous chapter, 'the ideal'. It is 'ideal' in both senses which the word bears in English: it is the 'ideal end', a perfection to be aimed at; and it is the end entertained as an 'idea', i.e. 'conceptually'. The point is that an actual entity is a process of becoming, and its prehensions or feelings, from their inception, must be guided by an 'idea of

---

[1] P R 56 [65].   [2] Cf. § 31.

itself' as it is to be, i.e. as an 'ideal'. This is necessitated by the notion of an actual entity as a process of self-creation, as has been shown. The necessity of having an 'ideal of itself' or 'subjective aim' is therefore a general metaphysical category applying to all actual entities. In other words, this 'idea of itself as superject' is the 'subjective aim' indispensable to the becoming of an actual entity.

What is of particular significance to us at the moment is that the 'subjective aim' is an 'idea' or 'concept'. Now a 'concept' or 'idea' must be a prehension, since the analysis of an actual entity reveals only prehensions.[1] But it cannot be a 'physical' prehension; this is the whole point of distinguishing the 'subjective aim' as an 'idea'. It is a prehension of a different kind, a 'conceptual' prehension. Thus in order adequately to understand the category of subjective aim and its role, it is necessary to investigate 'conceptual prehension' in general and its relation to physical prehension. It is also necessary to inquire whether the category of conceptual prehension is coherent with the other categories of Whitehead's system, and not a principle merely arbitrarily introduced.

We have already referred to conceptual prehension in contrast to physical prehension, defining it as prehension the datum for which is an eternal object.[2] However, from our previous discussion of the nature and existence of eternal objects it is not clear how there *can be* 'conceptual' prehension in addition to physical prehension. For although we can *distinguish* 'eternal objects' or 'forms of definiteness', by the ontological principle they *exist* only as determining the definiteness of specific actual entities.

There is no character belonging to the actual apart from its exclusive determination by selected eternal objects. The definiteness of the actual arises from the exclusiveness of eternal objects in their function as determinants. If the actual entity be *this*, then by the nature of the case it is not *that* or *that*. The fact of incompatible alternatives is the ultimate fact in virtue of which there is definite character.[3]

And further, when one actuality prehends another, it is an *actuality*

[1] § 28.   [2] § 31.   [3] P R 339 [367].

which is the datum of the prehension, the prehension accordingly being a 'physical' prehension.

This physical prehension is, however, mediated by eternal objects, for, as Whitehead says,[1]

the organic philosophy does not hold that the 'particular existents' are prehended apart from universals; on the contrary, it holds that they are prehended by the mediation of universals. In other words, each actuality is prehended by means of some element of its own definiteness. This is the doctrine of the 'objectification' of actual entities. Thus the primary phase in the concrescence of an actual entity is the way in which the antecedent universe enters into the constitution of the entity in question, so as to constitute the basis of its nascent individuality.

Thus in so far as eternal objects enter into this prehension, it is not as themselves data, but only as determinants of the definiteness of the data. How, then, can eternal objects as such be data, which they would have to be if there is to be 'conceptual' prehension as distinct from 'physical' prehension.

To understand this we must recall the previous analysis of the nature of an eternal object as dual. Antecedent actualities are objectified in physical prehension by means of the two-way functioning of eternal objects:[2] as determining the definiteness of the datum and that of the prehending subject. In this relational functioning the eternal objects are 'realized determinants'.

Now when we consider an actual entity in abstraction from the factor of 'acting' which constitutes it 'actual', we find that we are considering a 'realized determinant', that is, an eternal object as determining the definiteness of that acting. Thus in an important sense that 'realized determinant' *is* the actual entity in question. The relevant sense here of *is* ('being', 'to be') is not that of 'existing' in the full 'actual' sense; it is the derivative sense for which the word 'essence' was originally coined as meaning that by virtue of which a 'being', οὐσία, is *what* it is. Accordingly we can say that eternal objects, as 'realized determinants', *are* the actualities in the sense of the 'essence' of those actualities. It is to be noted that in this Whiteheadian position, 'essence' is *not* identified with 'act'

[1] P R 211 [230].　　　　　[2] § 31.

as it is in the Aristotelian doctrine;[1] on the contrary, the 'essence' of an actuality is constituted by the ingredient or 'realized' eternal objects as determining the definiteness of the 'act', and not as itself *being* the act. In Whitehead's doctrine the 'forms' are explicitly held to be 'eternal' in contrast to 'actual', i.e. 'acting'. It is because the eternal objects as 'realized determinants' *are* the actualities in the sense of 'being' their *essence* that physical prehension constitutes an 'objectification' of antecedent *actualities*.

But eternal objects, as we have seen, are not *merely* 'realized determinants'; in their nature they are not restricted to being the 'essences' of particular actualities. Even as a 'realized determinant' an eternal object retains its character of a 'general capacity for determination'. That is to say, even as a 'real potentiality' it has the aspect of a 'pure potentiality'. It is because of this that eternal objects are distinguished by Whitehead as a kind of entity standing in extreme contrast to 'actual' entities: the type of 'pure potentiality' is the strict contrary, as a kind of 'entity', to 'actuality'. In other words, we must admit the category of eternal object; eternal objects cannot be regarded as nothing but actualities, considered in abstraction from their 'activity'. Despite their *existing* as determining the definiteness of actualities, eternal objects are entities whose *nature* transcends the particular instances of their 'realization'. This dual aspect of an eternal object, as 'realized determinant' and as 'general capacity for determination', is necessarily involved in its nature, both as 'eternal' and as 'object'. It is by virtue of this dual character that

immanence and transcendence are the characteristics of an object: as a realized determinant it is immanent; as a capacity for determination it is transcendent; in both roles it is relevant to something not itself.[2]

We can now clarify the distinction between 'physical' and 'conceptual' prehension. In physical prehension the actuality which is the datum is felt through the ingredient eternal objects functioning relationally. That is to say, the eternal objects enter in physical prehension as 'realized determinants'. In conceptual

---

[1] Cf. § 14 above.   [2] P R 339 [366–7].

prehension, on the other hand, the datum is an eternal object, *not* as a 'realized determinant', but in its 'general capacity for determination'. In conceptual prehension, in other words, the datum is an eternal object in abstraction from the particular mode of its realization; the datum is an eternal object in its aspect as a pure, general potential. As Whitehead has put it,

a conceptual feeling is feeling an eternal object in the primary metaphysical character of being an 'object', that is to say, feeling its *capacity* for being a realized determinant of process.[1]

In other words,

a conceptual feeling is the feeling of an eternal object in respect to its general capacity as a determinant of character, including thereby its capacity of exclusiveness.[2]

§ 35

CONCEPTUAL VALUATION OR REPRODUCTION

We must now consider the relation between physical and conceptual prehension in the process of becoming of an actual entity. By the category of relativity, the process of becoming of an actual entity starts with prehensions whereby the antecedent actualities are objectively included in it. These initial prehensions are physical prehensions; they are the simple physical or causal feelings, and as we have seen,[3] they are 'conformal'. It is to be noted that the category of relativity and the ontological principle necessitate that the initial feelings be *physical*. The process of becoming cannot commence with conceptual prehensions; an actual entity must arise out of something definite 'given' to it. This means that it must arise out of a 'real potentiality'; it cannot arise out of mere abstract general potentiality.

[1] P R 339 [366]. Cf. also F R 26: 'It is the experience of forms of definiteness in respect to their disconnection from any particular physical experience, but with abstract evaluation of what they *can* contribute to such experience.'
[2] P R 339 [367].   [3] § 31.

Accordingly conceptual prehension must originate in a phase succeeding that of the initial physical prehension. Further, those initial simple physical prehensions are required as providing the data for the conceptual prehensions. These data are the eternal objects which determine the definiteness of the objectified data of the simple physical feelings. That is to say,[1]

from each physical feeling there is the derivation of a purely conceptual feeling whose datum is the eternal object determinant of the definiteness of the actual entity . . . physically felt.

The conceptual feeling is a reproduction of the ingredient eternal object. It must be clear that what the conceptual feeling reproduces, thereby constituting the 'concept', is the eternal object, not as a 'realized determinant', but as a 'general capacity for determination'. In other words, the conceptual feeling reproduces, not the objectified actuality as mediated by the eternal object, but that eternal object in abstraction from its particular instance of ingression.

This reproductive conceptual derivation is a metaphysical category; that is, it is a general metaphysical characteristic of all actual entities that they have reproductive conceptual prehensions in addition to physical prehensions. The reason is, as will be appreciated more fully as we proceed, that conceptual prehension is indispensable to the activity of self-creation of an actual entity. In part this has already been established with the recognition of 'subjective aim' as a metaphysical category. The entire process of the integration of feelings into the unity of a superject is dependent upon the subjective aim, the 'idea of itself'. In addition to this, as we shall see, the process of *integrating* requires other conceptual functioning as an indispensable ingredient.

Therefore, an actual entity is constituted, not only by 'physical' prehensions, but also by 'conceptual' prehensions. To be more specific,

in each concrescence there is a twofold aspect of the creative urge. In one aspect there is the origination of simple causal feelings; and in

[1] P R 36 [39–40].

The Analysis of Prehension

the other aspect there is the origination of conceptual feelings. These contrasted aspects will be called the physical and the mental poles of an actual entity. No actual entity is devoid of either pole; though their relative importance differs in different actual entities. Also conceptual feelings do not necessarily involve consciousness; though there can be no conscious feelings which do not involve conceptual feelings as elements in the synthesis.

Thus an actual entity is essentially dipolar, with its physical and mental poles; and even the physical world cannot be properly understood without reference to its other side, which is the complex of mental operations. The primary mental operations are conceptual feelings.[1]

All the more complex 'mental operations' depend upon the primary conceptual feelings, which are the feelings of conceptual reproduction. These feelings are primary in the sense of initiating the 'mental pole' by reproducing the eternal objects ingredient in the simple physical feelings, in their 'general capacity for determination'. Thus the primary conceptual feelings, like the primary simple physical feelings, are 'conformal'; they are a conformal conceptual reproduction of the physical pole; they are the conceptual 'registration' of the physical pole. The physical and mental poles of an actual entity are essentially bound up with each other.

The mental pole originates as the conceptual counterpart of the operations in the physical pole. The two poles are inseparable in their origination. The mental pole starts with the conceptual registration of the physical pole.[2]

That the primary conceptual feelings always derive from primary physical feelings, it will be noted, is necessitated by the ontological principle. To put this in another way, all 'concepts' or 'ideas' derive in the first instance from 'physical experience', i.e. direct experience of other actualities. As Whitehead observes,[3]

this category [of conceptual reproduction] maintains the old principle that mentality originates from sensitive experience. It lays down the principle that all sensitive experience originates mental operations.

[1] P R 339 [366].   [2] P R 351 [379].   [3] P R 351 [379].

181

But, he points out, 'it does not, however, mean that there is no origination of other mental operations derivative from these primary mental operations'.[1] On the contrary, there is necessarily such secondary conceptual derivation from the original conceptual reproduction. This secondary origination of conceptual feeling does not involve a contradiction of the general principle of the derivation of conceptual from physical prehension, as we shall show later.[2]

In upholding the principle of the origination of mentality from 'sensitive experience', Whitehead differs from most modern thought in one vital respect. This is in regard to the interpretation of what constitutes 'sensitive experience'. Most post-Cartesian philosophy, explicitly or implicitly adhering to the sensationalist theory, conceives 'sensitive experience' in terms of 'sensa', 'sense-data', 'impressions of sensation', etc., that is to say, in terms of 'mental entities'. These are the entities which, in Whitehead's analysis, constitute 'conceptual reproduction':

This conceptual registration constitutes the sole datum of experience according to the sensationalist school. Writers of this school entirely neglect physical feelings, originating in the physical pole. Hume's 'impressions of sensation' and Kant's sensational data are considered in terms only applicable to conceptual registration. Hence Kant's notion of the chaos of such ultimate data. Also Hume—at least, in his *Treatise*—can only find differences of 'force and vivacity'.[3]

Whitehead, on the contrary, conceives 'sensitive experience' in terms of 'physical prehension', that is, prehension of other actual entities whereby they are objectively in the constitution of the prehender:

'pure' physical prehensions are the components which provide some definite information as to the physical world; the subsidiary 'pure' mental operations are the components by reason of which the theory of 'secondary qualities' was introduced into the theory of perception. The account here given traces back these secondary qualities to their root in physical prehensions expressed by the '*withness* of the body'.[4]

---

[1] PR 351 [379].   [2] § 36.   [3] PR 351 [379–80].   [4] PR 88 [99].

In this way the solipsist difficulty, which haunts the sensationalist theory, is avoided.

This category of conceptual reproduction is also termed by Whitehead the category of conceptual 'valuation'. The reason is that a conceptual prehension, like a physical prehension, has a 'subjective form',[1] and that 'the subjective form of a conceptual feeling has the character of a "valuation"'.[2] But in order adequately to elucidate this our investigation must proceed a stage further.[3]

§ 36

PURE AND HYBRID PREHENSIONS

The process of becoming of an actual entity is constituted by a process of prehending activity whereby data are received and integrated into a new concrete unity which *is* the actuality in question. That is to say, the prehensions are analysable into primary 'physical' prehensions, whereby the data are received, and into the derivative supervening prehensions integrating the data. We have already indicated that this supervening process must be complex. A full analysis will reveal the various 'categoreal obligations' which this process must satisfy, and will distinguish the varieties or types of prehending activity entailed in such a process of integration. In this introductory book, however, we shall not enter into all this detail, but only such of it as is necessary for a general understanding of Whitehead's metaphysical doctrine.

For reasons which we considered in the last section, the primary physical feelings give rise to reproductive conceptual feelings. As we have seen, 'the two poles are inseparable in their origination',[4] and accordingly the reproductive conceptual feelings can also be regarded as 'primary'. Thus the reproductive

---

[1] See § 30 above.   [2] P R 340 [367].
[3] The notion of 'valuation' will receive further consideration in § 37.
[4] P R 351 [379].

conceptual feelings and simple causal feelings constitute the two main species of 'primary' feelings. All other feelings of whatever complexity arise out of a process of integration which starts with a phase of these primary feelings.[1]

Before going on to the analysis of the derivative feelings or prehensions, it is necessary to make an important distinction among simple physical prehensions. A 'simple physical feeling' is one which has as its datum only one actual entity; this is what constitutes the feeling in question 'simple', as we have seen. But such a simple physical feeling may be either 'pure' or 'hybrid'.

In a 'pure physical feeling' the actual entity which is the datum is objectified by one of its own physical feelings.[2]

All more complex pure physical feelings are analysable into such pure simple physical feelings as their components. In the interests of understanding this category of pure simple physical feelings it is worth noting a cosmological interpretation Whitehead makes of this category:[3]

Thus having regard to the 're-enaction' which is characteristic of the subjective form of a simple physical feeling, we have—in the case of the simpler actual entities—an example of the transference of energy in the physical world. When the datum is an actual entity of a highly complex grade, the physical feeling by which it is objectified as a datum may be of a highly complex character, and the simple notion of a transference of some form of energy to the new subject may entirely fail to exhaust the important aspects of the pure physical feeling in question.

The other species of simple physical prehensions is a 'hybrid' simple physical feeling:

In a 'hybrid physical feeling' the actual entity forming the datum is objectified by one of its own conceptual feelings.[4]

This distinction between 'pure' and 'hybrid' simple physical prehensions is necessary because a prehension by one actuality of the 'mental pole' of another cannot be a 'conceptual' prehension;

[1] P R 338 [365–6]. [2] P R 347 [375]. [3] P R 347 [375–6]. [4] P R 347–8 [376].

it is a 'physical' prehension, a prehension *of that actuality* as having a 'concept', and not a prehension of an eternal object as such. A conceptual prehension, as we have seen, can arise only from initial physical prehension. Thus a pure conceptual prehension also arises from a 'hybrid' physical prehension as the conceptual reproduction of that hybrid prehension. In the next chapter we shall see something of the metaphysical importance of hybrid physical prehensions. Here we might note that in cosmological theory this category provides the metaphysical basis for explaining 'the origination and direction of energy in the physical world',[1] of which an outstanding instance is 'conceptual feeling' in the form of 'desire' and 'volition', etc., passing into bodily deeds.

A 'complex', as opposed to 'simple', 'pure' physical feeling arises as the integration of two or more pure simple physical feelings; and by the subsequent integration of such complex feelings still further complex feelings can arise. Thus by integration there can arise feelings of any degree of complexity. An analogous derivation of 'pure' complex conceptual feelings is evidently also possible. These two species of prehensions, including their derivatives, constitute the two species of 'pure' prehensions.

There can, however, also arise feelings integrating physical and conceptual prehensions. Whitehead calls these derivative integrating feelings 'impure'. An 'impure' prehension or feeling is one having as its data both physical and conceptual feelings, integrating them into one new feeling. Whitehead has stated his doctrine as follows:[2]

The basic operations of mentality are 'conceptual prehensions'. These are the only operations of 'pure' mentality. All other mental operations are 'impure', in the sense that they involve integrations of conceptual prehensions with the physical prehensions of the physical pole. Since 'impurity' in prehension refers to the prehension arising out of the integration of 'pure' physical prehensions with 'pure' mental prehensions, it follows that an 'impure' mental prehension is also an 'impure' physical prehension and conversely. Thus the term 'impure' applied

[1] P R 348 [376].   [2] P R 44 [48–9].

to a prehension has a perfectly definite meaning; and does not require the terms 'mental' or 'physical', except for the direction of attention in the discussion concerned.

An 'impure' prehension is thus always one which arises in a later phase of the process of concrescence of an actual entity, since it arises from simple 'pure' prehensions, or from complex 'pure' prehensions, or from 'hybrid' physical and 'pure' conceptual prehensions. It is evident that 'impure' prehensions too may be of any degree of complexity.

§ 37

THE UNITY OF PREHENSIONS

We can now consider as a whole, and more fully, the concrescent process of an actual entity. This process is the becoming of the subject-superject as one epochal unity. By the ontological principle, 'the ground, or origin, of the concrescent process, is the multiplicity of data in the universe, actual entities and eternal objects . . .'[1] The genetic process itself is analysable into prehensions or feelings, starting with the 'primary' feelings, followed by phases of complex feelings involving integrations of feeling as in antecedent phases, and terminating in a completed unity of feeling, the 'satisfaction'.

It must be emphasized that although we analytically distinguish various phases and a variety of feelings, they are not in fact separate. The 'satisfaction', for example, is not a separate and distinct feeling; it is the 'consummation' of the antecedent feelings, and as such it is 'cumulative' of them. Nor are the antecedent feelings distinct from the 'satisfaction'. For the 'satisfaction' is the actual entity as 'superject', and the 'superject' is not distinct from the 'subject'. Nor is the 'subject' distinct from any of the antecedent feelings. On the contrary,

[1] P R 317 [343].

the subject is at work in the feeling, in order that it may be the subject with that feeling. The feeling is an episode in self-production, and is referent to its aim. This aim is a certain definite unity with its companion feelings.[1]

This unity is not merely a unity, i.e. some or other unity, but 'a certain definite unity'. The aim at that definite unity is the aim at the achievement of a certain experience, a certain intensity of experience. It is the aim at the 'realization' of something 'for its own sake'. By virtue of the prehending or experiencing activity of an actual entity being an activity of self-creation, the achievement of a certain definite unity in experiencing has a characteristic which we can express by the phrase 'for its own sake'. This attainment or realization of an intensity of experience 'for its own sake' is a basic factor in the notion of 'value'. Thus in *Science and the Modern World* Whitehead had insisted that 'what the fact of the reality of an event is in itself' is inherently bound up with the notion of 'value':[2]

... the element of value, of being valuable, of having value, of being an end in itself, of being something which is for its own sake, must not be omitted in any account of an event as the most concrete actual something. 'Value' is the word I use for the intrinsic reality of an event.

The achievement as such is not equated with 'value'; it is the 'achievement *of* value': 'realization therefore is in itself the attainment of value'.[3] The notion of 'value' is complex, but for our present purposes it is not necessary to enter into its analysis here. It is sufficient to note that it involves this factor of 'realization for its own sake'.

In the process of concrescence the data have to be assessed, 'evaluated', with a view to their compatibility for inclusion in the terminal unity, in accordance with the criterion constituted by the subjective aim. That is, the data are evaluated for maintenance or discard in accordance with the subjective aim dominating the activity of self-creation. We shall come to the discussion of subjective aim in this role in the next chapter. Here we must note

[1] P R 316 [342].   [2] S M W 116.   [3] S M W 116.

that this activity of 'evaluation' is the basic and essential activity of the 'mental pole'. In other words, conceptual prehension is in its nature an activity of evaluation. This evaluation commences with the primary conceptual prehensions, the conceptual reproductions, as evaluations of the 'what' of the data. This is why Whitehead refers to this conceptual prehension as 'conceptual valuation',[1] and speaks of this phase of conceptual activity, starting with the conceptual reproductions, as 'a ferment of qualitative valuation':

The intermediate phase of self-formation is a ferment of qualitative valuation. These qualitative feelings are either derived directly from qualities illustrated in the primary phase, or are indirectly derived by their relevance to them. These conceptual feelings pass into novel relations to each other, felt with a novel emphasis of subjective form. The ferment of valuation is integrated with the physical prehensions of the physical pole.[2]

The outcome of this prehending activity in a terminal 'satisfaction' is the realization or actualization of a certain definite 'value-experience'. It is beyond the scope of this book to enter into further details; I shall merely indicate the implications of this conception with one brief quotation:[3]

Everything has some value for itself, for others, and for the whole. This characterizes the meaning of actuality. By reason of this character, constituting reality, the conception of morals arises. We have no right to deface the value-experience which is the very essence of the universe. Existence, in its own nature, is the upholding of value-intensity. Also no unit can separate itself from the others, and from the whole. And yet each unit exists in its own right. It upholds value-intensity for itself, and this involves sharing value-intensity with the universe. Everything that in any sense exists has two sides, namely, its individual self and its signification in the universe. Also either of these aspects is a factor in the other.

[1] § 35.

[2] A I 269–70. The justification for the phrase 'or are indirectly derived by their relevance to them' is to be found in the category of 'conceptual reversion'. Despite its metaphysical importance, I have omitted discussion of this category as one of the 'details' we would not go into in this introductory exposition.

[3] M T 151.

CHAPTER XVI

God

---

§ 38

THE SOURCE OF SUBJECTIVE AIM

The being or existence of an actual entity, in terms of the categories of Whitehead's system, is constituted by its process of becoming. This process is one of the growing together or concrescence of data into a novel unity. In this epochal whole of activity the process of concrescence is governed by an aim at the achievement of that particular novel unity as its outcome or superject. The superject is thus the final cause in the process of becoming. This means that the process of 'concrescence moves towards its final cause, which is its subjective aim'.[1] It is to be noted that none of these are separate and distinct factors. Nor is the 'subject' something distinct from them.

The concrescence is dominated by a subjective aim which essentially concerns the creature as a final superject. This subjective aim is this subject itself determining its own self-creation as one creature.[2]

The point is that the subjective aim, as we have seen, is a prehension, and there can be no prehension without a subject. An actual entity must be conceived as one epochal whole of becoming.

[1] P R 298 [320].   [2] P R 96 [108].

Whitehead points out that

> this doctrine of the inherence of the subject in the process of its pro-
> duction requires that in the primary phase of the subjective process
> there be a conceptual feeling of subjective aim: the physical and other
> feelings originate as steps towards realizing this conceptual aim through
> their treatment of initial data.[1]

We have already explained that the subjective aim must be a
conceptual prehension; it is the 'idea of itself as superject'. In this
last passage Whitehead stresses that the subjective aim is required
from the beginning of the process in order to direct the concrescing
activity. There can be no activity without an aim. The aim must
be involved at the outset; it cannot be something 'generated' by
the activity.

The problem which now confronts us is that, by the ontological principle, the subjective aim must itself derive from somewhere—it cannot come into being from nowhere, 'out of nothing'
—and 'somewhere' must mean 'some actual entity'. To be more
specific on this point, since this subjective aim is a conceptual
feeling, and since it arises, as has been emphasized, in the primary
phase, it must be a primary conceptual feeling, i.e. a conceptual
reproduction. What then is the physical prehension from which
it arises? That is to say, which actual entity is the datum of that
prehension?

By the category of relativity there is a metaphysical necessity
that an actuality, upon achieving completion, shall be an object
for subsequent actualities; 'it belongs to the nature of a "being"
that it is a potential for every "becoming"'.[2] Completed actualities are *potential for* actualities in becoming. They must be
included as objects in those concrescing actualities; but 'how'
they are included does not depend on the past actualities, but on
the 'decision' of the concrescing actual entities. Moreover, each
past actuality is one among a vast multiplicity of data to be
synthesized by any one actual entity in becoming. They are the
data *for* synthesis; they cannot themselves effect that synthesis.

[1] P R 316 [342].   [2] P R 30 [33]. Cf. § 18 above.

Further, since each past actuality can be, and is, a datum in a vast number of different individual syntheses, it is evident that

these data in their own separate natures do not carry any regulative principle for their synthesis.[1]

Yet, by the ontological principle, that 'regulative principle', i.e. subjective aim, must derive from some actual entity.

This metaphysical situation, which is displayed by the foregoing argument, Whitehead maintains, requires the admission of a unique actual entity as the primordial source of the aim at definiteness. In other words, we have here a metaphysical problem which can be solved in only this way, namely, by the admission of a unique actual entity. Whitehead points out[2] that this problem is one which Aristotle faced at an analogous point in his philosophy and that he solved it in the same way. The significance of this reference to Aristotle is not only on account of his undoubted metaphysical insight, but even more that 'in his consideration of this metaphysical question he was entirely dispassionate; and he is the last European metaphysician of first-rate importance for whom this claim can be made. After Aristotle, ethical and religious interests begin to influence metaphysical conclusions'.[3]

The metaphysical problem which is involved here is, in general terms, that of the explanation of 'definiteness'. Not merely the explanation of why there should be *this* and not *that* definiteness, but the explanation of 'definiteness' at all. The problem is thus another aspect of the problem of 'being', of 'existence', for there can be no existence, no actuality, without definiteness. It was this which Plato and Aristotle appreciated in insisting that the basic metaphysical problem, the problem of the ultimate nature of things, is the problem of 'being'—and not, as many of their predecessors had maintained, 'what things are made of'. It was the recognition of this fundamental relationship of 'definiteness' and 'being' which led Plato and Aristotle, in their different ways, to the identification of 'being' and 'form'. The consequent development was that of the notion of 'pure being' as 'incorporeal', as

---

[1] A I 328.   [2] S M W 215–16.   [3] S M W 215.

'pure form', which was, in the final analysis, to be conceived as 'perfect being', i.e. the Divine Being or God.

We have seen in some detail that Whitehead rejects the identification of 'being' and 'form'. Likewise the conception of 'being' as 'eminent', as the divine, is unacceptable; this conception renders impossible a coherent application of the ontological principle. Whitehead holds that we must admit a multiplicity of actualities, i.e. entities which themselves are 'beings' in the full sense of 'actual'. The general metaphysical problem is that of the explanation of 'what' they are. We have shown that their 'whatness', their 'definiteness', is inexplicable by reference solely to themselves. Only one solution is possible, Whitehead holds, and that is to maintain, with Aristotle, that there is a unique actuality from which all definiteness is ultimately derivable. This must be explained in detail.

§ 39

GOD AS AN ACTUAL ENTITY

The argument of the previous section has been that no actual entity in the process of becoming can itself provide the 'regulative principle' indispensable to its process of concrescence. Nor is such a principle derivable from antecedent ordinary actual entities. To an actual entity in the process of becoming, these antecedent actualities constitute a mere welter of data. What is necessary is a criterion in terms of which a decision can be made between a wealth of alternatives, so that a definite concrescence of those data can begin. There must accordingly be a unique actual entity, Whitehead maintains, capable of providing that criterion. That is to say, this unique actual entity

is the principle of concretion—the principle whereby there is initiated a definite outcome from a situation otherwise riddled with ambiguity.[1]

[1] P R 488 [523].

God

In other words, it is Whitehead's doctrine that there must be a unique actual entity—which he identifies with the God of the higher religions[1]—having the metaphysical function of providing the subjective aims for the ordinary actual entities:

In this sense God is the principle of concretion: namely, He is that actual entity from which each temporal concrescence receives that initial aim from which its self-causation starts.[2]

Whitehead is fully alive to the danger of violating the coherence of his system by the introduction of a unique actual entity. It is essential that a *deus ex machina* be avoided. That is to say,

God is not to be treated as an exception to all metaphysical principles, invoked to save their collapse.[3]

On the contrary, Whitehead maintains, what is necessary is that 'He is their chief exemplification'.[4] In other words, God must be conceived, philosophically, in terms of the generic metaphysical principles applying to all actual entities; or, as Whitehead puts it,[5]

the description of the generic character of an actual entity should include God, as well as the lowliest actual occasion, though there is a specific difference between the nature of God and that of any occasion.

If God be treated as an exception to the metaphysical principles which a particular system is seeking to maintain, it means that the principles in question are not truly 'metaphysical'. The successful application of a categoreal scheme to God is, on the other hand, one of the crucial tests for its coherence which a metaphysical

[1] Whitehead's reason for the identification of this unique actual entity with the God of religion is to be found in the interpretation of religious phenomena in terms of his philosophical concepts. As he puts it, this unique actual entity 'is here termed "God"; because the contemplation of our natures, as enjoying real feelings derived from the timeless source of all order, acquires that "subjective form" of refreshment and companionship at which religions aim' (P R 43 [47]). The adequate appreciation of this is only possible when we have proceeded further in our analysis of the metaphysical nature and function of this actual entity.

[2] P R 345 [374]. It seems preferable to speak of 'ordinary' actual entities and a 'unique' actual entity rather than, as Whitehead does, of 'temporal' actual entities and a 'non-temporal' actual entity. His terminology here is apt to be misleading, for in one important respect, as we shall see (§ 41), God is no less 'temporal' than are other actual entities.   [3] P R 486 [521].   [4] P R 486 [521].   [5] P R 154 [168].

system has to undergo. It is accordingly necessary to inquire whether Whitehead is able consistently to conceive an actual entity which is unique, but which nevertheless exemplifies the metaphysical categories.

It is Whitehead's doctrine that the unique actual entity, God, is essential to the *existence* of the ordinary actual entities constituting the world. These actual entities cannot 'exist' without 'definiteness', and for this they are dependent upon God as the 'principle of concretion'. That is to say, the ordinary actual entities are only able to come into being, to 'exist', by virtue of receiving from God their subjective aims.

Therefore, 'in this sense, God can be termed the creator of each temporal actual entity'.[1] But, Whitehead points out, 'the phrase is apt to be misleading by its suggestion that the ultimate creativity of the universe is to be ascribed to God's volition'.[2] According to the categories of Whitehead's system, this cannot be; the conception of a supreme, transcendent God, creating the world *ex nihilo* is not consistent with Whitehead's scheme. We have seen[3] that in his doctrine creative activity or Creativity is the 'ultimate' of which each actual entity is an instantiation. Thus God does not 'create' the actualities by his own activity, for each is a process of *self*-creation. Also God must likewise be a process of self-creation. Whitehead accordingly maintains that

the true metaphysical position is that God is the aboriginal instance of this creativity, and is therefore the aboriginal condition which qualifies its action. It is the function of actuality to characterize the creativity, and God is the eternal primordial character.[4]

We must examine this in some detail.

That God must be the aboriginal instance of creativity is clear, since God is required by all other actualities as their 'principle of concretion', as the provider of their subjective aim. But in saying that God is the 'aboriginal instance of creativity', Whitehead does not mean or imply that God is in the past of all other actualities, in the sense that God was once the solely existing actual entity. A

[1] P R 317 [343].   [2] P R 317 [343-4].   [3] § 14.   [4] P R 317-18 [344].

consistent metaphysical pluralism cannot hold that creativity originally had only a single instantiation. Moreover, such a conception of God would constitute a violation of all the categories of Whitehead's system. By the ontological principle and the category of relativity, all actual entities require 'data'. Thus God as an actual entity can no more be without other actual entities than they can be without God. The respect in which God requires the other actual entities will be discussed later.[1] First we must consider God as required by the many actual entities constituting the world.

§ 40

THE PRIMORDIAL NATURE OF GOD

In the last-quoted passage Whitehead states that 'God is the aboriginal instance of this creativity, and is therefore the aboriginal condition which qualifies its action'. But if God be the 'aboriginal instance' of creativity, why does it follow that he is therefore the 'aboriginal condition which qualifies its action'? By the latter phrase Whitehead means more than that God 'conditions' creativity in being that instantiation which is God himself. Whitehead says (in the passage above) that 'it is the function of actuality to characterize the creativity'. Thus every actuality 'characterizes' the creativity; in other words, every actual entity 'conditions' the creativity. By the phrase 'God is the aboriginal condition which qualifies the action of creativity', Whitehead means that in addition to each ordinary actual entity 'conditioning' creativity, God also 'conditions' creativity in every instance of its individualization. This God does through his basic metaphysical role of providing the subjective aim for every actual entity. But what is the significance of saying that this conditioning by God is 'aboriginal'? To appreciate this we must investigate what must be the nature of God as a unique actual entity fulfilling the function of the 'principle of concretion'.

[1] § 41.

We can perhaps most conveniently approach this from a consideration of subjective aim. We have seen that in a concrescing actual entity the subjective aim is a 'concept', a conceptual prehension; more precisely, it is a primary pure conceptual prehension. As such it must have derived from a primary physical prehension. Now the datum of this physical prehension is God, since it is from God that the subjective aim is received. But in receiving the subjective aim from God, what the actual entity prehends is not God as such, in full concreteness, but only God as objectified by one of his 'concepts', namely the relevant subjective aim. Therefore, this physical prehension must be a 'hybrid' prehension—as we have seen,[1] 'in a "hybrid physical feeling" the actual entity forming the datum is objectified by one of its own conceptual feelings'.[2]

It is clear that God as the 'principle of concretion' must have conceptual prehensions of subjective aims relevant to particular actual entities. Now the data of conceptual prehensions are eternal objects. Thus subjective aims—whether in the prehension of the individual actual entities or of God—are analysable into specific selections of eternal objects. Therefore the various subjective aims, as in God's conceptual prehension, are eternal objects as potential for actualization by ordinary actual entities. In other words, God conceives or envisages eternal objects in their relevance for actualization by the actual entities constituting the world.

To hold that God conceives eternal objects 'in their relevance for particular actualization' implies in God an activity of selection, and also an 'urge towards realization of the datum conceptually prehended'[3]—which Whitehead calls 'appetition'.[4] Further, to 'select' certain eternal objects as relevant for actualization implies that there must be eternal objects available for selection. The problem is, in what way can eternal objects be thus 'available' to God? This 'availability' implies their 'existence'. Also, it must have reference to *all* eternal objects. Whitehead maintains that the only answer consistent with the ontological principle and the

---

[1] § 36.   [2] P R 347–8 [376].
[3] P R 43 [47].   [4] Cf. P R 43 [47–8], 45 [49], and F R 15–16, 26–7, 72.

other categories is that this 'existence' of all eternal objects must be constituted by a primordial conceptual realization of them by God. As he summarizes this argument,

the differentiated relevance of eternal objects to each instance of the creative process requires their conceptual realization in the primordial nature of God.[1]

We arrive at the same conclusion from a consideration of the nature of eternal objects as such. It has been shown earlier[2] that in their essential nature, in abstraction from their realization in ordinary actualities, eternal objects are 'pure potentials'. They are *pure* potentials because, though in their nature they are 'potential for' actuals, in themselves they are indifferent to the particular actualization they might happen to have. It is important to be clear that though eternal objects in their essential nature are 'abstract', and thus constitute the 'general potentiality' of the universe, as 'potential' they are *relevant to* the actual entities constituting the actual universe. Now the pure abstract, or general potentials must be 'somewhere'. As Whitehead puts it,[3]

everything must be somewhere; and here 'somewhere' means 'some actual entity'. Accordingly the general potentiality of the universe must be somewhere; since it retains its proximate relevance to actual entities for which it is unrealized. This 'proximate relevance' reappears in subsequent concrescence as final causation regulative of the emergence of novelty. This 'somewhere' is the non-temporal actual entity. Thus 'proximate relevance' means 'relevance as in the primordial mind of God'.

This factor of the 'relevance' of eternal objects is of vital signifi-cance. I have said that eternal objects are 'relevant' by virtue of their nature as 'potentials'. They can be 'potential for' actual entities only if they be 'relevant to' those actualities. But how is it possible for abstract eternal objects, unrealized in any actuals, to be 'relevant' and thus 'potential'? In Whitehead's words:[4]

In what sense can unrealized abstract form be relevant? What is its basis of relevance? 'Relevance' must express some real fact of together-

[1] P R 363 [392].   [2] § 19.   [3] P R 62–3 [73].   [4] P R 44 [48].

197

ness among forms. The ontological principle can be expressed as: All real togetherness is togetherness in the formal constitution of an actuality. So if there be a relevance of what in the temporal world is unrealized, the relevance must express a fact of togetherness in the formal constitution of a non-temporal actuality.

To state the argument more fully: unrealized abstract form can be 'relevant' only if it has some essential relationship to, some 'togetherness' with, forms or eternal objects which are realized. It follows that there must be an essential intrinsic 'togetherness' among eternal objects. That is to say:

An eternal object, considered as an abstract entity, cannot be divorced from its reference to other eternal objects, and from its reference to actuality generally; though it is disconnected from its actual modes of ingression into definite actual occasions. This principle is expressed by the statement that each eternal object has a 'relational essence'. This relational essence determines how it is possible for the object to have ingression into actual occasions.[1]

Now the ontological principle requires that this intrinsic togetherness among eternal objects be referred to some actual entity. The only possibility is the conceptual realization of eternal objects in the mind of God. It is by virtue of this that

there is a general fact of systematic mutual relatedness which is inherent in the character of possibility. The realm of eternal objects is properly described as a 'realm', because each eternal object has its status in this general systematic complex of mutual relatedness.[2]

We cannot in this book enter into detailed analysis of this notion of eternal objects as constituting a 'general systematic complex of mutual relatedness', important as it is. Our present concern is that on Whitehead's principles this togetherness of eternal objects exists as a primordial conceptual realization by God. Whitehead's doctrine is therefore that

the primordial created fact is the unconditioned conceptual valuation of the entire multiplicity of eternal objects. This is the 'primordial nature' of God. By reason of this complete valuation, the objectification

[1] S M W 198.   [2] S M W 200.

of God in each derivate actual entity results in a graduation of the relevance of eternal objects to the concrescent phases of that derivate
occasion. There will be additional ground of relevance for select
eternal objects by reason of their ingression into derivate actual entities
belonging to the actual world of the concrescent occasion in question.
But whether or no this be the case, there is always the definite relevance
derived from God.[1]

This conceptual valuation of the entire multiplicity of eternal
objects must be 'primordial', the 'aboriginal instance of creativity',
because all other individualizations of creativity are dependent
upon that unique conceptual valuation for their existence, as we
have seen. Further, as 'primordial' or 'aboriginal', that conceptual
valuation of all eternal objects must be 'unconditioned'. And, 'by
the principle of relativity there can only be one non–derivative
actuality, unbounded by its prehensions of an actual world'.[2] In
other words,

unfettered conceptual valuation, 'infinite' in Spinoza's sense of that
term, is only possible once in the universe; since that creative act is
objectively immortal as an inescapable condition characterizing creative
action.[3]

It is to be noted that Whitehead says God in his 'primordial
nature' is the primordial conceptual *valuation* of the entire multiplicity of eternal objects. The point is that God does not 'originate'
eternal objects, bringing them into existence 'out of nothing'.
Whitehead consistently insists that God

does not create eternal objects; for his nature requires them in the same
degree that they require Him. This is an exemplification of the coherence of the categoreal types of existence. The general relationships of
eternal objects to each other, relationships of diversity and of pattern,
are their relationships in God's conceptual realization. Apart from this
realization, there is mere isolation indistinguishable from nonentity.[4]

That is to say, God's primordial 'existence' *is* the act of complete
conceptual valuation of the eternal objects; God cannot 'exist'
and then set about creating eternal objects. Eternal objects are

[1] P R 42 [46].   [2] P R 44 [48].   [3] P R 349 [378].   [4] P R 363 [392].

inseparable from God's primordial existence; they are the primordial 'definiteness' apart from which no existence or creativity, even in the primordial instance of God, is possible at all. Whitehead is insisting here on the complete illegitimacy and futility of trying to conceive eternal objects or 'forms' as separate from existence or 'being'. But this does not mean that he *identifies* 'being' and 'form'. 'Being' requires 'definiteness' or 'form', and equally 'form' requires 'being'; and this relationship of mutual requirement is impossible if the two be identical.

Whitehead's doctrine is that the metaphysical situation demands a unique actual entity as the primordial source of all definiteness or form—without that no actual entity at all is able to *be*, to exist. As such this unique actual entity must, in one aspect at least, be the complete conceptual valuation of all potentiality. In Whitehead's words,[1]

such a primordial superject of creativity achieves, in its unity of satisfaction, the complete conceptual valuation of all eternal objects. This is the ultimate, basic adjustment of the togetherness of eternal objects on which creative order depends. It is the conceptual adjustment of all appetites in the form of aversions and adversions. It constitutes the meaning of relevance. Its status as an actual efficient fact is recognized by terming it the 'primordial nature of God'.

In this passage Whitehead makes it clear that this complete primordial conceptual valuation of all eternal objects involves (*a*) the 'basic adjustment of the togetherness of eternal objects on which creative order depends', and also (*b*) the 'conceptual adjustment of all appetites in the form of aversions and adversions'. These two 'adjustments' are interrelated, but it will be convenient first to consider the former in some abstraction from the latter.

The argument is that 'creative order' depends upon a 'basic adjustment of the togetherness of eternal objects', namely as a 'general systematic complex of mutual relatedness'. By 'creative order' Whitehead means the order exhibited in 'creation', i.e. actuality. Unless there be a factor of 'order', 'creation' or 'existence' is impossible. This is necessitated not only by each actual

[1] P R 44 [48].

entity as a concrescence, a growing together into a unity, which implies that it must have internal order; some basic factor of 'order' must also be exhibited by the relationship between actualities, for without it they could not be interrelated as is required by the category of relativity. Whitehead's point is that this 'creative order' must be dependent upon that primordial 'conceptual order' which is constituted by the eternal objects in the primordial nature of God. In other words, 'creative order' necessitates, finally, a single overriding adjustment of eternal objects in a 'general systematic complex of mutual relatedness' which is relevant to all actuality whatever. It should be noted that this 'general systematic complex of mutual relatedness' itself constitutes the illustration of certain completely general patterns or forms, i.e. eternal objects.

It is important to appreciate how order is established in the created world. We have shown that the 'being' or 'existing' of each actual entity is dependent upon the 'definiteness' derived from God as its subjective aim. That subjective aim is constituted by a selection of eternal objects. Now these eternal objects have a systematic relatedness to all other eternal objects, including the completely general forms. Thus by hybrid prehensions of God each actual entity acquires not only the specific character which constitutes it that distinguishable individual actuality, but also its generic character which it shares with all other actual entities.[1] Whitehead has expressed this as follows:[2]

This ideal realization of potentialities in a primordial actual entity constitutes the metaphysical stability whereby the actual process exemplifies general principles of metaphysics, and attains the ends proper to specific types of emergent order.

We have noted above that this primordial conceptual valuation of all potentiality involves not only the 'basic adjustment of the togetherness of eternal objects on which creative order depends', but also the 'conceptual adjustment of all appetites in the form of aversions and adversions'. It is important for an adequate under-

[1] Because of its complexity we must omit in this book the detailed analysis exhibiting metaphysical principles as eternal objects.   [2] P R 54 [64].

standing of God's primordial conceptual valuation to appreciate that it intrinsically involves the latter 'adjustment'. God's primordial conceptual valuation is constituted by a 'pure' conceptual prehension of all eternal objects; that is, the data of this prehension are 'pure' potentials, not 'real' potentials. But as 'potentials' they are 'relevant' to actuals. Pure abstract eternal objects have 'relevance' for actuals because God's pure conceptual prehension involves 'appetition', that is, the 'urge toward their realization'. Without this appetition eternal objects would be futile, 'a mere isolation indistinguishable from nonentity'. Whitehead points out[1] that 'appetition' must be regarded as an essential ingredient of all conceptual prehension; it is because of this that conceptual prehension has the character of 'valuation'.[2] Whitehead has expressed his doctrine as follows:[3]

If we consider these 'pure' mental operations in their most intense operations, we should choose the term 'vision'. A conceptual prehension is a direct vision of some possibility of good or evil—of some possibility as to how actualities *may* be *definite*. There is no reference to particular actualities, or to any particular actual world. The phrase of 'good or of evil' has been added to include a reference to the subjective form; the mere word 'vision' abstracts from this factor in a conceptual prehension. If we say that God's primordial nature is a completeness of 'appetition', we give due weight to the subjective form—at a cost. If we say that God's primordial nature is 'intuition', we suggest mentality which is 'impure' by reason of synthesis with physical prehension. If we say that God's primordial nature is 'vision', we suggest a maimed view of the subjective form, divesting it of yearning after concrete fact—no particular facts, but after *some* actuality. There is a deficiency in God's primordial nature which the term 'vision' obscures. One advantage of the term 'vision' is that it connects this doctrine of God more closely with philosophical tradition. 'Envisagement' is perhaps a safer term than 'vision'. To sum up: God's 'primordial nature' is abstracted from his commerce with 'particulars', and is therefore devoid of those 'impure' intellectual cogitations which involve propositions. It is God in abstraction, alone with himself. As such it is a mere factor in God, deficient in actuality.

[1] Cf. P R 44–46 [47–50].   [2] Cf. § 35 and § 37 above.   [3] P R 45–6 [49–50].

God

§ 41

GOD AS 'PRIMORDIAL' AND 'CONSEQUENT'

The last point made in the previous quotation is highly important. God is not to be identified with his 'primordial nature'; that is, God is not to be conceived as wholly constituted by a primordial conceptual valuation of pure abstract eternal objects.

Viewed as primordial, he is the unlimited conceptual realization of the absolute wealth of potentiality. In this aspect, he is not *before* all creation, but *with* all creation. But, as primordial, so far is he from 'eminent reality', that in this abstraction he is 'deficiently actual'— and this in two ways. His feelings are only conceptual and so lack the fulness of actuality. Secondly, conceptual feelings, apart from complex integration with physical feelings, are devoid of consciousness in their subjective forms.[1]

The primordial nature is only one aspect of God. We must be clear that in considering the primordial nature we are making an abstraction from God's complete actuality. We shall go astray in our conception unless we bear in mind the relation of this aspect to the other aspects of God.

On the other hand we shall equally get into difficulties if we do not make a definite distinction between the primordial nature of God, which is absolute, and God in other aspects in which he is relative. The failure to make this distinction is at the base of the unsatisfactoriness of most traditional conceptions of God.

But although the primordial nature is only an aspect of God, it is one which is absolutely fundamental to 'being', that is, to all actuality whatsoever. In this aspect God

is the unconditioned actuality of conceptual feeling at the base of things; so that, by reason of this primordial actuality, there is an order in the relevance of eternal objects to the process of creation. His unity of conceptual operations is a free creative act, untrammelled by reference to any particular course of things. It is deflected neither by

[1] P R 486 [521].

203

love, nor by hatred, for what in fact comes to pass. The *particularities* of the actual world presuppose *it;* while *it* merely presupposes the *general* metaphysical character of creative advance, of which it is the primordial exemplification. The primordial nature of God is the acquirement by creativity of a primordial character.

His conceptual actuality at once exemplifies and establishes the categoreal conditions.[1]

We have seen that a subjective aim is a categoreal requirement of all actual entities. God, as an actual entity, is not an exception to this. The primordial nature of God corresponds to what in ordinary actual entities is their subjective aim. The difference lies only in God's unique metaphysical function necessitating a unique subjective aim. By reason of his role, God's 'subjective aim', i.e. his primordial nature, is constituted by the complete conceptual envisagement of all eternal objects with the urge toward their realization in the actualities of the world. God's metaphysical function is exemplified in his aim, which is inherent in his appetitive valuation of eternal objects.

The primordial appetitions which jointly constitute God's purpose are seeking intensity, and not preservation. Because they are primordial, there is nothing to preserve. He, in his primordial nature, is unmoved by love for this particular, or that particular; for, in this foundational process of creativity, there are no pre-constituted particulars. In the foundations of his being, God is indifferent alike to preservation and to novelty. He cares not whether an immediate occasion be old or new, so far as concerns derivation from its ancestry. His aim for it is depth of satisfaction as an intermediate step towards the fulfilment of his own being. His tenderness is directed towards each actual occasion, as it arises.

Thus God's purpose in the creative advance is the evocation of intensities.[2]

In this passage Whitehead brings out the essential metaphysical interrelatedness of all actualities, including God. The ordinary actual entities are dependent upon God for their 'definiteness' in the form of their 'subjective aim'. An 'aim' implies 'purpose'. The

[1] P R 486–7 [522].   [2] P R 146–7 [160–1].

immediate purpose, as we have seen, is its self-creation into an actual entity. But its own 'being' is not wholly an end in itself. By the category of relativity, every 'being' is a potential for another 'becoming'. That is to say, its 'being' has a dual value: to itself, and to others.[1] This dual aspect is reflected in its subjective aim: to create a value-intensity for itself, and also thereby for others.

The subjective aim of each actual entity, since it derives from God, exemplifies also God's purpose—inherent in the primordial appetition whereby that particular subjective aim is relevant to that particular actuality. God's purpose, in regard to each particular actual entity, is the highest intensity of experience possible to it, which is to say, the maximum actualization of value in that instance. But that actualization of value-intensity is not only for that actual entity itself; it is also for others, including God. Thus in another aspect, God's purpose or aim for each actuality is for its 'depth of satisfaction as an intermediate step towards the fulfilment of his own being'.

It is to be noted that this conception involves that the category of process and the category of relativity apply equally to God. That is to say, God's 'being' is constituted by his 'becoming', and this necessitates his physical prehension of the world. God requires the other actual entities for the 'fulfilment of his own being'.

Thus, analogously to all actual entities, the nature of God is dipolar. He has a primordial nature and a consequent nature. The consequent nature of God is conscious; and it is the realization of the actual world in the unity of his nature, and through the transformation of his wisdom. The primordial nature is conceptual, and the consequent nature is the weaving of God's physical feelings upon his primordial concepts.[2]

The further elaboration of the nature of God, especially into its religious implications, is beyond the scope of this book. Our concern is metaphysical, the metaphysical nature of actuality. Whitehead has expressed his metaphysical conception as follows:[3]

Whitehead's Metaphysics

The notion of a supreme being must apply to an actuality in process of composition, an actuality not confined to the data of any special epoch in the historic field. Its actuality is founded on the infinitude of its conceptual appetition, and its form of process is derived from the fusion of this appetition with the data received from the world-process. Its function in the world is to sustain the aim at vivid experience. It is the reservoir of potentiality and the coordination of achievement. The form of its process is relevant to the data from which the process is initiated. The issue is the unified composition which assumes its function as a datum operative in the future historic world.

God's actuality is 'founded on' the infinitude of his conceptual appetition in an analogous sense to that in which the being of every ordinary actuality is 'founded on' its subjective aim. But to *be* actual, there must be the 'fusion of this appetition with the data received from the world-process', again analogously to the process of becoming of ordinary actualities. That is to say, the full actual being of God involves physical prehensions of the actualities of the world, and their unification into a new superject. Thereby God as 'consequent' is the 'coordination of achievement'.

This coordination of the achievement of the world is in terms of his primordial aim at intensity of value-experience. It is by reason of this integration of God's physical prehensions of the world with his pure conceptual prehensions that specific subjective aims for particular ordinary actualities are emergent. For God's pure conceptual prehensions involve only a *general* relevance to actuality. Physical prehensions of particular actualities are required to render the pure conceptual prehensions of specific relevance.[1] The outcome is God as a datum for new concrescing actual entities: 'The issue is the unified composition which assumes its function as a datum operative in the future historic world.' Whitehead has summarized his doctrine in the following passage:

God, as well as being primordial, is also consequent. He is the beginning and the end. He is not the beginning in the sense of being in the past of all members. He is the presupposed actuality of conceptual opera-

[1] The consequent 'impure' conceptual prehensions, the subjective aims, are 'propositions'. The analysis of 'propositions', however, lies beyond the scope of this book.

tion, in unison of becoming with every other creative act. Thus, by reason of the relativity of all things, there is a reaction of the world on God. The completion of God's nature into a fulness of physical feeling is derived from the objectification of the world in God. He shares with every new creation its actual world; and the concrescent creature is objectified in God as a novel element in God's objectification of that actual world. This prehension into God of each creature is directed with the subjective aim, and clothed with the subjective form, wholly derivative from his all-inclusive primordial valuation. God's conceptual nature is unchanged, by reason of its final completeness. But his derivative nature is consequent upon the creative advance of the world.[1]

We can now appreciate the sense in which God is both 'non-temporal' and 'temporal'. Like every other actual entity, the 'being' of God is constituted by a process of 'becoming'. In this respect, therefore, God is no less 'temporal' than other actualities: 'his derivative nature is consequent upon the creative advance of the world'. Moreover, in God, as in other actualities, there is the microscopic process, which is the epochal unit of becoming; and there is the macroscopic process, which is the 'transition from attained actuality to actuality in attainment'. Each unit of becoming in God's existence is objectively immortal in his succeeding units of becoming. In God each epochal unit of becoming initiates with a hybrid prehension of the primordial nature as subjective aim. 'Thus God has objective immortality in respect to his primordial nature and his consequent nature.'[2] But because of the aboriginal all-inclusiveness of the conceptual prehension constituting God's primordial nature, *it* is, in the strictest sense, 'non-temporal' or 'eternal'.

The full coherence of the metaphysical categories is exemplified in the mutual interdependence of God and the World. None is independent, 'requiring nothing but itself in order to exist'. On the contrary, each requires the other as a metaphysical necessity of its 'being'. Thus the World cannot be fully and adequately understood unless God be taken into account, and conversely. And this mutual interdependence of actualities cannot be under-

[1] P R 488 [523–4].   [2] P R 43 [47].

stood unless we conceive the universe as essentially a process of activity. In such a conception

there is no meaning to 'creativity' apart from its 'creatures', and no meaning to 'God' apart from 'creativity' and the 'temporal creatures', and no meaning to the temporal creatures apart from 'creativity' and 'God'.[1]

In this doctrine the actualities are individualizations of the ultimate creative activity. Each 'temporal creature' is the creativity individualizing itself in accordance with a particular subjective aim.

But the initial stage of its aim is an endowment which the subject inherits from the inevitable ordering of things, conceptually realized in the nature of God. The immediacy of the concrescent subject is constituted by its living aim at its own self-constitution. Thus the initial stage of the aim is rooted in the nature of God, and its completion depends on the self-causation of the subject-superject. This function of God is analogous to the remorseless working of things in Greek and in Buddhist thought. The initial aim is the best for that *impasse*. But if the best be bad, then the ruthlessness of God can be personified as *Atè*, the goddess of mischief. The chaff is burnt. What is inexorable in God, is valuation as an aim towards 'order'; and 'order' means 'society' permissive of actualities with patterned intensity of feeling arising from adjusted contrasts.[2]

One main topic of the next chapter will be the amplification of the last clause.

[1] P R 318 [344].　　　　　[2] P R 345 [373-4].

CHAPTER XVII

Creative Universe

---

§ 42

THE CREATIVE PROCESS

This final Part is concerned with a metaphysical description of the universe as Whitehead conceives it in terms of his categoreal scheme. So far we have concentrated mainly on the metaphysical nature of the individual actualities. Now, in this concluding chapter, we shall shift to a consideration of the universe as a whole, placing the emphasis on the interrelations of actualities.

It has been made sufficiently clear that in Whitehead's conception the universe is a process of creative activity. Actuality is constituted by individualizations of the ultimate creative activity or creativity. In other words, the creative process consists in individual epochal units of activity, the actual entities, perpetually superseding each other. 'The universe is thus a creative advance into novelty.'[1]

Since we had previously tended to emphasize the separate individuality of the actual entities, we must now stress the correlative intrinsic connection between the actualities. It then becomes clear that the creative advance takes place by the earlier actualities merging into the constitution of the later. 'The creative process is thus to be discerned in that transition by which one occasion, already actual, enters into the birth of another instance of experienced value'.[2]

[1] P R 314 [339–40].   [2] R M 99.

This is not as straightforward as it might appear, for Whitehead's conception of the creative advance of the universe differs in a vital respect from antecedent notions. Because of the prominence in our conscious experience of enduring entities, creative advance has usually been conceived as a single-line inheritance. For example, we ourselves, at the present moment, are evidently an inheritance from, or continuation of, ourselves at the immediately antecedent moment, and so on. It is therefore not surprising that previous thought has explicitly or implicitly generalized single-line inheritance as a metaphysical character of the creative advance.

Whitehead's system, however, involves the rejection of this conception of the creative advance of the universe. By the category of relativity this transition from actuality to actuality cannot constitute a simple single-line inheritance, for, as we have seen,[1] 'the data for any one pulsation of actuality consist of the full content of the antecedent universe as it exists in relevance to that pulsation'.[2] This means that the creative advance is highly complex; in Whitehead's forceful expression, 'the whole world conspires to produce a new creation'.[3] The creative process is a vastly intricate mesh of interrelationship, in which each individual actual entity, directly or indirectly, inherits from all its antecedents and adds its contribution to all its successors.

In this doctrine, therefore,

the creative action is the universe always becoming one in a particular unity of self-experience, and thereby adding to the multiplicity which is the universe as many. This insistent concrescence into unity is the outcome of the ultimate self-identity of each entity.[4]

It is of the greatest importance to be clear as to what is involved in this conception of each actual entity as a unification, or concrescence, of the many antecedent actual entities, each in turn becoming an object or datum for succeeding concrescences.

One aspect is brought out by observing that it constitutes Whitehead's solution to the problem of the One and the Many. Because it is the metaphysical nature of each actual entity that it

[1] § 18. [2] M T 121. [3] R M 99. [4] P R 78 [89].

is a process of concrescence, each actual entity is a One constituted by a unification of the Many. In this doctrine the Many are always becoming One, and the One always becomes one of the Many. The creative advance is a process of the rhythmical fluctuation between the Many and the One, and the One and the Many.

It should be noted that there is no single One. There are many Ones. But there is no One which is the complete totality of the Many. For each unification of the Many into One adds another to the Many. As Whitehead puts it:[1]

There is not one completed set of things which are actual occasions. For the fundamental inescapable fact is the creativity in virtue of which there can be no 'many things' which are not subordinated in a concrete unity. Thus a set of all actual occasions is by the nature of things a standpoint for another concrescence which elicits a concrete unity from those many actual occasions. Thus we can never survey the actual world except from the standpoint of an immediate concrescence which is falsifying the presupposed completion. The creativity in virtue of which any relative complete actual world is, by the nature of things, the datum for a new concrescence, is termed 'transition'. Thus, by reason of transition, 'the actual world' is always a relative term, and refers to that basis of presupposed actual occasions which is a datum for the novel concrescence.

By the very nature of actuality as a process of concrescence, the universe is a creative advance into novelty. There can be no static completion; the universe is perpetually adding to itself.

§ 43

VALUE AND ORDER

It would be quite incorrect to suppose that this conception reduces the universe to a dead level of ineffectiveness; that the mutual

[1] P R 299–300 [321–2].

immanence of actualities would eliminate all variety and distinction. The very contrary is the consequence of Whitehead's doctrine, and is secured by his categories of objectification and subjective aim.

The theory of objectification is 'the discussion of how the actual particular occasions become original elements for a new creation'.[1] That the category of objectification is at the core of Whitehead's scheme has been sufficiently displayed. The same is the case with the category of subjective aim. It remains here only to bring out an implication, not so far stressed, of the former category, especially when taken in conjunction with the latter.

Objectification is achieved in the process whereby an actuality in concrescence appropriates its data. In the previous two chapters it has been shown that this appropriation must of necessity be selective, and that the subjective aim provides the principle of selection. Thus objectification involves elimination,[2] elimination of incompatible elements. Another way of expressing this is to say that objectification involves abstraction. This means that antecedent actualities are objectified in a concrescing actuality under an abstraction, an abstraction determined by the subjective aim of the latter. This abstractive elimination constitutes the perspective of the antecedent actualities from the standpoint of the concrescing actual entity. With this outline statement of the principle involved, we can appreciate Whitehead's analysis of the process of objectification:

The objectified particular occasions together have the unity of a datum for the creative concrescence. But in acquiring this measure of connection, their inherent presuppositions of each other eliminate certain elements in their constitutions, and elicit into relevance other elements. Thus objectification is an operation of mutually adjusted abstraction, or elimination, whereby the many occasions of the actual world become one complex datum. This fact of the elimination by reason of synthesis is sometimes termed the perspective of the actual world from the standpoint of that concrescence. Each actual occasion defines its own

[1] P R 298 [320].
[2] By 'negative prehension'. The details of this process are omitted in this book.

actual world from which it originates. No two occasions can have identical actual worlds.[1]

With objectification and subjective aim providing the categoreal basis for variety among actual entities, we have but to take into account the role of God to complete the metaphysical picture. In the previous chapter[2] we have seen that God's 'function in the world is to sustain the aim at vivid experience';[3] in other words, that 'God's purpose in the creative advance is the evocation of intensities'.[4] That is to say, God is that unique actual entity from which is derived the element of τέλος in the universe, necessitated by the conception of the universe as creative *activity*. As Whitehead put it in the last quotation in the previous chapter: 'What is inexorable in God, is valuation as an aim towards "order".'[5]

The point is that God's aim in the world is the achievement of intensity of value-experience, and the procurement of this necessitates 'order'. We must accordingly examine the notion of 'order', and show what is involved in Whitehead's statement[6] that ' "order" means "society" permissive of actualities with patterned intensity of feeling arising from adjusted contrasts'.[7]

§ 44

ORDER AND SOCIETY

Objectification, we have observed, involves elimination of incompatibilities. Now if the data for an actual entity include many elements mutually incompatible, they frustrate each other in their role as objects, resulting in a lowering of intensity of experience in the prehending actual entity. As opposed to this, if the data be not only compatible, but also in *contrast*, the result is a heightening of intensity of experience. A ready exemplification of

[1] P R 298–9 [321].   [2] § 41.   [3] M T 128.   [4] P R 147 [161].
[5] P R 345 [373].   [6] See p. 208 above.   [7] P R 345 [373–4].

this principle is to be found in aesthetic experience, where intensity is very clearly the outcome of patterned contrasts; a mere harmony of pattern, devoid of contrasts, is dull.

Intensity of experience in any actuality is dependent upon the requisite contrasts obtaining among its data. That is to say, the data must exhibit a particular 'order'. The 'order' consists in a certain pattern of characteristics being displayed by the data in question. This means that the actualities constituting the data are dominated by certain characteristic features. In other words, certain complex sets of eternal objects are shared by these actualities, constituting common elements in their definiteness.

It is important to be clear about the notion of 'order'. In its metaphysical analysis 'order' is constituted by the dominance of some set or sets of characteristics in a group or nexus[1] of actual entities. In other words, 'order' exists to the extent to which certain characteristics dominate. This implies that the nexus also displays other, perhaps incompatible, characteristics. The latter characteristics existent in a nexus of actualities constitute the element of 'disorder' in the nexus. The dominance of particular characteristics to the exclusion of incompatible ones, constituting 'order' in a nexus, implies the retreat of 'disorder'. It is to be noted that 'order' and 'disorder' are thus primarily features of a *nexus* of actualities.

It is evident that in accordance with the categories of Whitehead's system the universe of actualities will be distinguished by nexūs displaying various kinds of 'order'. These kinds of order will be governed by the particular 'ideals' appropriate to the subjective aims of the actualities in question. The degree of 'order' will represent the degree of dominance in that nexus of the particular 'ideal'.

Now any nexus of actualities 'ordered' among themselves by virtue of a particular 'ideal' character dominating each of the individual component actual entities, is called by Whitehead a 'society'. 'The term "society" will always be restricted to mean a

---

[1] 'Nexus' (plural, 'nexūs') is Whitehead's term for any group of actual entities united by their being in interrelationship. Cf. A I 254, 258.

nexus of actual entities which are "ordered" among themselves.'[1] That is to say, a 'society' of actualities is constituted by the component members each displaying a determinate common character. That common character constitutes the 'order' exhibited. There is a 'society' in respect of that 'order'.

This means that 'order' is 'social order'. In other words, 'order' is brought into being only by a 'society' of actualities illustrating that 'order'. Whitehead's definitive statement is as follows:

A Society is a nexus which 'illustrates' or 'shares in', some type of 'Social Order'. 'Social Order' can be defined as follows: 'A nexus enjoys "social order" when (i) there is a common element of form illustrated in the definiteness of each of its included actual entities, and (ii) this common element of form arises in each member of the nexus by reason of the conditions imposed upon it by its prehensions of some other members of the nexus, and (iii) these prehensions impose that condition of reproduction by reason of their inclusion of positive feelings involving that common form. Such a nexus is called a "society", and the common form is the "defining characteristic" of that society'.[2]

It should be noted that this notion of a 'society' is much more than a mere class-concept. That is to say, not every group or nexus of actualities sharing a dominant common characteristic constitutes a 'society'. There is a 'society' only when the individuals share a common characteristic by virtue of the inheritance of that characteristic from each other. It is because of this factor of the genetic derivation of its defining characteristic that a 'society' is the vehicle for the procurement of value-intensity. The respect in which 'society' secures value-intensity is two-fold. The first is that 'order', which is the condition of value-intensity, is the outcome of mutual prehensions by members of a nexus, thereby raising that 'order' into prominence. Whitehead has expressed this as follows:

The point of a 'society' as the term is here used, is that it is self-sustaining; in other words, that it is its own reason. Thus a society is more than a set of [actual] entities to which the same class-name applies: that is to say, it involves more than a merely mathematical conception of 'order'. To constitute a society, the class-name has got to apply to each member, by reason of genetic derivation from other members of that same society. The members of the society are alike because, by reason of their common character, they impose on other members of the society the conditions which lead to that likeness.[1]

The second respect in which 'society' is the vehicle for value-intensity, thus making for the importance of the notion, is an implication of the former. The essential character of a society arises by virtue of the relation of genetic derivation pertaining among its members. If 'society' were a mere class-concept it would apply to a group of contemporary actualities,[2] in virtue of a common character. But it is the essential characteristic of contemporaries that they do not genetically derive from each other. By reason of genetic derivation, a 'society, as such, must involve antecedents and consequents. In other words, a society must exhibit the peculiar quality of endurance'.[3] Endurance, which is the special character of a 'society', is essential to procuring and maintaining value-intensity.

It is clear that the role of 'societies' is of the greatest importance in the universe, and it is accordingly not surprising that so much antecedent philosophy has mistakenly regarded societies as the actual entities. That is to say, most antecedent thought has conceived actual entities or substances as essentially enduring. But we have shown in an earlier chapter[4] that the entities which endure cannot be *actual* entities. In Whitehead's doctrine the 'things that endure are all societies. They are not actual occasions'.[5]

We have here a point of very considerable significance for philosophical thought. As Whitehead has put it:

It is the mistake that has thwarted European metaphysics from the time of the Greeks, namely, to confuse societies with the completely real things which are the actual occasions.[6]

[1] P R 124 [137]. Also A I 261.

[2] We have to omit in this book any detailed consideration of the relations of contemporary actualities. For our purposes a definition of contemporaries will suffice: 'It is the definition of contemporary events that they happen in causal independence of each other. Thus two contemporary occasions are such that neither belongs to the past of the other' (A I 251).

[3] A I 261–2.   [4] Chapter V.   [5] A I 262.   [6] A I 262.

This is at the root of the difficulty, which has haunted traditional philosophy, of being able to give a satisfactory metaphysical explanation of the relations of actualities. Actualities must have self-identity and individuality, and have therefore been conceived as 'requiring nothing but themselves in order to exist'. Relations then become purely accidental, and it is even difficult to see how there can be any relations at all. Yet the insistent fact is that enduring things are not only in interrelationship, but also that they are subject to change by virtue of that interrelationship.

Whitehead's doctrine solves these traditional difficulties, while at the same time making interrelationship metaphysically essential, and not merely accidental. This becomes clear by the supplementation of our previous discussion[1] by the theory of 'society'. The theory of actual entities as epochal units of concrescence provides, as we have shown,[2] a complete reconciliation of 'change' and 'changelessness'; and it makes relatedness as fundamental metaphysically as self-identity and unitariness. The classical notions of 'essential' and 'accidental' qualities are notions appropriate to the enduring things which are 'societies', and not to actual entities. As Whitehead expresses it:[3]

A society has an essential character, whereby it is the society that it is, and it has also accidental qualities which vary as circumstances alter. Thus a society, as a complete existence, and as retaining the same metaphysical status, enjoys a history expressing its changing reactions to changing circumstances. But an actual occasion has no such history. It never changes. It only becomes and perishes. Its perishing is its assumption of a new metaphysical function in the creative advance of the universe.[4]

[1] Chapter V.　　　　　[2] § 13.　　　　　[3] A I 262.
[4] Whitehead points out (fn. 1, A I 262) that 'this notion of "society" has analogies to Descartes' notion of "substance", cf. Descartes' *Principles of Philosophy*, Part I, Principles LI–LVII'.

§ 45

THE THEORY OF SOCIETY

It is highly important for the correct understanding of Whitehead's doctrine to be clear that it does not merely amount to the substitution of the notion of 'society' for the older concept of an enduring substance. That is to say, it is not simply the case that, analogously to the way in which in twentieth-century physics the old impenetrable atom has been found to be a composite of more elementary particles, Whitehead's theory regards as composite what had previously been held to be the fundamental unitary actual entity.

In Whitehead's doctrine all enduring entities, such as those we meet in ordinary everyday experience, are societies. But it does not follow from the definition of 'society' given in the previous section that all societies are of this kind. On the contrary, these enduring entities are but a special case of societies. To appreciate this we must elaborate the theory of society.

We shall start by making some distinctions in the concept of an 'enduring entity'. The enduring 'physical objects' of ordinary everyday experience are complex, not in that they are constituted by successive epochal actualities, but rather in that they are clusters of strings of superseding actualities. To illustrate this in terms of the concepts of modern physics: an ordinary 'physical object' is constituted by a multiplicity of molecules; each molecule is made up of a multiplicity of atoms; and each atom in turn is composed of electrons, protons, and other entities. Now each electron, etc., is an 'enduring entity' constituted by a route of electronic actualities—if electrons, etc., be not themselves in fact composite entities.

Now we have to analyse this in terms of the theory of society. It will be recalled that a 'society' is constituted by the genetic relationships of a nexus of actualities exhibiting a particular 'order'. This 'order' consists in the actualities in question sharing a particular 'defining characteristic'. Thus there is a 'society' in respect to that particular 'order'.

Consider, for example, the case of a route of electronic actualities. The route constitutes a 'society' in respect to its 'electronic' character. Further, this character is inherited by each member of the route from the antecedent actuality in the route. Thus not only does this nexus of actualities constitute a society, but the defining characteristic of that society, its 'order', takes a serial form. Now 'when the genetic relatedness of its members orders these members "serially" ',[1] Whitehead speaks of the society in question as having 'personal order'. It is thus evident that an 'enduring entity' 'is a society whose social order has taken the special form of "personal order" '.[2]

Whitehead points out that 'a society may (or may not) be analysable into many strands of "enduring objects". This will be the case for most ordinary physical objects. These enduring objects and "societies", analysable into strands of enduring objects, are the permanent entities which enjoy adventures of change throughout time and space. For example, they form the subject-matter of the science of dynamics. . . . A nexus which (i) enjoys social order, and (ii) is analysable into strands of enduring objects may be termed a "corpuscular society" '.[3]

It is to be noted that speaking of a society as 'corpuscular' means that the inheritance includes a dominant characteristic whereby the nexus of actualities forms one 'body'. But, as in the case of gases, the defining characteristics of the component enduring objects might predominate over any common pattern whereby they make up a single 'body'. There is a 'society' in respect of a certain volume of gas, but it is not a 'corpuscular' society—though the individual molecules will be 'corpuscular'.[4] Another form of variation in dominant characteristics is to be found in considering a wave of light in different stages of its career. Whitehead's analysis is as follows:

[1] P R 47 [51]. [2] P R 46 [50]. [3] P R 47–8 [52].
[4] This is a somewhat simplified analysis. A more adequate analysis will be in terms of the notion of 'structured' societies which include 'subordinate societies and nexūs with a definite pattern of structural inter-relations' (P R 137 [151]).

A train of such waves at all stages of its career involves social order; but in the earlier stages this social order takes the more special form of loosely related strands of personal order. This dominant personal order gradually vanishes as the time advances. Its defining characteristics become less and less important, as their various features peter out. The waves then become a nexus with important social order, but with no strands of personal order. Thus the train of waves starts as a corpuscular society, and ends as a society which is not corpuscular.[1]

The essential point to be appreciated is that there is a 'society' in respect of any particular element of 'order' genetically inherited. Thus a society can be analysed into components, themselves societies, and these component societies are also likewise analysable. An ordinary 'physical object' is an instance of a society made up of societies within societies. Furthermore, 'enduring entities', whether they be a single strand of personal order, or of the more complex kind of a corpuscular society, are not the only kinds of societies.

Even in the case of single-strand personal order, each actuality in the strand inherits not exclusively from the antecedent actuality in the series. By the category of relativity, it inherits from its entire 'actual world' of past actualities, and in particular from the contemporaries of its immediate predecessor in the strand. By virtue of its particular subjective aim, it has inherited its dominant or defining characteristic from certain of its antecedents; thereby it becomes a member of the society defined by that particular characteristic. But this does not preclude its subordinate inheritance of other features from other actualities, thereby constituting it a member of a wider society, or indeed of an indefinite number of wider societies.

Moreover, the existence of any more specialized society, such as one displaying 'personal order', implies the appreciable attainment of value-intensity by the actualities in question, and this is dependent upon a favourable 'order' pertaining among their data. In other words, any specialized society depends upon a favourable environment of social order, that is, of wider societies. This is a

[1] P R 49 [53-4].

point of vital importance and it is worth quoting Whitehead's statement at some length:

Thus a society is, for each of its members, an environment with some element of order in it, persisting by reason of the genetic relations between its own members. Such an element of order is the order prevalent in the society.

But there is no society in isolation. Every society must be considered with its background of a wider environment of actual entities, which also contribute their objectifications to which the members of the society must conform. Thus the given contributions of the environment must at least be permissive of the self-sustenance of the society. Also, in proportion to its importance, this background must contribute those general characters which the more special character of the society presupposes for its members. But this means that the environment, together with the society in question, must form a larger society in respect to some more general characters than those defining the society from which we started. *Thus we arrive at the principle that every society requires a social background, of which it is itself a part.* In reference to any given society the world of actual entities is to be conceived as forming a background in layers of social order, the defining characteristics becoming wider and more general as we widen the background. Of course, the remote actualities of the background have their own specific characteristics of various types of social order. But such specific characteristics have become irrelevant for the society in question by reason of the inhibitions and attenuations introduced by discordance, that is to say, by disorder.[1]

What is specially to be noted is the relationship of societies to their social environment, namely, that the specialized societies will form parts of the wider societies. That is to say, actualities with dominant characteristics, by virtue of which they are members of certain special societies, also exhibit characteristics of more general types of social order, in ever-widening generality. This means that the more general types of social order are presupposed for the more special types to be possible at all. For example, the very high-grade 'personal' society constituting a human 'self' is dependent upon a favourable environment of

[1] P R 125 [148] (my italics).

societies of everwidening generality: upon the complex society constituting the 'mind-body'; in turn dependent upon 'organic' societies of cells; which are dependent upon 'inorganic' societies of molecules, atoms, electrons, etc. The wider social environment is constituted by the very wide societies with electronic, protonic, etc., defining characteristics, and indeed also by societies of still greater generality with the defining characteristics of dimensionality, measurability, etc.

The importance of the characteristics of the wider social environment is evident. It is these which constitute the 'laws of nature'. These 'laws' will be of differing degrees of generality, depending upon the generality of the society in question. For example, the laws of physics are of wider generality than the laws of biology. What must be stressed is that in this doctrine what have traditionally been termed 'laws of nature' are formulations of the defining characteristics of certain very wide societies. Metaphysically considered,

the causal laws which dominate a social environment are the product of the defining characteristic of that society. But the society is only efficient through its individual members. Thus in a society, the members can only exist by reason of the laws which dominate the society, and the laws only come into being by reason of the analogous characters of the members of the society.[1]

The laws are 'causal' because of the factor of genetic derivation of the defining characteristics.

It will be noted that the incidence of particular laws is neither metaphysically necessary nor necessarily unvarying. Other characteristics, alternative to those in fact existing, might have existed. Also, the incidence of particular laws only means that certain characteristics are dominant; it does not imply that alternative characteristics cannot be exemplified by some actualities in a nexus. Further, there is no metaphysical reason to preclude a steady shift or change in the dominance of certain characteristics. With such a shift there will accordingly be a change in the prevalent laws of nature. As Whitehead insists,

[1] P R 126 [139].

there is not any perfect attainment of an ideal order whereby the indefinite endurance of a society is secured. A society arises from disorder, where 'disorder' is defined by reference to the ideal for that society; the favourable background of a larger environment either itself decays or ceases to favour the persistence of the society after some stage of growth: the society then ceases to reproduce its members, and finally after a stage of decay passes out of existence. Thus a system of 'laws' determining reproduction in some portion of the universe gradually rises into dominance; it has its stage of endurance, and passes out of existence with the decay of the society from which it emanates.[1]

This applies to all societies, even to the widest we can detect as at present prevalent, constituting the general character of the universe in this 'cosmic epoch'. As Whitehead illustrates this:

The arbitrary, as it were 'given', elements in the laws of nature warn us that we are in a special cosmic epoch. Here the phrase 'cosmic epoch' is used to mean that widest society of actual entities whose immediate relevance to ourselves is traceable. This epoch is characterized by electronic and protonic actual entities, and by yet more ultimate actual entities which can be dimly discerned in the quanta of energy. Maxwell's equations of the electromagnetic field hold sway by reason of the throngs of electrons and of protons. Also each electron is a society of electronic occasions, and each proton is a society of protonic occasions. These occasions are the reasons for the electromagnetic laws; but their capacity for reproduction, whereby each electron and each proton has a long life, and whereby new electrons and new protons come into being, is itself due to these same laws. But there is disorder in the sense that the laws are not perfectly obeyed, and that the reproduction is mingled with instances of failure. There is accordingly a gradual transition to new types of order, supervening upon a gradual rise into dominance on the part of the present natural laws.[2]

[1] P R 126 [139].   [2] P R 126–7 [139–40].

§ 46

COSMOLOGY

The concern of this chapter has been the universe in respect of its metaphysical generality. In so far as more special features have entered the discussion, it has been for the purposes of illustration. Thus, for example, it has been our intention to bring out that there will be 'cosmic epoch' constituted by the dominance of some or other very general types of order. This is a necessity of the metaphysical nature of the universe. But the particular type of order at any time actually reigning is not a metaphysical necessity.

Because of their contingency, prevalent types of order are discoverable only empirically. The enterprise having as its specific function the empirical discovery of special types of order has come to be called 'science'. Thus in Whitehead's doctrine science achieves understanding in terms of the features of order displayed by societies. But this scientific discovery and understanding of the prevalent types of social order cannot proceed in isolation from some conception of the completely general or metaphysical nature of things. Even within the scientific field, the understanding of special types of society presupposes some conception of the wider social environment within which those special societies exist. With regard to science in general, Whitehead points out that

in the absence of some understanding of the final nature of things, and thus of the sorts of backgrounds presupposed in such abstract statements [i.e. those of science], all science suffers from the vice that it may be combining various propositions which tacitly presuppose inconsistent backgrounds. No science can be more secure than the unconscious metaphysics which tacitly it presupposes.... All reasoning, apart from some metaphysical reference, is vicious.[1]

[1] A I 197–8.

What is of immediate relevance to science is not the complete generality of metaphysics as such, but rather a conception of the present stage of the universe in respect to its most general characters. That is to say, science requires an application of the categoreal notions, an interpretation of the universe as it is at present in terms of a metaphysical scheme of ideas. This philosophical enterprise of interpretation, of applying metaphysical notions to the present epoch of the universe, constitutes 'cosmology'. Thus cosmology, as Whitehead conceives it, 'is the effort to frame a scheme of the general character of the present stage of the universe'.[1] In other words, 'cosmology sets out to be the general system of general ideas applicable to this epoch of the universe'.[2] Further discussion of Whitehead's doctrine of the relations of philosophy and science is beyond the scope of this book. It must suffice merely to indicate here that it is Whitehead's view that consequently 'the cosmological scheme should present the genus, for which the special schemes of the sciences are the species'.[3]

A point of final relevance to the topic of this book is that cosmology is 'philosophy', and not 'science'. Cosmology is 'philosophical' because it is the endeavour to understand in terms of the completely general or metaphysical nature of things. That is to say, an enterprise is 'philosophical' in virtue of its seeking to understand in terms of the nature of *actual* entities.[4] This means that metaphysics is fundamental to all 'branches' of philosophy, and that 'all difficulties as to first principles are only camouflaged metaphysical difficulties'.[5] This is why Whitehead, in his later works, discussed the various major philosophical problems, epistemological, logical, ethical, aesthetic, etc., explicitly in terms of his metaphysical system.

[1] F R 61.
[2] F R 70. 'Cosmology' thus takes the place of the 'philosophy of science' of Whitehead's earlier works. [3] F R 61.
[4] Cf. e.g. Whitehead's comparison of Newton's *Scholium* with Plato's *Timaeus*, P R 131 [144]: 'But there is another side to the *Timaeus* which finds no analogy in the *Scholium*. In general terms, this side of the *Timaeus* may be termed its metaphysical character, that is to say, its endeavour to connect the *behaviour* of things with the *formal nature* of things.' [5] P R 267 [288].

Index

Index

Aesthetic feelings, 150
Affective tone, 149–52, 155
Agency. *See* Act, Acting, Activity
Alexander, Samuel, 107, 148
Animal faith, 26, 142
Appearance, 56
Apperception, 145
Appetition, 196–202, 206
Applicability, 39, 47, 48, 50, 165
Apprehension, 145
Aristotle, 109, 119, 134, 178, 191–2; on οὐσία, 17–23, 83–6 *passim*, 92; on problem of metaphysics, 17–22, 29, 54, 59; on being, 33–4; rejects Platonism, 60; and substance, 17–18, 61, 62, 63, 112; on matter and form, 82–6; theory of form, 85–6, 92; on potentiality, 96; on actuality, 115; on becoming, 115
Atomism, of actuality, 74–80, 81

Becoming: problem of, 60–3, 68–70, 71–80, 115; and process, 68–75, 80; atomicity of, 71–5, 75–80 *passim*; as epochal, 74–8, 79–80, 81, 88; as being, 93–4, 122–3; and being, 133–5, 205; as prehending, 147–8; activity of, 167–70, 171–4; process of, 179, 189, 217
Being: the problem of, 18–20, 53; meaning of, 18–20; ambiguity of, 19, 22–5, 26; in Aristotle, 33–4, 85–6; and becoming, 60–3, 68–70, 122, 133–5, 189, 205; as acting, 82–7, 88–90, 93, 100; and form, 92–3, 191–2, 200–2; as becoming, 93–4, 115, 190; as potential for becoming, 102, 103–8 *passim*; and essence, 177–9; and definiteness, 191–2, 194, 200, 201; pure, as incorporeal, 191–2; perfect, 192; and God, 194, 203; of God, 206–7

Bergson, H., 148
Body: and mind, 57–8, 128, 131, 185; and perception, 140–3, 182
Broad, C. D., 61

Categoreal obligations, 108, 183
Categories: scheme of, 50, 165; and Aristotelian logic, 62–3
causa sui, 66, 171
Causal efficacy, 140–3. *See also* Perception
Causal feelings, 157–62, 179, 180–1, 184
Causation, 138, 157–62, 222
Cause: efficient, 108, 110, 171–4; final, 170–4, 175, 189
Change: in Newtonian cosmology, 6–7; and changelessness, 59–67, 68–80 *passim*, 217; defined, 64, 80; and process, 64–7, 68–70, 71–80 *passim*; in becoming, 93; problem of, 115
Changelessness, 55, 59–63, 64–7 *passim*, 174
Coherence: in scientific theory, 11; in metaphysics, 30–1; as test of system, 34–8, 49, 50; defined, 35–9; and Occam's razor, 49; and monism, 55–6; test of applied, 55–9, 60, 66–7, 70, 71, 86–7, 111–12, 118, 134–5, 142, 166, 171–2, 176, 192, 193, 207
Collingwood, R. G., 149 *n.*
Conceptual prehension, 156, 159, 166, 175–88 *passim*, 190–202 *passim*; as evaluation, 183, 188
Conceptual registration, 181
Conceptual reproduction, 179–83, 183–8 *passim*, 190; as category, 180, 181
Conceptual reversion, category of, 188 *n.*
Conceptual valuation, 179, 183; un-

227

fettered, 199–200; primordial, 200–2, 203, 204

Concrescence, 154, 157, 167, 175, 177, 180–1, 183, 189–92, 192–5 *passim*, 201, 206–7, 211–13, 217; theory of, 88–90; as experience, 126, 133–5; activity of, 145–8, 148–52; process of, 186–8

Concreteness, 128–9, 155; of events, 13; defined, 89

Conformal feeling, 154–6, 157–62, 179

Conformal conceptual reproduction, 181

Conformation, to past, 88–90

Consciousness, 137, 145, 181, 203, 210

Consequent nature. *See* God

Contingency, 38

Continuity, 67, 72–80

Continuum, concept of, 72–5

Contrast, 213–14

Corpuscular society. *See* Society

Cosmic epoch, 223, 224

Cosmology, 30, 224–5; defined, 225

Creation, *ex nihilo*, 194

Creative activity, 213

Creative advance, 135, 172, 204, 207, 209–13 *passim*, 217

Creative order. *See* Order

Creative process, 174

Creativity, 88–90, 91–2, 97, 108, 171–2, 194–5, 199, 200, 208, 209, 211; category of, 81–7; defined, 84–7; and God, 194–5, 199, 200

Critical realist use of essence, 93 *n.*

Cumulative character of time, 162

Cumulative, actuality as, 186

Data: for becoming, 89–90, 91, 98–9, 101–3; for philosophical generalization, 119, 124; for prehension, 153–6, 156–62 *passim*, 165, 167, 183, 190–2, 210–13 *passim*, 213–17, *passim*; for process, 206

Decision, 172, 190; referable to actual entity, 26; in respect to potentials, 98–9, 100

Definiteness, problem of, 92, 94, 159, 191–2, 194, 200, 201, 204

Democritus, 117–18

Descartes, René, 69, 81–2, 118, 141–2, 149, 174, 217 *n*; on substance, 20, 48, 57–8, 59, 66; use of *res vera*, 21; subjectivism of, 26, 27, 28, 119–21, 124–5; incoherence in, 36, 49, 57–8, 58 *n.*, 67; on method, 41; on *inspectio and judicium*, 46; method of, 47, 57; dualism of, 57, 128; substance-quality metaphysics, 63; on duration, 65, 73–5; on experience, 116, 137–8; on formal and objective existence, 146; God in, 171

Desire, 185

Dipolarity, 181–2, 205

Disorder, 37, 214, 221, 223. *See also* Order

Divisibility, and actual division, 77, 168–70, 171–4

Dualism, 57–8, 125–30, 146–7

δύναμις, 115

Duration: analysed, 65–7; Descartes on, 65–7; as continuity of becoming, 73–5; defined, 80

Emotional experience, 149–52; in sensationalism, 138–40

Emotional feeling, 154–6

Empiricism: British, 28, 121; and metaphysics, 44–5

Endurance: self-identical, 6; characteristic of society, 216–17, 218

Enduring entity: not actual, 63–7; in materialism, 83

Enduring entities, 210; as societies, 216–17, 218–23; kinds of, 218–23

Energy, physical, transference of, 184–5

Index

Index

Whitehead's Metaphysics

defined, 214–15; corpuscular, 219; structured, 219 *n.*; personal, 221

Solidarity of world, 112

Solipsism, 26, 116, 121, 183

Space: in Newtonian cosmology, 6–7; theory of, 73–5

Space-time, 8, 12

Speculation, metaphysical. *See* Metaphysics

Spinoza, Benedictus de, 20, 41, 56, 84, 87, 171, 199

Subject of prehension, 153–6, 157–62, 169–70, 171–4, 189–90

Subject-superject, 165–70, 173–4, 186–7, 208

Subjective experience, as datum for philosophical generalization, 119–23

Subjective immediacy of actual entities, 108–9, 116, 134–5, 154–6, 208

Subjective aim, 170–4, 176, 187, 189–92, 193, 195, 196, 201, 206, 208, 212–13, 214; as category, 180, 204

Subjective form, 154–6, 183, 184, 202, 203

Subjectivism: form in which rejected, 28; in post-Cartesian philosophy, 124

Subjectivist principle, the reformed, 119–23, 124, 126, 127, 130, 134, 136

Substance: as category, 17–18, 53–4, 138; Aristotelian, 17–18, 61–3, 118; term unsatisfactory, 22–3; transformed into actual entity, 27; Cartesian, 36, 48, 57–8, 59; as self-identically enduring, 61–7; by generalization from macroscopic things, 62–4, 119; as stuff, 62–3, 71; monistic, 83–4, 86, 87, 171; traditional doctrine criticized, 111–12, 116–18, 119–21, 124, 174; as enduring, 216–17, 218

Superject, 173–4, 175, 180, 189–90. *See also* Subject-superject

Sympathy, 154

System: in metaphysics, 30–1, 34, 39; construction of, 48–50

Thought, 138, 144, 145, 174

Time: conception of in Newtonian cosmology, 6–7; theory of, 72–80, 88; epochal theory of, 74–8, 88; irreversibility of, 162

Togetherness: concrete, 89; experiential, 126–7, 130, 197–8, 200

Transcendence, and immanence, 178

Transition, 64–6, 88–90, 93, 207, 209, 211; involves agency, 64–6, 70; continuity of, 72–80

Tredennick, H., 18

Ultimate, category of, 81–7, 88–90

Unconscious perception, 140–3

Universality: of principles, 38–9; of eternal objects, 92

Universals, 93, 117, 177

Universe, 86–7

Unity, unitariness, 23, 55, 59–63, 175, 183, 210–11, 212, 217; prehensive, 12; of actual entity, 71–80 *passim*, 173–4; of prehensions, 186–8

Unmoved mover, 86

Vacuous actuality, theory of, 125–30

Vacuousness: character of abstract entities, 128–30

Valuation, 183, 183 *n.*, 208; and God, 198–202

Value, 187–8, 205, 209; and order, 211–13

Value-intensity, 215–16, 220. *See also* Intensity

Volition, 185

Working hypothesis: in metaphysics, 45–8

Zeno: paradoxes of, 72–8